Enid Candlin

BROADWAY!

BROAD

HOLLIS

W A Y !

125 Years of Musical Theatre

ALPERT

MUSEUM OF THE
CITY OF NEW YORK

INCLUDING:

LITTLE JOHNNY JONES

LEAVE IT TO JANE

LADY, BE GOOD

OH, KAY!

ANYTHING GOES

PAL JOEY

GUYS AND DOLLS

THE KING AND I

WEST SIDE STORY

CAMELOT

CABARET

EVITA

CATS

LES MISÉRABLES

ARCADE
PUBLISHING
NEW YORK
LITTLE, BROWN
AND COMPANY

The author of the text wishes to acknowledge the valuable
assistance of Dr. Lynn Doherty, curator of the
Theatre Collection of the Museum of the City of
New York, and her staff.

First Edition

Alpert, Hollis
    Broadway! : 125 years of musical theatre / text by Hollis Alpert.
— 1st ed.
        p.   cm.
    Companion text for the IBM-sponsored show drawn from the
collections of the Museum of the City of New York and opening at the
IBM Gallery of Science and Art in New York City in May, 1991.
    Includes index.
    ISBN 1-55970-092-0
    1. Musical theater — New York (N.Y.) — Exhibitions.   I. Museum of
the City of New York.   II. IBM Gallery of Science and Art.
III. Title.
ML1711.8.N3A46   1991
792.6'09747'10747471 — dc20   90-49222

Published in the United States by
Arcade Publishing, Inc., New York,
a Little, Brown company

10   9   8   7   6   5   4   3   2   1
Designed by Robert Reed

RAI-WI

Published simultaneously in Canada
by Little, Brown & Company
(Canada) Limited

Printed in the United States of America

Picture Credits

All photographs are courtesy of the Museum of the City of New York, except for the following:

Hampden Booth Theatre Library, 11; Collection of the Lincoln Center Library of the Performing Arts, 31, 60, 80, 98, 114, 115, 151, 173, 174, 186, 200, 201; Schubert Archive, 69; The Rare Book and Manuscript Department, Columbia University, 96; Collection of Mrs. Sylvia Lupas, 132; Loomis Dean, *Life Magazine* © Time Warner, Inc., 168; Mark Kauffman, *Life Magazine* © Time Warner, Inc., 208; John Dominis, *Life Magazine* © Time Warner, Inc., 210; Collection of Mrs. Lisa Aronson, 215, 224; Triton Gallery, 224; Martha Swope Photography, Inc., 226, 231, 235, 237; Clive Barda Photography, 236, 240, 241. Costumes in 100–101 and 190–191 courtesy of the Museum of the City of New York, except, in 100–101, Victor Moore tailcoat from *Of Thee I Sing* courtesy of the Collection of Miles White; in 190–191, Cecil Beaton ball gown for *My Fair Lady* courtesy of the Collection of Paper Mill Playhouse, Milburn, NJ; backdrop painted by Nolan Studios, NYC. Photography by Arie deZanger as follows: ii–viii, 6, 10–20, 21–27, 27–33, 33–38, 41, 43, 46–47, 49–51, 53, 54–55, 57, 59–70, 71–76, 76–86, 88–91, 96–98, 99–115, 117–120, 122–125, 128–129, 131–140, 144–148, 149–159, 163–167, 170–174, 176–177, 180, 183, 185–194, 198–200, 202–207, 209, 210–213, 214–218, 224–225, 228, 230, 231–234.

Contents

BROADWAY!

George L. Fox, whose pantomime *Humpty Dumpty* (1868) rivaled *The Black Crook* in popularity.

Foreword

"Give my regards to Broadway, remember me to Herald Square. Tell all the gang at Forty-second street that I will soon be there." The young George M. Cohan sang this memorable tune in his 1904 production of *Little Johnny Jones*. For more than a century and a quarter the world has given its regards to Broadway and its singular contribution to the human spirit, the American musical. Like the nation and the city that it reflects, the Broadway musical evolved from diverse traditions that merged in nineteenth-century New York. From this amalgam sprang a new art form that took its name from Broadway, the historic avenue that traverses the length of Manhattan. Today the Broadway musical remains one of America's proudest achievements.

The story of Broadway is marked by milepost productions and a galaxy of men and women who have sung and danced and strutted their way to immortality. *Broadway! 125 Years of Musical Theatre* is the tale of these productions, from *The Black Crook* of 1866 to *The Phantom of the Opera* of 1988 and *Miss Saigon* in 1991. It also tells of the many talented people who wrote the music, lyrics, and books; designed the costumes and stage sets; choreographed the dances; turned up the lights; and raised the curtain. This book has been done in collaboration with the Museum of the City of New York, which also organized the exhibit of the same name. Both the book and exhibition draw upon the Museum's extraordinary Theatre Collection, which numbers more than two million items and which continues to grow through the generosity of all those who love American theatre.

The Museum of the City of New York is grateful to those whose assistance and support have made the book — and accompanying exhibit —possible. Of particular note is the work of author Hollis Alpert, who managed to coalesce a vast mountain of disparate material into a cogent and charming book; and of the exhibit's curator, Dr. Lynn Doherty, whose talents and energies lent excellence to the project. The generous grant from International Business Machines, Inc., supporting the exhibition, exemplifies the best of the corporate-private sector partnership that has so often benefited American culture. Finally, the Museum thanks the men and women whose contributions to American musical theatre have enriched our lives.

Robert R. Macdonald

DIRECTOR, MUSEUM OF THE CITY OF NEW YORK

vii

Hello Dolly

Introduction

While the operetta, musical comedy, and musical play have existed in Britain and Europe for a great many years, it has been said that the American variety of the above, named "the musical," has been America's only original contribution to the art of the theatre. This declaration has opened up a rich field of analysis, starting with the very definition of the musical.

Just what is this American musical theatre, so often identified with that place, and state of mind, known as Broadway? In bygone days, entertainments with music bore several labels. Opera-bouffe came from the French; comic opera from the English; operetta from the German-speaking countries. All three terms were used by theatre managers for musical works too light, too frothy and cheerful, to be dignified as operas. There were differences between them, for instance, between Offenbach's *La Belle Hélène* (opera-bouffe) and *H.M.S. Pinafore* (comic opera). For a sample of pure operetta we need seek no farther than *The Merry Widow*.

But these weren't American musicals. The strictly American form of musical theatre developed for the most part during this century. The distinction was subtle, perhaps, but it was there, and it mainly had to do with the libretto,

the play, taking on a larger function. American musicals told a story with music, instead of the other way around. They also dealt with native themes and characters, and matters familiar to contemporary audiences, and they came to be known as musical comedies. And eventually, because they weren't always comedic, as musicals.

A few years ago, James B. Graves, in the *Journal of Popular Culture*, a publication known for taking the less serious very seriously, decided that where the musical was concerned there was a distinct lack in the area of theoretical formulation. After much reference to the philosophical ponderings of Suzanne K. Langer, he found that it was the comedic element in our musicals that distinguished them from other forms, such as those mentioned earlier. He pointed to the fact that, unlike opera or operetta, classically trained singers were not required to carry along the musical burden of the story.

The point seems reasonably well taken. But, as it happened, he went directly counter to prevailing orthodoxy — that it was music that made the musical go round, whatever it was and whatever it was called. Some years before, British critic Kenneth Tynan, in discussing American musicals, had written, "What the drama frequently lacks is poetry. The musical helps us rise above the prosaic, to express what we are feeling in a form more heightened than plain talk. In the hands of the musicians the drama takes off and soars. The key man is he who writes the music." All hail, then, Victor Herbert, Jerome Kern, George Gershwin, Frederick Loewe, and Marvin Hamlisch.

Deems Taylor, a musician himself, would have generally agreed with Tynan. He enunciated his basic Broadway equation as follows: brilliant score plus brilliant lyrics equals success; brilliant score plus dull lyrics equals success; dull score plus brilliant lyrics equals failure.

One can almost hear the ghosts of such lyricists as Larry Hart, Oscar Hammerstein II, Ira Gershwin, and Alan Jay Lerner rising up in protest, not to mention the discomfited shades of choreographers Bob Fosse and Michael Bennett, along with the very much alive Agnes de Mille and Jerome Robbins. And what about the book writers? The above-mentioned Hammerstein and Lerner, and Abe Burrows, P. G. Wodehouse, George S. Kaufman and Moss Hart? Well, at least they'd have Mr. Graves on their side, especially when they were funny.

Yet, without the contributions of all involved in the fashioning — librettists, composers, lyricists, choreographers, producers, directors — would we have as a living legacy the musical masterpieces that are the subject

The Ziegfeld Theatre, designed by Joseph Urban, which opened in 1927.

of this book? We do applaud the work of scholars and historians who, indeed, add to our theatre knowledge and help us understand and appreciate subtleties that might well have escaped some of us. But a look at the development of the American musical stage shows not one distinct species, but many.

What is noticeable is that theorists prefer to deal with what they call "the modern musical," which is supposed to have evolved from more primitive forms. The dates of the emergence of this *modern* musical vary. For some it began in the late twenties with *Show Boat*, regarded as a necessary revolt against the earlier twenties musicals which had, in the words of the dyspeptic George S. Kaufman, "the kind of tunes you go *into* the theatre whistling."

On the other hand, that fine critic and blessedly good writer Walter Kerr just loved those twenties musicals, and in particular *No, No, Nanette*, which he saw when he was ten, and again in a latter-day revival, even though after curtain's rise he heard that inevitable comic maid grumble on her way to the front door or the telephone. He also reminded us that the so-called twenties musical stretched back to the preceding decade, when the celebrated Princess Theatre musicals were being turned out by Jerome Kern, P. G. Wodehouse, and Guy Bolton.

But here's where the historians are most helpful, pointing out that there wouldn't be a modern musical without all that came much earlier. The date *they* fix on is 1866, and it's one we'll accept, because *The Black Crook* of that year gave Broadway its first great hit and made it the all-but-official center of extravagant entertainment.

One wonders, too, whether there would be the musical as we know it today if it were not for Broadway, that long thoroughfare which, in the mid-1800s, stretched from the Battery as far north as the city limits at 42nd Street. New York City was then a thriving center with a constantly expanding population, leading to a building boom and a spate of hotels on Broadway and its surroundings to cater to travelers and transients. The greater their number, the more the need for nightly entertainment, and this led to the construction of theatres in the same area. The crowds came, and eventually there was that all-important support, the audience.

There was, of course, musical theatre in other cities besides New York — Philadelphia and Charleston, for instance — but Broadway was where it took hold, where the largest audience existed to patronize the greatest number of theatres. Consequently, New York had the largest cadre of performers, and although much of the rest of the country saw the same shows, New York was where the grandest entertainments were born, and where the touring companies came to rest. As Manhattan expanded northward, the theatres moved, too, but huddling close always to Broadway. By 1900 the theatre center had left its downtown base and moved to 14th Street; from there it soon ventured to 42nd Street and beyond.

Broadway had its greatest years between the two world wars. After that began the decline in numbers of theatres and productions. Today, "Broadway" in the theatre sense runs seven or eight blocks north and south, and only two east and west. Yet, this small area is still the mecca for the talents that make the musicals that are still our best-loved theatre form, and where the great hits play on and on.

Attempting to pin down the essential nature of the musical is complicated, if only because there is so vast an area to define. If the criterion is the demands of the music, we can see the order descending from opera to operetta, to musical comedy, to revue, to vaudeville. It's a ragged order, however, because all these forms overlap.

We have to account, too, for other forms, faded into history, that had their influences — the traditional English pantomime, for instance, and the minstrel show, very much an original American form. The latter was a sort of variety show performed by whites in burnt cork makeup, and consisted of little skits, jokes, and songs, structured in three parts, but with little or no attempt to tell a coherent story. First seen in New York in 1841, minstrel shows were popular for about half a century, providing a training ground for performers and composers in other musical genres.

Another form of variety, soon to be known as vaudeville, challenged the minstrel show in the 1850s. First performed in saloons in the Bowery area, these bills, made up of song, dance, and skits, had an unsavory reputation because of the presence of the easily available "waiter-girls" who thronged the premises. An enterprising manager, Tony Pastor, cleaned up the acts, so to speak, and opened his famous music hall in 1865, where all family members could safely come, and where a good many

performers, thanks to Pastor's gift for picking talent, made their first impressions and their names.

Concurrently popular with minstrelsy and vaudeville were the spectacle shows known as extravaganzas. Their best-known exponent was the Ravel Family, whose shows featured acrobatics, ballets, one-act farces, and *tableaux vivants*, a mélange that remained popular from the 1840s to the 1860s.

Then in 1866, through a combination of circumstances, a most spectacular extravaganza, so called then, brought together dances with scores of pretty girls, songs, spectacular scenes, bound them all together with a story, and so entranced audiences that it lasted longer on the stage than any previous show. The era of the American musical had begun.

Clearly, our musical theatre evolved out of a multitude of influences. It took offerings from the Old World and fused them with elements from native social and cultural milieus. It responded to changes in audience taste, welcomed the creative contributions of composers, writers, choreographers, and designers, and benefited from the shrewd instincts of producers. To performers who struck the public fancy, it gave bright stardom and unstinted adulation.

If we can't fully categorize the musical as a single species or breed, we can assume that its primary mission has always been far less to edify than to entertain us with song, dance, wit and comedy, scenic dazzle, and, yes, a story. And, by the evidence herein, how well it has done so over the years!

In this book, we do not attempt to

be encyclopedic. There are other histories that detail the thousands of productions that have played their moments, long or brief, and disappeared. Our focus here is on those that have gleamed most brightly in the theatrical firmament, that have added to the possibilities and richness and artistry of the form. It is a large story with a large and glittering cast. This selection, we feel, is representative of an entrancing legacy.

Mary Martin and friends in *South Pacific* (1949).

I *Early Enchantments, 1866–1900*

The Black Crook (1866): Sheet-music cover showing dancers performing the "Amazon's March," which provided an opportunity for the ladies of the ensemble to appear in abbreviated attire.

NIGHT OF THE FIRE

The Academy of Music was opened in 1854 and won much praise for the magnificence of the building which seated more than thirty-five hundred and the "gorgeousness" of its red and gold appointments. On the evening of May 21, 1866, the opera *La Juive* was given there to a full house, and the theatre was late in closing. A Mr. D'Arcy had been at the theatre and, after a supper, was returning to his home near 14th Street and Second Avenue. As he recounted it: "I noticed in passing the Academy that one of the Irving Place doors was still open. It was very late, and curious as to what was going on, I went into the lobby, in which the gas was burning brightly, and peered through the glass doors down to the auditorium. By the light of half a dozen torches I could see some men with axes trying to tear up the flooring of the parquet very near the stage. There was so little smoke in the house that the thought of fire never occurred to me, until as a big board was wrenched away, I saw a thick jet of smoke burst out and shoot up halfway to the ceiling. Apparently, until then, no one had thought of sending for the firemen. I stood in the lobby watching, until driven out by the smoke and flames." The theatre was totally destroyed by the conflagration, but was rebuilt in less than a year.

The Academy of Music on 14th Street and Union Square represented the northernmost border of the theatre district. Built as a grand opera house, it soon added drama, concert, and spectacle to its presentations in order to survive. However, it did maintain its reputation for fine offerings of serious music into the twentieth century.

During the night of May 21, 1866, New York's largest theatre, the Academy of Music on Union Square, was destroyed by fire. A case can be made — and several have made it — that this conflagration was the key element in the development of the American musical theatre. The Academy had been leased by two enterprising producers, Henry C. Jarrett and Harry Palmer, who had gone to Europe in search of a Continental attraction and had brought back a troupe of ballet dancers to appear in a current Parisian ballet success, *La Biche au Bois*. Back in New York they found themselves with thirty-five English, French, and Italian dancers, including a few noted prima ballerinas, who were demanding salaries and support. They desperately needed a theatre.

The next largest theatre, with nearly three thousand plush seats, was Niblo's Garden at Broadway and Prince Street, then managed by William Wheatley. William Niblo's Garden had once been a park where there were refreshments and outdoor concerts. Before his retirement, Niblo had built two theatres on a plot on the northeast corner of Broadway and Prince Street. By the mid-1850s the "garden" had become a fashionable entertainment complex — a grand theatre with adjoining saloon, a ballroom, and a family refreshment room. Then a large luxury hotel, the Metropolitan, was built around it. By this time Broadway was already *Broadway*. The street and its neighborhood contained more places of amusement, it was said, than any district of equal size in the world.

Wheatley, too, had his problems. He had engaged the ordinarily popular Ravel Family for a bill that included ballet, pantomime, and acrobatics, but they were not filling the theatre, having become, after some twenty years, rather old hat. To take their place he contracted to put on a fanciful melodrama by Charles M. Barras called *The Black Crook*. At which time Jarrett and Palmer came along.

They managed to convince Wheatley that they'd all benefit by joining forces and combining ballet numbers with Barras's play. The author was displeased by what he regarded as the ruination of his play, but was mollified with a royalty arrangement for each performance, and was to benefit enormously.

Once embarked on the project, Wheatley went all out. Barras's melodrama, originally designed as an opera libretto and containing noticeable echoes of *Faust* and von Weber's *Der Freischutz*, allowed for many scenic effects: a mountain storm, a flaming chasm, a grotto of golden stalactites, gilded chariots and angels descending through mist and clouds, and, not the least, a grand masquerade ball. The wildly convoluted story need not be told here other than to say that the title character had the responsibility of delivering a human soul to the "Arch Fiend" by a certain midnight, that another character was a dove that turned out to be Queen Stalacta of "the Golden Realm," and that the chief comic figure's name was Von Puffengruntz.

With post–Civil War reconstruction under way, the times were reasonably prosperous, and Mr. Wheatley was willing to invest more than normally in what would be a spectacle to outdazzle all others. The then unheard-of sum of fifty thousand dollars was spent on the production, which included redesigning the Niblo's stage so drastically that it caught the interest of the *Times*. Such a stage, it reported, was never seen in this country before. Every board slid on grooves and could be taken up, or pushed away, or slid entirely out of sight. Entire scenes could be dropped into the enlarged cellar below. Wheatley, in addition, imported new stage machinery and props from England, and more costumes, too. For he had decided to augment the ballet corps with another forty-five dancers who would march around in the "Amazon" drill formations currently popular.

Elaborate as these preparations were, they were innovative more in degree than in kind. American theatregoers had long been treated to scenic spectacle in opera, masques, and pantomime, mostly accomplished with paint and canvas. In *The Black Crook*, it was the sum of the not unfamiliar parts — the mélange of melodrama, spectacle, ballet, music, and songs — that caused a sensation, and created the first of the great Broadway hits.

Jarrett and Palmer acknowledged that while in Europe they had chosen to bring ballet to New York because it revealed the grace and beauty of female legs. "Legs are staple articles," said Jarrett, "and will never go out of fashion." Even "the surfeited New Yorker" would "open his eyes and pocketbook and hold his breath in astonishment."

And astonishment there was. New Yorkers saw more female legs on the Niblo's stage than had ever been seen before — some eighty pairs of them. More, they were amply revealed by pink tights, so close to flesh color that some thought they were seeing nude. Was there no shame in Messrs. Jarrett, Palmer, and Wheatley? The dancers, a reviewer noted severely, were fitted with "exceedingly short drawers extending very little below the hips." And worse. "The attitudes were exceedingly indelicate — *ladies* dancing so as to make their undergarments spring up, exposing the figure beneath from the waist to the toe." Thus was created the first great American leg show, the precursor of the *Follies, Vanities,* and *Scandals* of a later time.

The interior of Niblo's Garden in the mid-nineteenth century.

Nevertheless, most of the press approved of what it saw that evening of September 12, 1866, and so did the audience. The curtain was raised at 7:45 and did not descend for five and a half hours. New York had never enjoyed the

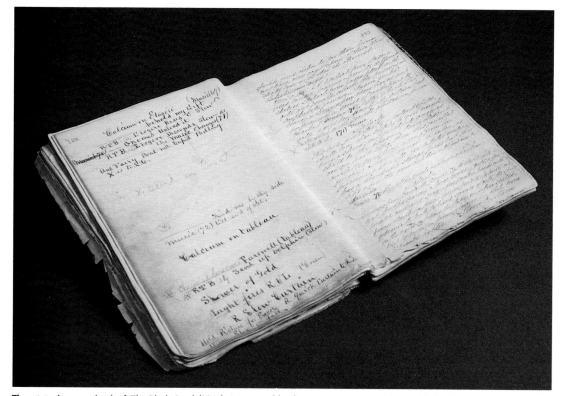

The original prompt book of *The Black Crook* (1866). It was used by the stage manager to call cues; his handwritten notations appear opposite the dialogue.

presence, said the *World*, "of so beautiful, varied, graceful, and thoroughly captivating a corps de ballet as [the] one herein introduced." Even though the *Times* critic dismissed the book as trash, he extolled the show's combination of "youth, grace, beauty and elan." Of particular mention was "the bewitching Pas de Démons, in which the Demonese, who wear no clothes to speak of, so gracefully and prettily disported as to draw forth thunders of applause." The scenic effects impressed, too: "hurricanes of gauze blew through the Harz mountains," and "cascading girls poured down the wild glens."

But along with a rush to the box office came stern reaction from the forces of morality. Soon editorials denouncing the "extreme nudity" appeared in the same papers that had earlier deemed *The Black Crook* as the most wondrous and startling entertainment ever seen in this country. Preachers railed against it; one took a hall a block away to fulminate against the indecent spectacle. Even the usually tolerant *Police Gazette* worried that pure-minded women would be shocked if not corrupted by "the postures throughout the piece," and the "suggestive nude display." It also noted that even some of the men in the audience turned pale and had to avert their eyes.

This, of course, was a publicist's dream, and Wheatley capitalized on the furor by spending five thousand dollars (again a huge amount) to further promote the show. It ran for a record 475 performances, earned more than a million dollars, and was reprised again

GOLDEN TRASH
From the review of *The Black Crook* in the *Times*, September 13, 1866:

"The first act is trashy, but offers ample scope for a fine spectacular display, and introduces the English and French ballet troupes, who were received with enthusiasm. Mlle. Fontani, the premier danseuse, is light as a feather, and exceedingly graceful; she was encored twice during the Pas de Fleurs. The Pas de Sabot is also a charming arrangement in which Mlle. Rose Delval received the well merited applause of the house. Miss Milly Cavendish was encored in her song of 'The Naughty Men.' The act closed with a grand incantation scene laid in a wild glen, whose weird and unholy look was quite apropos to the devilish business therein enacted. . . .

"The features of the second act were the dances held in the gorgeous grotto of Stalacta. The full ballet appeared in the Pas de Naiads, after which came the ballet success of the night, the bewitching Pas de Démons, in which the Demonese, who wear no clothes to speak of, so gracefully and prettily disported as to draw forth thunders of applause. No similar exhibition has been made in an American stage that we remember."

Lithograph printed by F. Mayer and Co., which shows the extraordinary variety of fanciful costumes created for the production.

Program of the original production of *The Black Crook.* Note the producers' unblushing reference to the staggering sums spent on the big transformation scene.

and again in the following decades, often with new material and newly conceived sets and costumes. *The Black Crook* is now remembered more for its shock effect and its stimulus on the theatre of its time than for its story or songs — the latter quite unremarkable and mostly gathered from contemporary compositions. Unlike other well-remembered musical productions, no song "hits" were created to provide nostalgia for later generations.

One star born of the success of *The Black Crook* was a petite fifteen-year-old Italian ballerina, Marie Bonfanti, who danced the part of Queen Stalacta. She remained with the show throughout its long run, and only two weeks after its close she was on the same Niblo's Garden stage in another production, *The White Fawn*. Wheatley, Jarrett, and Palmer, having made fortunes for themselves with the previous show, immediately tried for another. They dusted off the ballet, *La Biche au Bois*, that had been booked for the ill-fated Academy of Music (which had been rebuilt almost at once), gave it something of a story that involved a princess changed into a white fawn, and back into a princess again in a marvelous transformation scene at show's end.

Bonfanti remained under the management of Jarrett and Palmer, and to present her to full advantage in *The White Fawn* they brought over the Viennese Ballet Troupe, numbering forty dancers. Spectacles were alternated with ballets. Children and midgets, acting as laborers, built an actual tower on the stage. An enchanted-lake scene featured a firefly ballet. The forty ballet dancers exhibited an enticing amount of leg. A problem in

the first performance was the cumbersome stage machinery, which kept the show lumbering until two in the morning.

Nevertheless, Bonfanti gave the show enough cachet to keep it on the boards for a solid if not spectacular 175 performances. The little dancer so caught the fancy of audiences that after the final curtain the stage door at Niblo's was crowded with theatregoers waiting to see her exit. The shy, ladylike girl was frightened by the attention; she had to be smuggled out of her dressing room and through the streets to her home. In 1870 she returned to *The Black Crook* in a new production, and thereafter remained on the stage in opera and ballet until the 1890s.

A star of a quite different kind was George Lafayette Fox, a comedian whose specialty was pantomime. Born in Boston in 1825 to a family of actors, he barnstormed until the early 1860s, when he began presenting season-long pantomimes such as *Jack and the Beanstalk* at the Bowery Theatre. In 1868 he moved uptown to Broadway, where he presented a spectacular pantomime, *Humpty Dumpty*, that rivaled the popularity of *The Black Crook*.

If one is willing to stretch the point, pantomime in its English form, and as continued in America, was a forerunner of musical comedy in that it contained songs, dances, burlesque sketches, and dialogue, usually based on a Mother Goose tale, but in which the characters at the end are transformed into the traditional Harlequin, Pantaloon, and Columbine.

Fox, whose pointed nose made

THE LITTLE BONFANTI

The Italian-born Marie Bonfanti, who made so sensational an appearance in *The Black Crook*, was determined from early childhood to be a dancer. Though her well-off Milanese parents were not especially encouraging, they could only marvel at her intense four-hour-a-day practice sessions. Her first public appearance was at thirteen in Madrid, where Queen Isabella saw her and asked that "the little Bonfanti" be brought to her box. Marie thought she had caused too much excitement with her dancing and was crying so much that the queen had to soothe her. Her fame spread quickly, and she was performing at Covent Garden in London when Harry Palmer persuaded her to give up her next engagement in Paris and to come to America.

After her appearances in *The Black Crook* and *The White Fawn*, she journeyed to San Francisco, chaperoned by her sister, and, after a success there, came back to New York for a revival of *The Black Crook*, in which she headed a new dance called "Le Ballet des Ferns." She had lost "none of her magnetic power to sway audiences," said a critic. Her long subsequent career included her engagement as the premiere danseuse of the ballet corps of the Metropolitan Opera. She hung up her toe shoes in 1894 and taught the art of ballet to others thereafter.

(*opposite*)

Lithograph of Marie Bonfanti as Queen Stalacta. She subsequently married one of the young men who nightly filled the first row of the orchestra, bearing bouquets. As an elderly woman, she told an interviewer of crowds thronging the street in front of the theatre every night, begging her to appear on the balcony. She also noted, "The idea that some people have that women who dance on the stage in the ballet costume are of necessity impure, is absurd. Some of the best and purest women I ever knew were dancers. And no one has ever dared to say a word against me."

George L. Fox, star of *Humpty Dumpty* (1866). This great clown could mold a pleasant, rather ordinary face into an endless succession of bizarre expressions.

him resemble his namesake, had great control of his facial muscles; his mugging and miming, along with the kind of slapstick engaged in by clowns in pantomime, made him enormously popular. His *Humpty Dumpty* had little to do with the Mother Goose rhyme, but was in fact a grand-scale musical variety show. It featured circus acts, a troupe of roller skaters, Mlle. Tita Sangalli, an Italian prima ballerina, ballad singers,

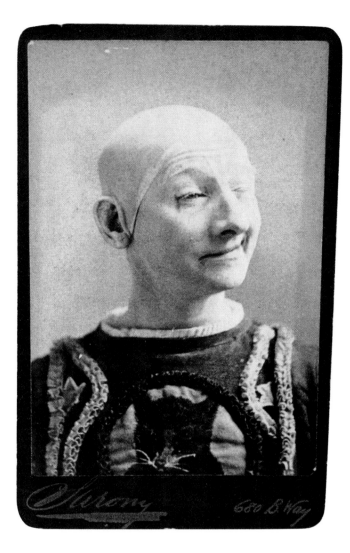 

and such scenic spectacles as a Valley of Fertility, a skating pond by moonlight, and a marketplace in Naples, complete with a tarantella by a corps of dancers.

Aided by Fox's cavortings and popularity, the show ran nearly a year and a half, and was remounted again and again over the next two decades. In a following manifestation, *Humpty Dumpty Abroad*, Fox included such innovations as a "Grand Chinese Divertisement de Dance," which took place in the "Celestial Empire — China," a ballet of "Charivari and Instruments," and an "Ocean Yacht Race" in the Bay of New York. Among the rich range of characters encountered by Humpty Dumpty were Belline, "the village belle," Cutler, "a butcher," and Chin-Pan-Seen, "Mandarin of the Red Button." (There were also mandarins of yellow, blue, and green buttons.) Later in his career, Fox began to develop some peculiar symptoms: on one occasion he leaped off the stage, into a stage box, and banged a lady on the head with a loaf of property bread. In 1873, after several other similarly odd incidents, he was judged insane and sent to an asylum, where he died a few months later.

His legacy, however, was clear: large audiences were ready and waiting to patronize musical entertainments that catered to popular tastes.

At about the time that Fox departed this world, a young Harvard graduate, J. Cheever Goodwin, decided to try his hand at burlesquing Longfellow's wearyingly long narrative poem *Evangeline*. Its heroine, it may be remembered, was separated from her fiancé, Gabriel, when both were exiled from their homes in Nova Scotia. The two then sought each other for years on end, from one end of the continent to the other, until, nigh unto death, they were reunited for a brief moment in, of all

places, Philadelphia.

One can understand Goodwin's need to satirize this woefully sad tale, which was mandatory reading for schoolchildren of the period. Goodwin turned Longfellow's work into a world-ranging comedy. Evangeline and Gabriel were still united in the end, but their adventures took them as far as the diamond fields of Africa, and not only was the heroine pursued by a whale, but she also danced with her pet heifer. Goodwin found a companion in literary crime, and a producer, in another Bostonian, Edward E. Rice, who had done some acting and whose musical gifts included playing the piano by ear. Goodwin wrote the book and lyrics, and Rice the score — not at all bad, by contemporary accounts — and, as a result, the truly American musical was created.

Its plot was mainly a prop for a series of ballads, duets, jigs, waltzes, and marches, intermixed with puns and gags. The first presentation (July 27,

Program from the original production of *Humpty Dumpty*. It illustrates the nineteenth-century tradition of adding new material and performers throughout the run.

A scene from *Evangeline* (1874).

Edward E. Rice, composer of *Evangeline*. He wrote all the songs, an unusual feat during these years when the music was almost invariably the work of several composers.

LONG LONG TRAIL A-WINDING

Longfellow's lengthy narrative poem *Evangeline, A Tale of Acadie* was based on a purportedly true story. Perhaps not as familiar now as in the past are the following majestic lines from the poem:

Ye who believe in affection that
    hopes and endures and is
    patient,
Ye who believe in the beauty and
    strength of woman's devotion,
List to the Mournful tradition
    still sung by the pines of the
    forest;
List to a tale of love in Acadie,
    home of the happy.

1874) was for a limited run of only two weeks during a summer lull at Niblo's Garden. Forced out of Niblo's, the show traveled to Boston's Globe Theatre; eventually it returned to New York and for the next thirty years it was the nation's most enduring and endearing show, its dancing heifer a perennial favorite.

Rice, at first, labeled the show an "American opera-bouffe," but since this did not fairly describe the kind of family entertainment he had in mind, and eschewing "burlesque," he advertised it as "Rice's Extravaganza Combination." By the time it reappeared in New York, it was a "refined musical extravaganza." One critic of the time, attempting to distinguish between the forms of burlesque and extravaganza, chose *Evangeline* as an illustration of the latter. "The traits of extravaganza," he said, "are mirth, melody, quaint fancy, and innocent diversion." It required "intelligence, a distinct idea, abundant good humor . . . clearly defined characters by the author, and not left to be rounded out by the whims or talents of the performers."

19

William S. Gilbert, who wrote the lyrics and libretto for *H.M.S. Pinafore.*

Sir Arthur Sullivan, the comic opera's composer.

Illustration for "The Baby" *Pinafore,* which featured a company of children.

One can see the concept being formed. And, indeed, Rice also sought to clarify his intention, which, he said, was "to foster a taste for musical comedy, relieved of the characteristic and objectionable features of opera-bouffe." As far as can be ascertained, this was the first time anyone had mentioned the term "musical comedy."

While Rice and Goodwin were enjoying their phenomenal success, as well as concocting other elaborate musical entertainments, Gilbert and Sullivan came along and reestablished British preeminence in America's musical theatre. The principal vehicle was their comic opera *H.M.S. Pinafore,* which made its London bow, under the management of Richard D'Oyly Carte, on May 15, 1878, and which was playing, only six months later, at the Boston Museum (a theatre so named to take the curse off the musical attractions that played there).

The remarkable partnership of W. S. Gilbert, who had deserted law for the professions of journalism and playwriting, and Sir Arthur Sullivan, England's most highly regarded composer of choral music, began in 1875 (after a hardly remembered joint work that had failed in 1870) with *Trial by Jury,* done as a forty-minute curtain-raiser for D'Oyly Carte. Sullivan regarded his true vocation as the composition of serious music, but the witty lyrics and nonsensical upside-down Gilbertian views of British institutions were impossible for him to resist. When Gilbert sent him the libretto for *Pinafore,* he came up with a sprightly score that

helped make the two of them the darlings of London — and also quite rich.

The frolicking send-up of the First Lord of the Admiralty and the Queen's Navy got off to a slow start because of a spell of bad weather in London, but it wasn't long before headlines were shouting *PINAFORE MANIA!* Sheet music of the piano score was published and snatched up, and among the purchasers were several American theatre managers who, because reciprocal copyright agreements did not yet exist between the two countries, felt free to appropriate it for their own use.

In Boston, *Pinafore* was a far greater success than any previous production, including the beloved *Evangeline.* Soon other productions opened in San Francisco and Philadelphia, and on January 15, 1879, it came to New York, where *Pinafore* mania struck again. By early May no less than eleven major New York theatres were playing the piece. The *Dramatic Mirror* wondered, half seriously, if the show was ultimately going to take over all of New York's theatres.

Not a dollar of this box-office windfall reached Gilbert and Sullivan, or D'Oyly Carte. Gilbert announced: "I will not have another libretto of mine produced if the Americans are going to steal it. It's not that I need the money so much, but it upsets my digestion."

Catch phrases from the comic opera swiftly crossed the entire nation. A newspaper editor in New York called a meeting of his reporters and informed them he had found "What, never? Well, hardly ever" used twenty times in the previous day's issue. "Never let me see it used again!" he commanded them.

A reporter couldn't resist. "What, never?" he asked.

"Well, hardly ever!" the editor shot back.

D'Oyly Carte crossed the Atlantic to survey the situation. He discovered that Philadelphia had a Negro version, and that in Boston the chorus was made up of fifty members of church choirs, assembled at the suggestion of one of the city's newspapers. Much to D'Oyly Carte's displeasure, he found that the *Canal Boat Pinafore* was being put on in New York at Tony Pastor's burlesque house.

D'Oyly Carte sent a distressed message to his London colleagues. The voices he had encountered, he said, were good, but they hadn't the remotest idea of how to play the piece. "The acting, costumes, time of music, etc. were too atrociously bad for words to express." The "business" invented by Gilbert and his actors had never been done. On his return, he advised them to bring over a company with the original orchestrations and the "business," and put on a genuine representation.

The expedition was mounted forthwith, and when its ship, the *Bothnia*, reached Sandy Hook, it was given a reception by a fleet of steamers hired by the various local companies playing the opera. "Every vessel in the motley squadron," the *Musical Times* reported, "was dressed with American and English flags and had on board a *Pinafore* band and chorus."

The authors were extensively interviewed, and one question asked was if Gilbert had ever expected quotations

Souvenir dish made in England during the *Pinafore* mania that swept both Europe and America.

from the libretto to become the catchwords of the day.

"Never," Gilbert replied emphatically.

"What! Never?"

"Well, very seldom," he said, judiciously.

Gilbert's authentic production at the Fifth Avenue Theatre impressed the

---

Program for a children's performance of *H.M.S. Pinafore*. This production apparently combined three groups of child performers.

21

New York critics. They admired the realistic shrouds with sailors clambering up and down, the divisions of the chorus, some on the gun deck, others on the quarterdeck. The most noticeable difference, however, was in the orchestration, its breadth, color, and tone, and its blending with the choral elements.

For New York audiences, and theatre professionals, seeing the real *Pinafore* was eye-opening. Here was exceptional musical theatre in which the book, lyrics, and music, along with delightful stage business, coalesced into an artistic whole. The literate wit, the humor, subtle even when most absurd, was a far cut above anything produced to date by native Americans. It took time, but *Pinafore* and others that followed led to distinct improvement in the efforts of American librettists, lyricists, and composers.

Curiously, no matter how much admired, Gilbert's New York production did little to diminish the patronage for the local productions. They continued to play, and without royalties to the authors. By now Gilbert and Sullivan had a new opera ready — *The Pirates of Penzance*. This time they had figured out how to forestall American piracy: open the work simultaneously in England and New York. To this end they arranged for a copyrighting performance by an English touring company in a tiny theatre in South Devon, and a day later, on December 31, 1879, by their *Pinafore* company at the Standard Theatre in New York. Unfortunately, the scheme did not end the piracy. What it did accomplish was American profits for Gilbert and Sullivan, and, through extensive touring, a persuasive example of how their works should be played.

At about the same time that *Pinafore* came to New York, the team of Harrigan and Hart, two former vaudevillians, opened (January 13, 1879) their comic play with music, *The Mulligan Guards' Ball*, one of a series that continued for more than a decade. If one likes to apply a theory of evolution to American musical theater, *Mulligan* and its offspring represent an important mutation in the American species.

For one thing, there were no discernible British or French influences in the plays; they were American to the core, portraying a New York City teeming with Irish, Italian, German, and Jewish immigrants, a city of pushcarts, tenements, ward heelers and grasping landlords.

Edward Green Harrigan grew up in a neighborhood overflowing with Irish immigrant families near where the Brooklyn Bridge now joins Manhattan. At eighteen, he left home and began a career as a song-and-dance man in variety houses. In 1871 he joined Tony Hart (born Anthony J. Cannon), a youthful song-and-dance artist, to form an act. Harrigan was a talented writer of vaudeville sketches in the tradition of farce-comedy; he also wrote lyrics for songs to go along with them, and to which a transplanted Englishman, David Braham, wrote the music. Soon, Harrigan and Hart (who, because of his short size and baby face, often played female roles) became the most popular duo in vaudeville.

Sheet music written by David Braham, principal composer for the *Mulligan Guards* plays of the late 1870s and '80s, starring the team of Harrigan and Hart.

In the photograph on the left, Edward Harrigan and Tony Hart in one of their most popular plays, *Ireland vs. Italy*. Hart is once again in female dress. On the right, Harrigan and Hart working as blackface comics early in their careers.

If Harrigan changed the direction of our musical theatre, the turning point was a song he wrote with Braham in 1872 called "The Mulligan Guards." It satirized a New York institution: the fraternal organizations, or clubs, known as "target companies." These had sprung up when immigrants, Irish and otherwise, were not allowed to join recognized city militia groups. They formed their own pseudo-military outfits, and usually named them in honor of some local politician.

Every now and then they would get together for a day of target practice. This meant marching off with muskets and their target, a sort of large standard with their political patron's name emblazoned on it, to a nearby picnic ground. These were festive occasions, and by the time the men got to the shooting range a good many of the marchers were so drunk they were as likely to hit one another as their target.

Harrigan's song ran:

We shouldered guns,
*   And marched, and marched away,*
From Jackson Street
*   Way up to Avenue A,*
Drums and fifes did sweetly, sweetly play,
*   As we marched, marched in the Mulligan*
*   Guards.*

There were, of course, no Mulligan Guards. Harrigan and Braham sold the sheet-music rights to the song for fifty dollars, and also used it in a variety sketch. In September 1878, Harrigan developed a longer, forty-minute version, *The Mulligan Guards' Picnic*, which was so successful that Harrigan decided to carry it further.

There were no Mulligans in the early sketch, and the "guards" then consisted of a contingent of three: a captain, played by Harrigan; Hart, carrying a musket, as his army; and as the target carrier a small black youngster they had found on the street lugging a target for a real group. But for the full-length *Picnic* and its sequel, *The Mulligan Guards' Ball*, Harrigan created the Mulligan family.

Dan Mulligan, as the head of the family in *Ball*, ran into problems putting on a ball for his guards — now more numerous — because the hall he booked was also committed to a black target company, the Skidmore Guards. The impasse was worked out when the blacks took the upstairs and the whites the downstairs, but the black celebration was so lively that the whole party came crashing through the floor (Harrigan, who staged the plays, used dummies) on the Mulligans below. A subplot had to do with Dan's disapproval of his son's romantic involvement with the daughter of a German family, the Lochmullers.

The unique quality of the series was its emphasis on real rather than stereotyped characters and situations, and an ethnic mix. Scenes took place in the neighborhood streets, the Mulligans' dining room, a barbershop (owned by a black member of the Skidmores) where Mulligan and others of the neighborhood gathered on Sunday mornings to talk over the local sporting news. The ballroom of the climactic action bore the name of the Harp and Shamrock. The accents of the players came from the streams of the various immigrant groups (a fourth of immigrants at the time were Irish) and of blacks moving up from the South. Songs were not simply stuck in, but used to advance the stage happenings.

Harrigan found much of his inspiration on the streets. His sharp eye and ear picked up the foibles of the Tammany Hall politicians, the landlords, and the slum dwellers. Nedda Harrigan, the youngest of his ten children, who married director Joshua Logan, remembered him actually following people around, learning their walks and observing how and where they lived. He would buy people's clothes off their backs, she said, to use for costumes.

The popularity of the *Guards*, and Harrigan's deepening exploration of the Mulligan family, bred a series that included *The Mulligan Guards' Chowder*, *The Mulligan Guards' Christmas*, and *The Mulligan Guards' Silver Wedding*. Their popularity remained high for years, and each of the shows ran for a hundred or more performances. Among Harrigan's

(opposite)
Scene design of a New York street painted by Charles Witham for *The Leather Patch*, an 1885 Harrigan and Hart production.

admirers was novelist and theatre critic William Dean Howells, who dubbed Harrigan a social realist on the order of a Dickens or a Zola.

Charles H. Hoyt, who created *A Trip to Chinatown* (1890).

Whether or not Harrigan was his direct inspiration, Charles Hoyt, a playwright and lyricist, followed his lead by using identifiable American types in his plays with music he called farce-comedies. By far the most successful of these (a record 650 performances) was *A Trip to Chinatown*, first presented out of town in 1890, and brought to New York late the following year. The plot was mundane: two tourist couples in San Francisco try to avoid each other on excursions to Chinatown, but wind up in the same restaurant, and still try to avoid each other. Characters had names such as Welland Strong (a hypochondriac hoping an earthquake will rejuvenate him), Rashley Gay, Ben Gay, and Norman

Blood. A pretty and spirited widow helps to keep the action muddled. The innocent, broadly comic fun was interlarded with musical numbers.

Hoyt's method was to revise his shows as they played, and *Chinatown* was well honed by the time it got to the Madison Square Theatre in New York. The songs, with music by Percy Gaunt, were not only notable for their popularity, but proved that, transferred to sheet music, they could bring large additional profits.

Before the show's arrival in New York, a songwriter, Charles K. Harris, paid a member of the cast to sing his "After the Ball" during the second act. Through three verses and three choruses, the audience sat silent, and Harris thought he had a dud. But at the finish, as he recounted it, "For a full minute the audience remained quiet, and then broke loose with applause. The entire audience, standing, applauded wildly for five minutes." The five million sheet-music copies sold made Harris a millionaire.

A few months after the New York opening, a new performer, who proclaimed herself an "artist of the dance," was inserted in the show. Named Loïe Fuller, she hailed originally from Fullersburg, Illinois. After several years of acting and performing in variety shows in London and Paris, she took up dance, and was an early precursor of Isadora Duncan and Ruth St. Denis. She believed in natural movement and the visual impressions made by the interplay of motion, light and color, costume, and sound.

A New York audience saw her dance for the first time in January 1892,

A scene from *A Trip to Chinatown*.

Metal statuette of a dancer in the show.

Miss Loïe Fuller
Souvenir des Folies Bergère.

in *Uncle Celestin*, a French comedy with music by Edmond Audran. Clad in a silken costume, she elicited an awed report from a member of the New York press:

"Suddenly the stage is darkened, and Loïe Fuller appears in a white light which makes her radiant, and a white robe that surrounds her like a cloud. She floats around the stage, her figure now revealed, now concealed by the exquisite drapery which takes forms of its own and seems instinct with her life. . . . It will be the talk of the town."

Loïe Fuller in one of her butterfly dances.

Scene from *The Passing Show* (1894), the first American revue.

(*opposite*)

Detail of an oil painting of Thomas D. Rice performing his "Jump Jim Crow" routine in November of 1833. Rice was an itinerant performer who supposedly copied the shuffling dance of an elderly black stablehand. He became very successful, as the overflow crowd on stage illustrates. He also set the pattern for white-only minstrel performances, which lasted until the mid-1850s.

Soon she was, and Hoyt then hired her as the "Première Danseuse" in *Chinatown*, at three times her previous salary.

Her specialty was a "butterfly dance," in which she flitted around the stage and used her skirts as the butterfly's wings. Audiences loved it, and a vogue for so-called skirt dancing was created. Fuller stayed with the show for only four months: Paris and its artistic ferment were too strong for her to resist, and she returned to France.

Vaudeville, a cut above burlesque, became more elegant in 1894 when *The Passing Show*, advertised as a "topical extravaganza," was presented at the Casino Theatre, home to some of Broadway's best musical theatre. The show's producers, George Lederer and Sydney Rosenfeld, were well aware that they were breaking with precedent by

putting on variety at higher than usual prices and in a tonier setting; they were perhaps less aware that they were breaking new ground in Broadway's musical theatre, that, in fact, they were creating the first American revue.

Instead of a variety bill filled with individually booked acts and sketches, changed weekly, they mounted an entire production, with all its material specially commissioned. Performers did not do their turns and vanish, but reappeared throughout the evening. Dialogue and songs were written for them. Sketches satirized well-known actors of the day. One comic sketch was called "Round the Opera in Twenty Minutes." The huge cast of one hundred (performing labor was cheap then) included ballet dancers, a bevy of chorines, and some remarkable comic acrobats, the Tamale Brothers.

Undoubtedly the inspiration for

28

Carved wooden minstrel figure. Late nineteenth century.

The Passing Show came from Paris, where the topical revue was already well established. In fact, one critic used the French word *revue* in describing the show. Not that he was unduly impressed by what seemed to him a lot more of the same, but he had no way of knowing that in the next decade, and for decades thereafter, Broadway would be brightened and glamorized by similar shows called *Follies*, *Scandals*, and *Vanities*.

During the 1880s and 1890s, minstrel shows performed by blacks gained popularity, and large troupes were organized that toured throughout the country. The shows were a caricature of Negro life, and they had the unfortunate effect of fixing "a tradition," as James Weldon Johnson wrote, "of the Negro as only an irresponsible, happy-go-lucky, wide-grinning, shuffling, banjo playing, singing, dancing, sort of being." Even so, they provided a training ground and theatrical experience for many black performers. Somewhat of a departure from the strict minstrel format was the *Creole Show*, which played in several cities in the early 1890s and almost reached the "Broadway zone" in New York, where it played in a theatre in Greely Square.

One talented member of the *Creole Show*, Bob Cole, played an important part in the development of black participation in American theatre. He was a versatile playwright, performer, and stage manager. While he was developing a minstrel show in New York for two white managers, an argument broke out over pay and working conditions, and Cole walked out. Cole and his sympathizers

were subsequently boycotted by other white managers, at which point Cole issued what amounted to a manifesto by black performers.

"We are going to have our own shows," he announced. "We are going to write them ourselves, we are going to have our own stage manager, our own orchestra leader, and our own manager out front to count up. No divided houses — our race must be seated from boxes back." He was as good as his word. In 1898 he created and organized *A Trip to Coontown*, and in so doing made a firm break with the minstrel tradition. It was the first musical show to be produced entirely by blacks, the first to have continuity and a plot — in essence, the first all-black musical comedy. But obstacles had to be overcome. White managements rejected the show, and, along with threats to performers who appeared in it, virtually every theatre in the country was closed to it. However, Canada had been overlooked by the boycotters, and soon enough word came from up north of the show's success. The firm of Klaw and Erlanger defied the lockout and brought it to New York.

A Trip to Coontown's story about the efforts of a con man to fleece an old black man out of his pension was not particularly original, but its songs were "admirable," the *Times* said, and of the performers: "their lightness of foot and distinction with which they carry themselves, place these artists high above the average white face comedy level." Cole and his partner, Billy Johnson, later collaborated on other Broadway plays (not necessarily black) and wrote a string of popular hits, among the most

Billy Johnson (left) and Bob Cole (right), stars of *A Trip to Coontown* (1898).

remembered of which is "Under the Bamboo Tree."

A few months later another all-black musical broke through the white barrier to Broadway. Its composer was Will Marion Cook, a musician who had studied at Berlin's *Hochschule* and with the great violinist Joseph Joachim. He saw new musical possibilities in the use of Negro harmony and tempo, and what was then called ragtime. Recruiting the black poet Paul Laurence Dunbar for the lyrics, Cook wrote a sketch called *Clorindy, or The Origin of the Cakewalk*, and rounded up twenty-six of the best black dancers and singers he could find. That, however, was less than half the battle.

Edward E. Rice (of *Evangeline* fame) was then one of Broadway's most prominent theatrical producers. Cook

White ceramic pitcher encircled by painted minstrels. Late nineteenth century.

THIRD AVENUE THEATRE.

Third Avenue, 30th and 31st Streets.

S. DEVRIES..Business Manager

LADIES WILL KINDLY REMOVE THEIR LARGE HATS.

Week Commencing Monday, April 4, 1898.

POPULAR PRICE MATINEES WEDNESDAY AND SATURDAY.

Reserved ORCHESTRA AND BALCONY. **25 and 50 cents.**

BOB COLE AND BILLY JOHNSON

In the Roaring, Racy, Rollicking Musical Comedy

A Trip to Coontown

Supported by a Select Company of Colored Artists.

Cast of Characters.

Willie Wayside, who has seen better days.	BOB COLE
Jim Flimflammer, a bunco Steerer.	BILLY JOHNSON
Silas Green, Sr., with a $5,000 pension	Robert A. Kelley
Silas Green Jr., his wayward son...... }
A Sly Cop of the Coontown police force }	J. A. Shipp
Billy Binkerton, a detective.... }
Rube. .... }
Italian............. }
Hebrew............. }	Tom Brown
Chinaman............ }
Capt. Fleetfoot, of the gallant 54th of Mass.	Walter Dixon
The Black DeReske of the Coontown Opera Co.	Lloyd G. Gibbs
Sam, a waiter	Geo. Brown
Reverendly. .... }
Bill Pulaski, a razor inspector . }	Hen Wise
Mrs. Fannie Brown, a widow with a boarding house	Vincent Bradley
Fannie Brown, her daughter.	Pauline Freeman
Florinda.	Lena Wiser
Rotinda.	Marguerite Rhodes
Lucinda.......... }
Flotinda.......... }	May Wynder
Marinda.	Sadie Robinson
Aminda.	Bell King
Balinda.	Clara Freeman

Boarders, Pleasure Seekers, etc.

Time—Present time.   Place—Suburbs of New York.

Programme Continued on Second Page Following.

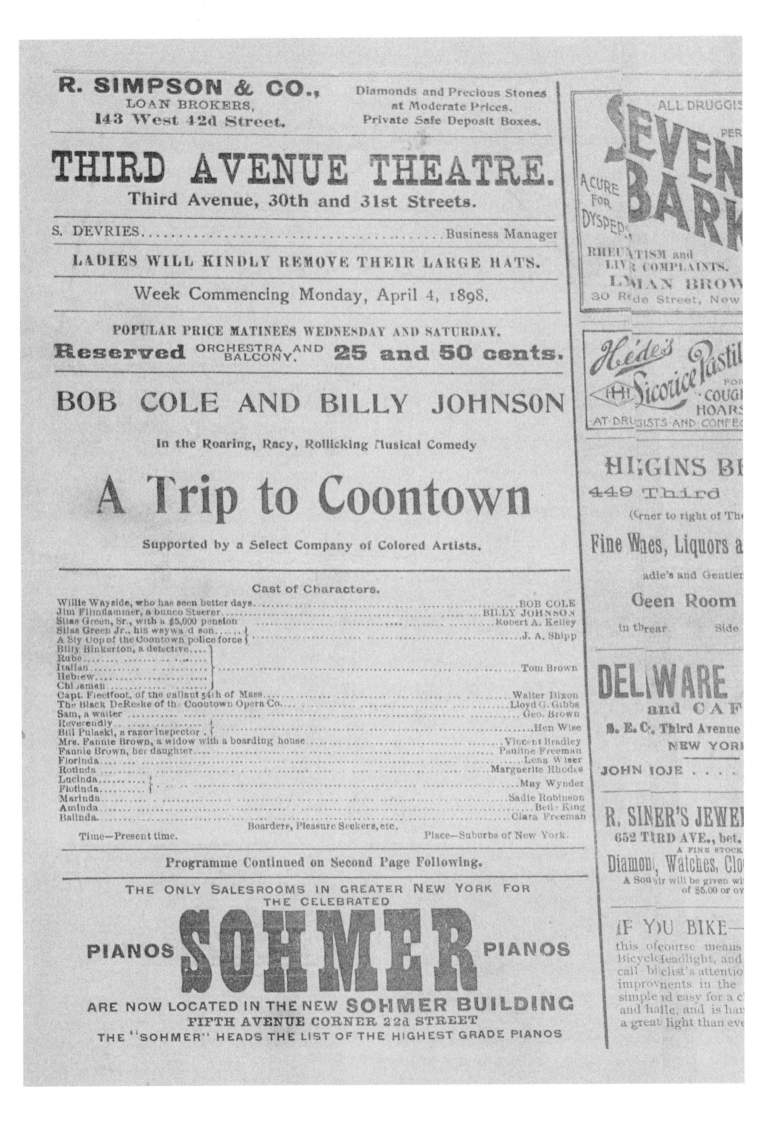

went to see him and asked for the chance to present his show, but Rice kept putting him off. One day Cook overheard Rice telling members of an act to show him their material at the Casino Roof Top Garden above the Casino Theatre during rehearsal time the next day. Cook quickly gathered his company, lied to them that a booking was imminent, and herded them into the auditorium before the arrival of Rice. When Rice got there he heard twenty fine voices ringing out "Darktown Is Out To-night." He agreed to put *Clorindy* on as an afterpiece to the regular show playing in the Roof Top Garden. The all-white audience, augmented by patrons leaving the Casino Theatre below, cheered the first performance wildly. As Cook wrote of the heady experience later: "Negroes were at last on Broadway, and were there to stay."

He was a little too optimistic, for it took five years before another musical, written and staged by black talent, came to Broadway. This was *In Dahomey*, a full-length production, with music and arrangements by Cook and Will Vodery, and starring the prominent vaudeville team of Bert Williams and George Walker.

It opened at the New York Theatre, in the heart of the Times Square theatre district. Williams and Walker played, respectively, a lethargic rube and a slick city con man. Williams, because of his light color, had to use blackface (Walker did not), and both employed traditional Negro stage dialect. The songs, though, had an authenticity that came from characters and situation. After a modest run in New York, *In Dahomey* went to London, where it played for

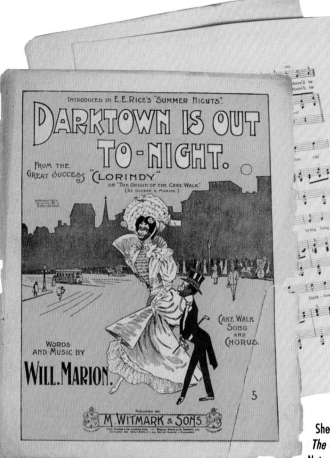

Sheet music from *Clorindy, or The Origin of the Cake Walk* (1898). Note the omission of composer Will Marion Cook's surname.

seven months so successfully that the company received a royal command for a performance at Buckingham Palace in honor of the ninth birthday of the son of the Prince of Wales. The cakewalk dance, a highlight of the show, became the rage of England.

The song that helped Bert Williams to establish the woeful stage persona he frequently used to great comic effect.

Scene from *In Dahomey* (1903). Left to right: Hattie McIntosh, George Walker, Ada Overton Walker, Bert Williams (in blackface), and Lottie Williams.

(opposite)
Program for the original production of *A Trip to Coontown* of 1898. Cole used whiteface makeup to play the old tramp, Willie Wayside.

Oil painting of Victor Herbert. Artist unknown.

Despite such exceptions, America's musical theatre — and its drama, too — was at the turn of the century largely one of import, adaption, and revival. By and large Americans were striving, without much success, to imitate the gay melodies and never-never land of the European operetta. It was not until Victor Herbert came along that America had a competitor to Offenbach, von Suppé, and Gilbert and Sullivan.

Born in Ireland in 1859, Herbert received his musical training in Germany. He came to the United States in 1886 when his wife, a singer, was invited to the Metropolitan. Herbert, a cellist, landed a job in the orchestra pit, but he soon moved onward and upward, first as an army band leader, and then a symphonic conductor. He also had a deep-seated desire to write for the musical theatre. His first attempt was an 1894 operetta called *Prince Ananias*, composed for the Boston Light Opera Company. It was sung on Broadway by a group called The Bostonians, descendants of the church-choir chorus formed in 1879 to sing *Pinafore.*

That first operetta was a dismal failure, but the two that followed were much more successful. One of them, *The Fortune Teller*, which opened on September 26, 1898, revealed Herbert's musical talent in its most delectable form. It was a romantic and quite inane tale of Gypsy love and mixed identities, with both heroines played by the lovely singer Alice Nielsen. But it was the music that captivated audiences and critics alike. The quintessence of operetta is found in "Gypsy Love Song," and Gypsy music, too, in "Romany Life" and "Czardas." For

Alice Nielsen in *The Fortune Teller* (1898). The young opera singer formed her own company to produce the show, which Herbert wrote for her.

some strange reason, it lasted only five weeks in New York. But on tour it was immensely popular and long-lived. As the century drew to a close, Herbert was already famous. But his most remarkable accomplishments and triumphs still lay ahead of him.

In the early years of the new century, American musical theatre had little recognition as an art form, one reason being a lack of definition. There were operettas, European in flavor if not in conception; there was musical vaudeville, and musical farce. The operettas, with their formula plots, mostly imitated other operettas; the farce-comedies of Hoyt (and Harrigan before him) had rough vigor and some authenticity as to types and costume, but they, too, were simplistic, the humor broad and predictable.

Broadway at century's end, as Brooks Atkinson said, "was provincial and parochial . . . artistically trivial, but it had charm and a kind of disarming

The original Florodora Sextet.

simplicity." He might have been thinking of *Florodora*, an English import, which opened on November 11, 1900, after running a year in London. It was a huge hit (505 performances) and traveled so extensively that the whole country seemed to be singing or whistling, "Tell me, pretty maiden, are there any more at home like you?"

The reference was to the six willowy members of the Florodora Sextet. (Florodora was not a girl's name, but that of a perfume named after an island in the Philippines.) The story is too fusty to tell; in any case it was the sextet that made the show.

A good many of the seeds for a new American art form were planted during the nineteenth century, but what was badly needed to make the American musical great was vitality, vigor, and creativity. All three would appear in the person of a brash young man: George M. Cohan.

Cohan with Sam Harris. They produced forty-four shows in a partnership formed by a handshake. It ended in 1920 when Cohan, embittered by the actors' strike of the previous year, decided to retire from producing. He changed his mind a few months later, and was back on the boards within a year.

II *Cohan Comes Marching In, 1901–1917*

LITTLE JOHNNY JONES

FORTY-FIVE MINUTES FROM BROADWAY

GEORGE WASHINGTON, JR.

THE MERRY WIDOW

NAUGHTY MARIETTA

FOLLIES OF 1907

WATCH YOUR STEP

NOBODY HOME

VERY GOOD EDDIE

HAVE A HEART

OH BOY!

LEAVE IT TO JANE

George M. Cohan and family. Age four and on the road.

Cohan Comes Marching In, 1901–1917

In 1902, the *New York Times* warned that "In the not far distant future the musical comedy and its kin will be found among the 'have beens' so far as concerns New York. Nearly all agree that the cycle is dead." Theatre managers and producers, the *Times* said, thought the public was ready for a change toward the serious — if not to tragedy, then at least to melodrama.

George Michael Cohan, for one, refused to take the warning seriously. There has been argument over whether he was born on the Fourth of July, as he and his parents claimed, or on July 3, 1878, according to his birth certificate. A mistake by the registrar, his mother said firmly. For George, it was a matter of supreme importance.

He was impressed, he said, "with the fact that I had been born under the Stars and Stripes, and that has had a great deal to do with everything I have written." Patriotism was not a last refuge for him, but an inspiration. "Yes, the American flag is in my heart, and it has done everything for me."

He was also born to the stage. His parents were vaudeville performers, and from age eight on George's youth was spent traveling the country by train with his family. In 1889, his father, Jerry Cohan, formed an act billed as "The Cohan Mirth Makers — The Celebrated Family of Singers, Dancers and Comedians with their Silver Plated Band and Symphony Orchestra." The "Singers, Dancers and Comedians" were four in number. George and his younger sister, Josephine, did most of the dancing and some of the singing. As for the symphonic accompaniment, that varied from eight instruments to a single piano, depending on the place and the size of the audiences.

In time, "The Four Cohans" became one of the country's most popular vaudeville acts. By his late teens, George was the principal performer as a song-and-dance man, and wrote much of the sketch and song material. People loved the eccentric buck-and-wing dance he created, and it was imitated and used by other dancers to milk applause from the audience. Harrigan and Hart were his admired models when he wrote his first musical comedy in 1901. The show, *The Governor's Son*, was expanded from a vaudeville sketch written for the family act, but lasted only 32 performances. Another sketch, *Running for Office*, was turned into a full-length show, and was also a failure.

Ambitious, aggressive, abrasive, the young man was not easily deterred. His first two shows were produced at small downtown theatres. Now he wanted to move to larger theatres uptown. The idea for his next show came to him when he read of the exploits of an American jockey, Tod Sloan, who rode a royal mount in the 1903 English Derby. As Johnny Jones, Sloan's fictional counterpart, Cohan, at five feet six and 135 pounds, had a role for which he was physically suited.

For this more ambitious musical he needed the financial help of a partner, and he turned to a theatrical producer, Sam H. Harris. Each had an abiding love for the theatre. Harris had come up the hard way; he had been a newsboy, delivery man, cough-drop salesman, and manager of a prizefighter.

"The Four Cohans" take the stage. Left to right: George, Josie, Jerry, and Helen.

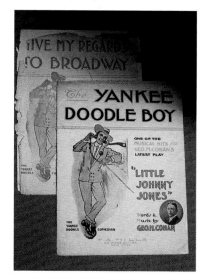

Two American song classics from *Little Johnny Jones* (1904).

41

COHAN AND CRITICS

When George M. Cohan's *Little Johnny Jones* opened in November 1904, many critics were slow in appreciating the breakthrough from operetta convention, and the freer American qualities it represented. Closest to the mark was the critic for the *Daily News*, who saw the show as "a new departure in musical comedy . . . with the customary insanity eliminated. The actors speak and move like really and truly human beings, and while there is no pretense at seriousness, there is no lapse into horse play or imbecility in straining after fun." Other critics complained, though, that the show was more "musical melodrama than musical comedy," and thought unseemly his use of contemporary expressions in his dialogue.

Cohan's singing, derived from his vaudeville style, was not universally admired. One critic thought he showed "divine courage in attempting to sing!" Another gave a derisive description: "With the very first note of the orchestra, Mr. Cohan sends his eyes up to heaven, lowers one side of his mouth almost to the ground, and then sings — through his nose!" The mixed and mixed-up notices shortened the first run of *Little Johnny Jones*, but Cohan brought it back the next year for a warmer and much longer welcome.

Harris, though, did not have enough money to produce the show, which came as a surprise to Cohan.

"When Sam and I went into business together," he later wrote, "I naturally thought he had a lot of money. We didn't talk about that until we were in the middle of rehearsal . . . when he told me he was broke. He seemed as much surprised as I was, when I told him I was broke, too. And the members of the company were very much surprised when they found out we were both broke!"

The surprise must have been considerable, since there were a hundred people in the company. Nevertheless, the necessary money was somehow found and *Little Johnny Jones* had its out-of-town premiere in Hartford, Connecticut. It electrified the audience.

In the first act, Cohan, as the brash, irrepressible jockey in England, surrounded by a double sextet of girls, describes himself:

> I'm the kid that's all the candy,
> I'm a Yankee Doodle Dandy.
> I'm glad I am.

To which the girls agree in chorus: "So's Uncle Sam."

Thus was the patriotic note struck resoundingly in the American musical. The song contained Cohan's favorite biographical note, too:

> I'm a Yankee Doodle Dandy,
> A Yankee Doodle do or die,
> A real live nephew of my Uncle Sam
> Born on the Fourth of July.

Cohan came at just the right moment. No one, wrote Oscar

Hammerstein II, was more representative of his time. "The whole nation was confident of its superiority, its moral virtue, its happy isolation from the intrigues of the old country, from which many of our fathers and grandfathers had migrated."

The song also had the virtue of being well integrated into the plot, of which there was doubtless too much. Most of it was set in England, which the American characters hold inferior to the good old U.S.A. When one American is asked: "What makes the Americans so proud of their country?," the answer is: "Other countries."

Johnny resists a villain's effort to make him throw the Derby, and when he loses anyway, he is falsely accused of doing it deliberately. During the course of the action, an amusingly drunken detective meanders about making quips; Johnny's fiancée, Goldie Gates (from San Francisco, of course) disguises herself both as a Parisian midinette and an English lord (!) and Johnny's reputation is at stake until the third act, which travels all the way to San Francisco's Chinatown to set things right.

With its twenty musical numbers,

Scene from *Little Johnny Jones* (1904).

the show ran almost five hours. But Cohan had a way of avoiding boredom. He was impatient with what he regarded as the indolent ways of operetta, and defined the basic element in his own shows as "Speed, speed, speed. Perpetual motion." A reviewer noted this. "One situation follows another with such rapidity," he wrote, "that the spectators barely have time to draw their breath between laughs."

Another of his contributions to the musical was contemporary slang. A girl was a "bird," to "soak" was to hit; "getting loaded" was getting drunk. His dialogue struck 1904 audiences as both fresh and hilarious, although maybe one had to be there to appreciate it. A sample:

WAITER: Do you feel like a cup of tea, sir?
CUSTOMER: No, I don't feel like a cup of tea.
　　Do I look like a cup of tea?

　　Or:

— Shall I call you a hansom, sir?
— Call me anything you like.

The show had its greatest moments at the close of the second act. Johnny is at the pier in Southampton, ready to board a liner for home. His pal, the detective, tells him he feels sure he can find evidence to clear him aboard the ship and there is no reason for him to leave. On finding the evidence he'll fire a rocket from the ship. So Johnny stays, and sadly sings a song that is probably close to immortal:

　　Give my regards to Broadway,
　　Remember me to Herald Square.
　　Tell all the gang at Forty-second Street
　　That I will soon be there . . .

The stage darkens, and as Johnny walks away, the ship in miniature, its lights twinkling, appears against the ocean backdrop, moving in the harbor. Then, after a tension-filled interval, a white rocket blazes up from the ship. Johnny returns to sing his regards to Broadway in a much happier frame of mind, needless to say to tumultuous applause.

A good many of the New York critics were not overly impressed, however, and the show lasted only 52 performances at the Liberty Theatre. Cohan, though, was determined to make it a hit, and he took it out on the road to improve and hone it. His faith was justified, and the following year he brought it back to Broadway for two long runs.

A. L. Erlanger, a leading theatrical producer of the time, was impressed by the lively spirit of *Little Johnny Jones* and asked Cohan if he could write a play without a flag in it. Cohan's answer was *Forty-five Minutes from Broadway*, the idea for which came when a friend remarked that his little town, New Rochelle, was a peaceful retreat, although only three-quarters of an hour by train from New York. Cohan built his story around a missing will, a maid who had hoped to inherit her crotchety employer's wealth, and a nice young relative who would inherit the estate unless a will is found. Mary is the maid's name, and she was played by the popular burlesque comedienne Fay Templeton. Another comic part was a tough but sentimental Broadwayite played by Victor Moore, who went on to enduring popularity. The show opened in New York on New Year's

Fay Templeton with Victor Moore in *Forty-five Minutes from Broadway* (1906).

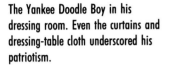
The Yankee Doodle Boy in his dressing room. Even the curtains and dressing-table cloth underscored his patriotism.

Day of 1906 and was successful both there and on the road. From it came the long-lasting title number, and "Mary's a Grand Old Name."

Cohan wasted little time in moving from the quiet streets of New Rochelle to Washington, D.C., for a story revolving around the title character of his next musical, an excessively patriotic young man who, in his zeal, renames himself George Washington, Jr. One of the show's high moments was a song about the American flag, first called "You're a Grand Old Rag." Cohan had run into a veteran of the Civil War who referred to it that way. Some superpatriots immediately objected to the description, and Cohan quickly changed "rag" to "flag."

His success, along with his combative manner, caused a critic to call him "a youthful egotist." The charge bothered him enough for him to reply in the house organ he put out with Sam H. Harris about their productions. "For the benefit of some damned fools I've met," he wrote, "let me say that my success comes from the fact that I know and have studied the business in which I manage to knock out a very good livelihood. I write my own songs because I write better songs than anyone else I know of. I write my own plays because I have not yet read or seen plays from the pens of others that seem as good as the plays I write. . . ."

No egotism there, obviously.

To Fannie Fair, a journalist with a musical comedy name, we owe this 1905 portrait:

Picture to yourself a very thin young man with a thin, shrewd face, self-contained, emotionless. Mr. George M. Cohan has an impersonal gaze, a modest manner, and the direct simplicity which belongs to men who are too keen to be bombastic.

Was there ever such a voice? Fearful and fascinating. All the whine of the street, the taunt of the disillusioned gamin is in it. It is so bad that one wonders.

Egotist or no, Cohan was the dominant showman — as actor, writer, composer, and producer — of his generation. The musicals he put on with Sam H. Harris for more than a decade were filled with exuberance and vitality and were deservedly popular. As Brooks Atkinson said about him: "Cohan's songs, both words and music, were sublimations of the mood of their day. They said what millions of people would have said if they had Cohan's talent."

In the summer of 1907, *Theatre Magazine*, forecasting the coming season, stated that Broadway would be cool to imported shows that reflected foreign life. True, the vogue for Viennese comic opera had declined almost to the vanishing point. But what the writer had apparently not noticed was that just about everyone in New York was playing or whistling the music of a Viennese operetta that was due to open that very same season. In fact, because of the lack of copyright, sheet music of "The Merry Widow Waltz" was being sold on sidewalks for five cents a copy. And when advance tickets went on sale for *The Merry Widow*, for five weeks long queues stretched down 42nd Street from the New Amsterdam Theatre.

The Merry Widow (Die lüstige Witwe) had been all the rage in Europe since its Vienna premiere on December 30, 1905. Had it not been for the lack of popularity of operetta here, even those of Johann Strauss, Jr., Colonel Henry W. Savage, who picked up the American production rights, would have brought it over sooner. For, when he saw it in Vienna, he was altogether taken by what he called "its essence of youthfulness." But would it translate well into English?

At age thirty-five, Franz Lehar was a relatively unknown violinist and bandmaster when, so the story goes, he watched thirteen-year-old Elizabeth Stein skating on the Prater rink where the band played. He wrote a waltz tune for her, to which she skated daily. Her father

happened to be Paul Stein, a well-known Viennese librettist. He and a lyricist, Victor Leon, were looking for a composer for an operetta, based on an old French comedy to which they were giving a modern twist. Through his daughter, Stein met Lehar and offered him the job of composing the score. Another story — probably with more substance — has it that the protagonist Danilo was based on the Parisian playboy prince of Montenegro, whose antics were causing quite a stir on the Continent. In the original version, Danilo is a count, but in the English version that enchanted London he became a prince. The translator also changed his small, nearly bankrupt Balkan country, Pontevidrinia, to Marsovia, and the delightful and rich widow, Hanna Glawari, to Sonya.

The lovely melodies of *The Merry Widow* were contained in a book that had charm in its own right. The story revolves around a scheme of the Marsovian ambassador to Paris to solve his country's financial problems by promoting a romance and marriage between the dashing Prince Danilo and the merry young widow of a banker. It turns out, though, that Danilo and Sonya had once been lovers, but he had been unable to marry her because his uncle would have disowned him. When they meet again, though love-stricken, the playboy prince still won't marry her, this time because she is so rich. Sonya now tells him she'll lose all her money if she remarries. This relieves him greatly, but, after he has proposed, Sonya has a surprise for him: her late husband's will stipulates that all her money will belong to her new husband. They, and

Donald Brian and Ethel Jackson in the New York production of *The Merry Widow* (1907).

Sheet music from *The Merry Widow* (1907).

presumably Marsovia, will live happily ever after.

The Merry Widow came at a time when, at least on the surface, middle Europe was enjoying a long peace, and when Paris was assumed to be the capital of the rich and favored. The plush restaurant Maxim's was a sort of headquarters where monarchs dallied with courtesans: the Clo-Clos, Zo-Zos, Fi-Fis, and Lo-Los of Lehar's engaging song. Here was a gorgeous musical confection that had glamour, romance, and a touch of naughtiness. When, in June of 1907, Savage saw *The Merry Widow* become an immediate smash in London, he brought it to America. Before long, some one hundred companies were playing it around the world.

Savage cast a little-known musical comedy soprano, Ethel Jackson, as Sonya, and persuaded George M. Cohan to release his handsome leading man, Donald Brian, for Danilo. He sent Ethel

Jackson to Paris to choose her costumes, and for one of them she spent the huge amount of four hundred dollars.

The standing-room-only opening night in New York was an event. Ticket scalpers were so numerous that Klaw and Erlanger, the owners of the New Amsterdam, hired a dozen guards to shoo them out of the lobby.

"It was one of the most brilliant audiences to attend a New York first night in years," Richard Aldrich reported the next morning in the *Times*. "The applause was almost terrifying in its intensity." And most so during the rapturous waltz scene at the conclusion of the second act. Danilo and Sonya moved slowly at first, to the strains of a melody hinted at throughout, then went

faster and faster into a whirl about the stage. The intimacy, the freedom of the movements, affected dance in musicals thereafter.

Fashion was affected, too, by a Merry Widow craze. There was a Merry Widow hat based on the one worn by Ethel Jackson — a creation topped by a bird of paradise, with a rose under the brim. There were Merry Widow gloves, corsets, shoes, candies, even cigars. Broadway marquees glittered with great names that season: Ethel Barrymore, Maude Adams, Henry Miller, Otis Skinner, the winsome Billie Burke, but it was Ethel Jackson who was the toast of Rector's, Shanley's, and Churchill's. She was driven to the theatre each night in her own horse-drawn brougham by a

Commemorative cigarette case given to Franz Lehar on the occasion of the four hundredth worldwide performance of *The Merry Widow*.

Orville Harrold, Emma Trentini,
Maria Duchene, and Edward
Martindell singing "Live for Today"
from *Naughty Marietta* (1910).

uniformed coachman, and attended by a red-and-gold-jacketed footman. Donald Brian became both a matinee and evening idol. Mrs. W. K. Vanderbilt welcomed him into Society when she invited him to a large tea dance at which debutantes battled for a chance to waltz with him.

For the next half-dozen years, Viennese operettas were the reigning musical fashion on Broadway. In quick succession came *A Waltz Dream*, composed by Oskar Straus, a Viennese rival of Lehar (who was also turning them out en masse), *The Chocolate Soldier*, also by Straus, *The Dollar Princess* (Leo Fall), followed by *The Balkan Princess* and other Princesses, not to mention *The Midnight Girl*, *The Sunshine Girl*, and *The Pink Lady*.

The best of the home-grown operettas came in November 1910, with Victor Herbert's *Naughty Marietta*, destined to become a classic of the operetta form. Herbert wanted and was encouraged to compose a grand opera on an American theme, and had contracted with Oscar Hammerstein, the famous

and colorful opera and theatre impresario, to write one for presentation at the latter's Manhattan Opera House. Hammerstein, a lover of opera, had built his house, and engaged a company to inhabit it in 1906, in direct conflict with the well-established Metropolitan Opera. For four years, a highly newsworthy battle for dominance ensued between Hammerstein and the management of the Metropolitan. The Manhattan Opera Company won the artistic battle, but the Metropolitan, with its far greater resources, won the financial; Hammerstein was bought out, with the proviso that he would not produce opera for the next ten years.

The settlement left Herbert without a place for his opera (*Natoma*) and it was shelved temporarily. But Hammerstein was not barred from presenting operetta, and he quickly contracted with Herbert for a comic opera to be called *Little Paris*. Somehow, a change came while Herbert was at work with the librettist, Rida Johnson Young, and *Naughty Marietta* came out instead. It came to New York after a brief tour — playing at the New York Theatre, which had once been owned by Hammerstein and which he was now forced to rent.

Hammerstein had some fine singers available to him from his defunct opera company, and the vocal and orchestral forces were superior to those of other operettas of the day. The libretto, for all its sentimentality, had verve and dash, and Herbert's music was acclaimed as the best by any American composer.

Acclaimed, too, in the title role was Emma Trentini, a diminutive Italian with a temperament far greater than her size. Perhaps Marietta was to have been French during the writing of the story, and it may well have been the casting of Trentini that changed her to an Italian contessa who has avoided an unhappy forced marriage by fleeing to eighteenth-century Louisiana.

There she meets handsome Captain Dick of the Rangers, who arrives on stage booming out his signature song, "Tramp! Tramp! Tramp!" Before true love can reach its fulfillment, several of Herbert's finest songs are heard. They have continued to be heard ever after on stage, in movies, and in recordings — notably "I'm Falling in Love with Someone," " 'Neath the Southern Moon," "Italian Street Song," and, of course, "Ah! Sweet Mystery of Life."

The melody of the latter song has haunted Marietta's dreams so compulsively that she won't marry anyone who can't finish the tune. Dick indeed manages to do so, and finds suitable words for it, too, in the operetta's finale. Contractual commitments confined the run to 136 performances, after which it went on a successful tour.

Trentini had been discovered by Hammerstein in a Milan cabaret in 1906 while he was searching out singers for his Manhattan Opera. It was his son Arthur who persuaded Oscar that the vivacious little singer was better suited to operetta. Before resuming the tour in the fall of 1911, Trentini, now a full-fledged star, returned to Italy for a summer vacation, during which she forgot most of the English she had learned. On her return she became exceedingly eccentric. She would refuse to give encores, or to sing whole numbers, and there were

times when her managers had to go to her hotel to persuade her to come to the theatre.

She thus contributed greatly — and justifiably so — to popular lore about the magnificent egos of prima donnas. "I surely did have a terrible time with this woman," one of her managers wrote rather pathetically.

She also managed to insult Herbert, the man who had most contributed to her stardom. A gala anniversary performance of *Marietta* was held in the spring of 1912, in honor of the twenty-fifth anniversary of Hammerstein's theatre-building career. Herbert himself came to conduct. All

Oscar Hammerstein.

went well until Trentini sang the "Italian Street Song," which was applauded vociferously. Herbert thereupon gave her a signal for an encore, but all she would do was bow to the audience. Herbert signaled her again and raised his baton for the orchestra to begin. Trentini simply gave him a haughty look and walked off the stage. Herbert was so angry and mortified that he handed the baton to the assistant conductor and left the orchestra pit, refusing to return. Moreover, he refused to write the music for her next show.

Was Trentini suitably punished for her churlish behavior? Not at all. She quickly found her way into Rudolf Friml's melodious *The Firefly* and scored another hit.

The same year *The Merry Widow* arrived to create the long-lasting operetta wave, another show of a very different kind opened that had signal consequences for Broadway's musical theatre: Florenz Ziegfeld's *Follies of 1907* (his name was not yet attached to the title). In view of the later lavishness of the *Ziegfeld Follies*, this first of the breed was relatively unpretentious. Bankrolled by the monopolistic theatre owners Klaw and Erlanger for a mere $13,000, it opened as a summer attraction (July 8, 1907) at a small garden stage atop the New York Theatre, renamed temporarily by Ziegfeld the Jardin de Paris.

As a revue, the *Follies* bore some resemblance to the *Folies-Bergère* (and Ziegfeld had certainly taken notice of that lively perennial as had his common-law wife, the beauteous Anna Held), but the name came rather from a column

called "Follies of the Day," written by one of Ziegfeld's librettists, Harry B. Smith. Why not "Follies of the Year"? was Smith's suggestion for the show. Ziegfeld was superstitious; he liked the titles of his shows to have exactly thirteen letters. In this case he settled for thirteen letters and numerals.

Ziegfeld at this time was in his fortieth year. The son of Dr. Florenz Ziegfeld, president of the Chicago Musical College, his first contact with show business was the appearance of Buffalo Bill and Annie Oakley in 1883, which impressed him mightily. Ten years later, his father was appointed musical director for the city's Columbian Exposition. The junior Ziegfeld persuaded his father to send him to Europe for performers, and, with the extravagance that later marked his career, he brought back a military band from Hamburg, several French and Russian acrobats and jugglers, and a strange English dancer, Maggie Potts, who called herself Cyrene. The show was a disaster, but he achieved his first coup when he brought from New York "The Great Sandow," a man with remarkable muscles.

He moved on to New York, where his first producing venture was a revival of a Charles Hoyt musical, *A Parlor Match*. For this he felt it necessary to seek new faces in Europe. In London, at the Palace Theatre, Ziegfeld saw a dark-haired beauty, Anna Held, and decided he wanted her not only for the show but himself.

There was a hindrance: she was already married and had a child. But she came to New York and made a brief

Playbill for the *Follies of 1907*.

(opposite) The young Florenz Ziegfeld.

SANDOW, THE GREAT

Ziegfeld first revealed his showman's instinct and flair for publicity when he presented the strong man known as "The Great Sandow" at the Chicago Columbian Exposition. The twenty-three-year-old Sandow had previously appeared in New York at the Casino Theatre with little success, though his act attracted some notice. His abdominal muscles, according to one account, "produce a wonderful checkerboard arrangement of fibres, the existence of which modern anatomists deny, though plainly visible at a distance of thirty feet."

Wearing silk trunks, he presented a series of "art poses" and then performed some awesome feats of strength, such as allowing a man to sit, suspended, on the palm of his hand. He would raise a huge dumbbell, then, putting it down, would reveal that each of the balls held a man. His finale was to have three horses walk across a plank laid atop his chest. In Chicago, Ziegfeld reaped publicity by having prominent people come backstage and feel the marvelous muscles. (The socially prominent Mrs. Potter Palmer ran her fingers over Sandow's huge chest and confessed to having been "thrilled to the spine.")

When the fair closed, Ziegfeld took Sandow on tour around the country. In San Francisco, Ziegfeld arranged a fight between Sandow and a lion. The ticket sale was brisk, but the fight was a flop. The lion had been "tranquilized" earlier by some blows to the nose, and on reaching the ring just lay down and went to sleep. Nevertheless, Ziegfeld and Sandow collected eighteen thousand dollars.

appearance as a beguiling ghost in *A Parlor Match*. The *Times* critic thought her more successful as a spectacle than a singer. She had a sweet voice, he admitted, but he wasn't sure about her performing abilities. As a sight to see, however, she was something else: "Her eyes are long, narrow, and heavily circled; her nose is straight; her mouth perfect; and, as for her chin, people might go some ways to see it without regretting the experience." The reference to her chin is a bit puzzling; photographs don't show it to be particularly unusual.

She was about twenty-three when Ziegfeld met her, and there was already an element of mystery about her. Born in Paris of Polish-Jewish parents, she claimed that when she was only eight she sang for *sous* on the streets of Montmartre. An orphan at twelve, she went to London, where she became a chorus girl. By the time she was fifteen, she was a soloist in Amsterdam, and she appeared in revues in several countries. In Paris music halls, she was known for her singing of:

Won't you come and play wiz me
As I have such a nice little way with me.

The implications, in view of her exquisite little figure, were not very obscure, and Ziegfeld was not averse to playing up this aspect of her personality. When he presented her in a second show, *Papa's Wife*, she titillated audiences with a song, "I Just Can't Make My Eyes Behave."

Ziegfeld would gladly have married her if it were possible, but Anna Held's husband, a Catholic, had refused

her a divorce. As it was, they lived together in what was eventually judged to be a common-law marriage. He lost little time in building her career, and was even more inventive than he had been with "The Great Sandow." Anna Held was his willing accomplice. Automobiles had appeared, and she claimed to be one of the fastest woman drivers alive. In Europe, she boasted, she had driven ninety miles in less than three and a half hours. She challenged any woman to beat her in a race from New York to Philadelphia. There were no takers, Ziegfeld said.

He was on his way to becoming a master publicist as well as a master showman. Held made carefully planned headlines when she supposedly stopped a runaway horse while riding her bicycle. The milk bath she was purported to take every morning in their hotel suite was also grist for his publicity mill: Ziegfeld let it be known that forty gallons of milk were delivered to her every day; and he invited a group of reporters to view her up to her neck in her milk-filled bath. "The milk she preserve zee creamy complexion," Anna told them.

The sensational news traveled through the country and to Europe as well. Ziegfeld added fuel to the liquid story. He declared that his dairyman was delivering sour milk and refused to pay the bill. The dairyman was persuaded to sue, with more resultant newspaper space. Then a French beauty threatened to sue Ziegfeld because she claimed he had stolen his milk-dip idea from her own well-publicized habit. For a time, milk sold in larger quantities than normal, as fashionable women attempted

Anna Held and Florenz Ziegfeld.

to emulate Anna Held's creamy complexion.

It was she who persuaded Ziegfeld to try a revue along the lines of the *Folies-Bergère*. By this time he had mounted several shows for her, in which she appeared gorgeously gowned and accompanied by a dozen or more American beauties. She had no fear of the competition. In one of these, *The Little Duchess* (1901), a French importation, she appeared in a bathing suit, but without causing any undue alarm. More was caused, though, when a dozen chorines unrolled their stockings in a boudoir scene. No wonder the shows were regarded as scandalous, and, while on tour, were sometimes threatened with censorship.

Things were almost out of hand in 1906 when Ziegfeld presented her in *The Parisian Model*. One of the scenes took place in an artist's studio. Several chorus girl "models" entered wearing long cloaks which, after stepping behind easels, they removed, revealing bare shoulders and legs. More inventiveness

came when the girls, wearing bells on their ankles, reclined on a revolving stage and kicked their legs in a shimmer of silvery sound. Hollywood would eventually borrow such ideas for its own musicals.

But it was always Anna who held center stage, in gowns designed for her that were sometimes said to have cost thousands. In one of her numbers in *The Parisian Model*, she sang six choruses and wore a different gown for each. For a later show, *Miss Innocence*, one of her gowns was designed in Paris and encrusted with genuine diamonds.

She did not appear in *Follies of 1907*, perhaps because the paucity of the budget did not allow for her accustomed extravagance. Instead, there were fifty pretty chorines who were called the "Anna Held" girls. One of these, Annabelle Whitford, was featured in stockings and bloomers as a "Gibson Girl Bathing Beauty," and reaped some Ziegfeld-sponsored publicity. Since these were follies of the day, the battle of the opera impresarios — Oscar Hammerstein, and Heinrich Conrad of

Nora Bayes, one of the stars of the *Follies of 1908*.

Scene from the *Follies of 1907*.

the Metropolitan — was satirized by a staged duel with swords, with the company joining in. The great tenor Caruso had recently been accused of pinching a woman in an unseemly manner in the monkey house of the Central Park Zoo. In the *Follies* he was put on trial and convicted.

Sheet music for "Shine on, Harvest Moon."

Musical numbers had topical references, too. In "If a Table at Rector's Could Talk," Nat Willis sang of the kind of talk that supposedly occurred over dinner tables at the fashionable restaurant. A comedian, Dave Lewis, sang "I Oughtn't to Auto Anymore." Critics, on the whole, applauded, one saying, "The action of the *Follies* is so fast that a state of delirious acquiesence is induced." The show ran through the summer, and then moved to the Liberty Theatre, and to runs in Baltimore and Washington. All told, the profits came to a smart $120,000 (equivalent to several million dollars today).

The *Follies* returned in 1908 to the Jardin de Paris. This time Ziegfeld's name was on the marquee, but it was not until three years later that he actually added his name to the title. The 1908 edition gave Adam and Eve in their garden an opportunity to see the results of the civilization they had inaugurated — a view, for instance, of a tunnel being dug beneath the Hudson River. The Anna Held girls were back and outfitted as taxicabs, which is to say that their otherwise skimpy outfits included taxi meters on their shoulders, red tin flags, signs reading "for hire," and headlamps that beamed out to the audience. They also paraded as "The Merry Widows of All Nations," a tribute to the operetta

Mae Murray in the *Follies of 1908.*

that was charming much of the nation.

The comedienne Nora Bayes introduced a song she wrote with her husband called "Shine On, Harvest Moon," thus providing ammunition for numberless hayrides and countless barbershop quartets. Ziegfeld presented his newest beauty in the person of Mae Murray, who impersonated Nell Brinkley, a popular magazine cover girl.

Soon the *Follies*, now established as an annual affair, became a showcase for young talent and a vehicle to stardom. In the 1909 version, Ziegfeld presented the Most Beautiful Woman in the World: Lillian Lorraine, who by contemporary accounts merited the title. Born poor in San Francisco in 1890, she was promoted by Ziegfeld into a dazzling, albeit brief, career. In the 1908 *Follies* she made a most unusual appearance. The audience saw her high above their heads, seated in a little biplane, scattering roses, while onstage chorines, costumed as airplanes, sang "Up, Up, in My Aeroplane." Lorraine also sang a song, "Nothing But a Bubble," while partly immersed in a pool of soap bubbles, and, later in the run, a long-lasting song, "By the Light of the Silvery Moon."

To augment her glamorous image, Lorraine wore diamonds and ermines onstage and off. How she accumulated them only she knew. Ziegfeld was so fascinated by her that he provided her a suite in the Ansonia, the same hotel in which he and Anna Held lived. Anna bore with the competition for a while, though complaining plaintively to members of the press that her husband now seldom spoke to her. Finally, in 1912, she filed for divorce.

Lorraine lived recklessly. Her life was a round of parties, a good many of them wild, at which she sometimes undraped herself entirely. She had a penchant for fostering scandal, something as innocuous as being the first to wear an ankle bracelet on Broadway, and, more serious, causing a quarrel between an airman and a New York socialite over the favors she dispensed. The socialite shot and killed the airman. She married, divorced, remarried, and divorced again. She drank herself into alcoholism, went bankrupt, had to sell her jewel collection, and while drunk one night set fire to her boardinghouse room, nearly killing herself. Not for nothing, then, was she known as Broadway's "broken butterfly."

But meanwhile she flourished in the *Follies.* In the 1910 edition she soared on a swing singing "Swing Me High, Swing Me Low"; in 1911 she shared the beauty spotlight with Vera Maxwell, who was billed by Ziegfeld as "The Spirit of the Follies." However, the 1910 version was historic for quite another reason — two, in fact — for this was the year that Bert Williams and Fanny Brice made their first appearances in the show and gave it two of its brightest and longest-lasting stars.

Williams was already famous for his vaudeville act with George Walker, and for their appearances together in a series of Negro musicals. After Walker died in 1909, Ziegfeld took the bold step of employing Williams in the *Follies* — bold because other than in vaudeville, black performers had never appeared with whites in a major Broadway musical.

Lillian Lorraine in the *Follies of 1909.*

Egbert Austin Williams was born in the West Indies in 1876. His grandfather had been a Danish consul who married a woman of mixed Spanish and African descent. When Bert was a small boy, his father moved the family to California, where, after high school, Bert studied civil engineering for a time. His talent for singing and comedy led him to join a group of boys and tour California, after which he appeared in minstrel shows and, later, with George Walker in a popular vaudeville act.

He was a remarkably gifted pantomimist, and sang his songs in a way that mingled humor, pathos, and poignance. The most famous of these, "Nobody," was written by Will Marion Cook, with lyrics by Alex Rogers. He sang, with just the right lugubrious touch, "I ain't never done nothin' to nobody . . . I ain't never got nothin' from nobody . . . No time."

A routine performed mostly in pantomime with Leon Errol — a rubber-legged comedian and dancer Ziegfeld introduced in the 1911 show — was probably the most hilarious of that season, or at least funny enough to be recounted in theatre histories. It had Williams as a Grand Central Station redcap, and Errol as a nervous tourist, made more so because the station is in a mess of subway construction. Errol kept falling from the girders into space, and Williams kept pulling him up until, at last, Williams became so dissatisfied with his measly five-cent tip that he stopped saving him.

Fanny Brice was just nineteen when she came into the *Follies*. Born on New York's Lower East Side in 1891 to saloon-keeper parents, she moved first to Newark, then to Brooklyn, where at age thirteen she won an amateur-night contest. At sixteen she was hired for the chorus of a George M. Cohan musical, but was quickly fired. She could sing, but as a dancer was a better clown, which she soon proved in burlesque. It was Irving Berlin (then Israel Baline) who provided her with a needed specialty number, "Sadie Salome, Come Home."

As she recalled in a memoir, "Irving took me into a back room, played a ragtime song, and sang it in a Jewish accent. I had never had any idea of doing a song with a Jewish accent, didn't even understand Jewish. But I thought, if that's the way Irving sings it, that's the way I'll sing it." Ziegfeld took in a performance, and quickly hired her for the *Follies* at what was for her a generous seventy-five dollars a week.

Fanny Brice, an elegant woman offstage and a raucous comic in performance.

Bert Williams and company in the *Follies of 1910*.

She was one among many in the 1910 *Follies*, and she almost blew her first great opportunity. Anxious to shine, she persuaded two black songwriters, Joe Jordan and Will Marion Cook, to come up with a number for her, which she sang at a rehearsal attended by A. L. (Abe) Erlanger, the show's backer. What she sang was "Lovey Joe," a "coon song" as they were called. When she sang the line "I jes' hollers for mo'," Erlanger wouldn't have what sounded to him like burlesque, and commanded her to sing it unaccented. She refused, and he ordered her out of the show.

Ziegfeld, though, told her to stay, and keep out of Erlanger's way. On opening night, she sang "Lovey Joe," with the song's proper accent, and stopped the show. The audience demanded twelve encores. Erlanger was there and wisely did not enforce his earlier ban. She had another show-stopper in "Goodby, Becky Cohen" provided her by Irving Berlin, and sung in a Jewish dialect.

It was Brice's claim throughout her career that there was a communication between her and the audience, a kind of secret both understood. She had skinny, though

reasonably shapely legs, but they were not typical showgirl legs. So, when she lifted her skirts and did her version of a can-can, the audience howled. When this happened, Fanny made the most of it.

"I never worked out any business ahead of time," she would say later. "It would only happen when I hit that audience, because they speak so much louder than my mind. They would tell me what they wanted." After that, she was in control.

In 1913, the *Follies* moved to the New Amsterdam Theatre, one of the most magnificent of its day. It had opened in 1906, and played host to *The Merry Widow*. Its Art Nouveau decor blended sculpture, painting, and architecture; its predominant colors were delicate shades of red, green, and gold. The stage and its equipment allowed for spectacular effects, and Ziegfeld began to take advantage of the possibilities. With Anna Held gone from his life, the dancing and singing chorus became "The Ziegfeld Girls," and their numbers increased to seventy-five. A new *Follies* star, Ann Pennington, emerged. An important song contributor was Gene Buck, who became a longtime assistant to Ziegfeld. Leon Errol, while holding up his errant pants, attempted to teach the entire cast a dance called "The Turkish Trot," based supposedly on a new ballroom craze, the turkey trot. The more sober finale was a salute to the opening of the Panama Canal.

The 1914 premiere took place on June 1. As though anticipating the Great War that would break out that summer, the entire cast gave a rousing rendition of "The Star-Spangled Banner."

Ann Pennington, who starred in the *Ziegfeld Follies of 1913*.

By the time Irving Berlin was twenty-five, he was well on his way to becoming America's most popular songwriter. Born in Russia the youngest of eight children, he came to the United States at age four, to a tenement on New York's Lower East Side. He was eight when his father, a rabbi and cantor, died, and the little boy left school after only two years to help earn money for the family. In Horatio Alger fashion, he had a newspaper route, and sang on street corners for pennies. At fourteen he left home with the idea of making his fortune. He sang in saloons for tips, and at one point guided a blind beggar about the streets of the Bowery, sharing the pennies thrown at them. He slept on park benches or, when he had the money, in cheap lodging houses. He became a singing waiter in the Pelham Cafe, a Bowery hangout. Joe McCarthy, who eventually wrote the lyrics to "Alice Blue Gown," worked there, as did George Weitz, a hoofer who later became the George White of the *Scandals*. "Izzy Baline" was fired for falling asleep at the cash register, so he moved uptown to the Union Square Saloon, where he served drinks. In 1907, he wrote his first song, "Marie from Sunny Italy," with music by a piano player at the saloon. The typographer for the sheet music got his name wrong: it came out as I. Berlin, which Israel preferred to Baline. Later he changed his first name to Irving. He was musically illiterate, but when a publisher liked his words to a song and asked for the music, he picked it out himself on the black keys. He never did learn to transpose keys, and to go from one key to another he used a sliding keyboard he had purchased for a hundred dollars.

In 1908, his song "Dear Little Girl" was heard in a show called "The Boys and Betty," and in 1909 his "Sadie Salome" (words only) became a hit with the help of Fanny Brice. One day in 1911, "out of the air," as he said, he plucked a tune which he wrote in eighteen minutes: "Alexander's Ragtime Band." Introduced in a show called "The Merry Whirl," it sold more than a million and a half sheet-music copies. It was almost inevitable, after his success as a songwriter and contributor to musical revues, that Berlin would be invited to provide a complete score for a musical. Charles Dillingham, a noted producer

who had been a drama critic and a press agent for Charles Frohman, came to Berlin in 1914 for *Watch Your Step*. The librettist was the prolific Harry B. Smith, whose concoction of a story was so thin that when crediting himself he labeled it "Plot (if any)." It had to do with a millionaire's will that specified his two-million-dollar fortune would go to a relative who could prove he or she had never been in love. Naturally, the complications made this difficult, but also provided excuses for some lively and graceful dancing by the team of Vernon and Irene Castle, who were then the darlings of the ballroom dance craze then sweeping the country. New dances came along so frequently, it seemed there was a fresh one every week: the fox trot, the maxixe, the grizzly bear, the turkey trot, the tango, and the one-step, to mention only the most popular. Ragtime, with its

The 1911 Irving Berlin song that started the rage for ragtime and opened the door for jazz.

Irving Berlin as a young man.

Telephone, { 5230 } 18th
          { 5231 }
Cable Address, "Markstern"

New York, *Feb 18* 190*8*

Mr *I. Berlin City*

=== "ROYALTY" ACCOUNT ===

WITH

JOS. W. STERN & CO.

PUBLISHERS AND IMPORTERS

34 EAST 21st STREET, NEW YORK

From	To	Number of Copies.	TITLE.	Royalty.	$	c.
190 *Jan* 1908		1 *20*	*Marie From Sunny Italy*	.01	*1*	*20*

Received *from JOS. W. STERN & CO., the sum of* *One 20/100* *Dollars ($ 1 20/100)*

in full settlement to date, the foregoing royalty statement having been examined by me and found accurate and correct in all respects.

Feb 18/08

Kindly acknowledge receipt.   *Signed,* *I. Berlin*

Receipt for royalties of $1.20 for sales of twelve copies of "Marie from Sunny Italy," in January of 1908.

Original set design for *Watch Your Step* (1914) by Helen Dryden and Robert McQuinn.

syncopated off-beat, was a prevailing rhythm, and *Watch Your Step*, labeled as a "syncopated show," leaned heavily on the new dances and American rhythms, predominantly those carried up from the South in the black migrations.

For the dance numbers Berlin composed "Show Us How to Do the Fox Trot," and "The Syncopated Walk." He moved easily to ballads such as "A Simple Melody," and for a musical sequence, "Old Operas in a New Way," he set new lyrics and a ragtime beat to arias from *Aïda*, *La Bohème*, *Carmen*, and *Rigoletto*. He, incidentally, paid his respects to ragtime by saying he was not the originator of its modern use. "Ragtime," he said, "is the one distinctive American contribution to the musical materials of

the world." He did say that "I have established the syncopated ballad and proven that the metre can be 'chopped up' to fit the words."

A good deal of the show was reminiscent of vaudeville, and, indeed, vaudeville performers were present in Harry Kelly, whose dog stubbornly refused to do tricks, Frank Tinney, a comedian who liked to go to the footlights and address the audience, and the comic dance team Elizabeth Brice and Charles King.

The show opened on December 9, 1914, at the New Amsterdam and broke the theatre's previous record for box-office receipts. The Castles won all-out raves from the critics. Despite the show's success, the critics had trouble labeling it. Just what was this nearly plotless wonder with its lavish sets, sumptuous costumes, sparkling performers, and its irresistably modern dances and music? Certainly it was fresh, lively, and distinctly in tune with popular taste. The *New York Times* wearily gave its muted blessing: "So many things have been called musical comedies that *Watch Your Step* might as well be called one."

A note: A comedian and juggler, W. C. Fields, was to be in the show, but his scene was cut. Not to worry, though; he was immediately hired by Ziegfeld for his next edition of the *Follies.*

In 1912 a small theatre, unpretentious outside but a jewel box inside, was built on the south side of 39th Street just west of Sixth Avenue. Seating only 299, it was called the Princess, and at first it was to be devoted to one-act plays. These did not attract much of an audience, however, and the policy was quickly changed — this on the advice of Elisabeth Marbury, an important agent who represented actors, playwrights, and composers, among the last-named, Jerome Kern. She suggested to the manager, Ray Comstock, that the house would be perfect for a small-scale musical. No lavish sets or crowds of ornately costumed girls: the concentration would be on the story and a well-integrated musical score.

(opposite)
Oil painting of Irene Castle by Nikol Schattenstein.

(below)
Vernon Castle, who was English born, enlisted in the Canadian army during the First World War. He became a trainer of fighter pilots and was killed in an air crash.

BROADWAY!

LEARNING FROM KERN

The young George Gershwin, while attending an aunt's wedding at the Grand Central Hotel in downtown Manhattan, heard a song being played by the orchestra that so impressed him he asked the leader what it was and who had written it. The song was Jerome Kern's "You're Here and I'm Here" from *The Girl from Utah*. Then he was taken by another song, which turned out to be Kern's "They Didn't Believe Me." Gershwin said later that it was Kern who made him realize that musical comedy music "was made of better material" than most popular music of the day and turned him away from Tin Pan Alley.

Similarly, Richard Rodgers felt he owed a great debt to Kern. As a boy, he saw Kern's *Very Good Eddie* on the subway circuit (the group of theatres that booked shows in the New York boroughs after their Broadway runs) and "was so captivated by the score it made me a Kern worshipper. The sound of a Jerome Kern tune was not ragtime, nor did it have any of the middle European influence of Victor Herbert. It was all his own — the first truly American theatre music — and it pointed the way I wanted to be led."

Guy Bolton and Jerome Kern were commissioned by Comstock and Marbury to revise a ten-year-old British musical, *Mr. Popple of Ippleton*, for American tastes. To save expense, instead of a tryout tour they put on a special performance for an invited audience. It was disastrous. Bolton and Kern were put to work to redo the play entirely, give it an American setting and new characters, a mostly new score, and a new title, *Nobody Home.*

Bolton, born in England of American parents, was thirty, schooled as an architect before he became a playwright. Kern, also thirty, had written songs since his high-school days, and was more theatrically experienced than Bolton. But most of his composing had been done as interpolations in shows assigned to others. Bolton and Kern met in 1914 when they worked together as librettist and composer, respectively, for *Ninety in the Shade*, a show that opened in January of 1915 and closed soon after, when the producers lacked the money to pay the actors.

A contemporary of Irving Berlin, Jerome David Kern had no need to go from rags to riches. He came from a relatively prosperous Jewish family, Bohemian on his mother's side, German on his father's. He was born on East 56th Street near what is now Sutton Place, but was then a neighborhood ringed by breweries. His high-school days were in Newark, where his father moved the family when he took over a large general store. Kern's mother was musical, and encouraged her son's musical bent. By sixteen he was composing for high-school music shows. He never graduated, but

went to Germany for training, then returned to New York for further studies. At nineteen he was working in a music-publishing house, playing the piano at Wanamaker's, and publishing his own songs.

His father had tried to turn him away from something so unproductive as songwriting by employing him in the family business. The store occasionally sold a piano, and Kern's father sent Jerome to a piano warehouse to pick out two for stock. Somehow the younger Kern blundered: when two hundred pianos arrived at the store, it was decided that Jerome could take his own path.

By the time he came to the Princess Theatre he had been called upon so often to add new numbers to shows both in New York and in London that he was described by the *Dramatic Mirror* as "long famous as chief aid to anemic scores." He was also called a "Red Cross Society to imported musical comedy." Apparently he did not mind this role, even when his rescue efforts involved redoing the larger portion of a score, which was the case for *The Girl from Utah*, an import from Britain by Charles Frohman that premiered in New York during the fateful month of August 1914. Kern, often used by Frohman for his shows on both sides of the Atlantic, was asked to provide additional numbers.

His songs, lyrical and graceful, lifted the show into a huge hit. One of these, the magnificent "They Didn't Believe Me," was the reigning song of its year, and rewarded Kern with a large sheet-music sale and an augmented reputation that led to commissions for complete musical scores.

Rehearsals went on day and night while Bolton and Kern wrote and rewrote *Nobody Home*. The plot now had to do with the efforts of a "society dancer," Vernon Popple, to marry the well-born and well-guarded Violet Brinton. The mixture of characters included Violet's snobbish aunt, the aunt's Italian husband, and Vernon's former inamorata, a Broadway star whose apartment, where most of the plot's second act complications take place, is up for sublet. The only other setting is the luxurious Hotel Blitz, known, obviously, as the "Blitz."

The new musical was announced as having a "real story and a real plot, which does not get lost during the course of the entertainment." Thus the critics came to opening night (March 4, 1915) looking for something different. The critic for the *Dramatic Mirror* acknowledged that the songs were "bright and tripping," but he was not otherwise overwhelmed. The *Sun*'s critic, while finding the show entertaining, doubted that Broadway's musical farce was much reformed, and he saw little that "could have been called important from any point of view." Still, *Nobody Home* played 115 performances, enough to convince the producers to try another.

The career of Jerome Kern might have ended shortly thereafter — the loss to American music would have been incalculable — if two months after the opening of *Nobody Home* he had kept a date to travel with Charles Frohman to England. The ship he was booked to sail on was scheduled to depart at noon. Kern, an habitual late sleeper, failed to get up on time, and literally missed the

boat. So the *Lusitania* left without him. It was torpedoed without warning by a German submarine on May 7, 1915; Charles Frohman was one of the many passengers who perished.

Kern went on to do the score for the next Princess show, *Very Good Eddie*, the title of which needs a bit of explanation. In vaudeville, the dummies used by ventriloquists were called "Eddies" — this because an often-used line by the ventriloquist when his dummy scored was, "Very good, Eddie." In the play adopted from a farce entitled *Over Night*, by Philip Batholomae, the hero is one Eddie Kettle, a mild little man married to, and henpecked by, a woman of Amazonian proportions. His name is meant to suggest the idea of a manipulated dummy. An idea of the handling of Eddie's marital relationship can be gained when a steward on the boat says, "Say, boss." Eddie asks, "Are you speaking to me?" The steward replies, "I was speaking to *her*." Another key character is a cute little woman married to a giant of a man. All four manage to get into severe mix-ups during the course of a trip on a Hudson River Dayline excursion boat.

By the end, though, Eddie has managed to tame his recalcitrant wife, and at the curtain's fall, the entire cast shouts with approval, "Very good, Eddie!"

During the show's upstate New York tryouts, it became obvious that it needed more work. Guy Bolton was called in to help Bartholomae with revisions, and the remodeled show opened at the Princess two days before Christmas of 1915. Clever publicity had

The *New York Evening Sun* headline reporting the death of Broadway producer Charles Frohman in the sinking of the *Lusitania*.

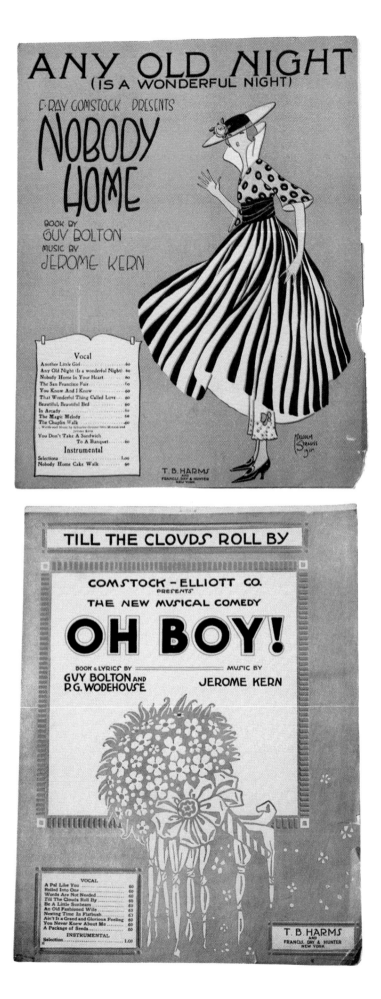

64

clearly given the show a cachet, for the opening-night audience was sprinkled with Astors, Pulitzers, and Vanderbilts. Also in the audience was the English writer P. G. Wodehouse, whom Kern introduced to Bolton. It turned out to be a felicitous meeting.

The show was greeted warmly and became a hit, playing through the spring of 1916 and then moving to a larger theatre, the Casino. Out of it came another Jerome Kern classic, "Babes in the Wood." But the show's important influence came from its "book," with its plot plausibility, its comedy created by recognizable characters, and songs that fitted smoothly into the plot context.

Pelham Grenville Wodehouse joined Bolton and Kern for later Princess shows, and his presence was discernible in the wittier lines and lyrics than the predecessors had. He was English born (1881), and after avoiding a career in finance, became a newspaperman, drama critic, and novelist. He also wrote lyrics for some of Frohman's London musicals, and it was on one of these that he had met Kern.

The triumvirate's first effort was *Have a Heart*, built around a couple's attempt to save their marriage by going on a second honeymoon. The Princess Theatre being booked, it opened at the Liberty. Although it was regarded favorably by critics as a Princess kind of musical, with the expected melodious score by Kern and a witty, if inconsequential, story, it nevertheless languished; the authors and composers followed up only six weeks later (February 20, 1917) at the Princess with their smash hit *Oh Boy!*, which the *New York Times* proclaimed a musical comedy "as good as they make them."

The Wodehouse-Bolton story told of the not-unfamiliar problem (in musicals) of a young man who has married without consulting his rich guardian aunt (Edna May Oliver), who is on her way to lecture him on the subject. His new wife must therefore leave on their bridal night, and in no time at all his apartment is invaded by an assortment of playboys, girls, and policemen, with all sorts of mix-ups of identity.

The panegyrics went to the fast-paced humor, the witty lyrics, and above all to Kern's melodious score, in which "Till the Clouds Roll By" was the most delectable and long-lasting. It was only six months later that the same three had another hit, *Leave It to Jane*, a college musical that had to open uptown at the Longacre Theatre because *Oh Boy!* was still going strong at the Princess. The style was now firmly established, and its success bred imitators, although few were able to achieve the sheer stylishness of the Bolton-Wodehouse-Kern combination. Kern was now incontestably the greatest songwriter of the era. Two youthful songwriters, George Gershwin and Richard Rodgers, heard, admired, and were moved to emulation.

From left: Guy Bolton, P. G. Wodehouse, and Jerome Kern.

(opposite)
Sheet music for the Princess musicals: *Nobody Home* (1915), *Very Good Eddie* (1915), *Oh Boy!* (1917), and *Oh Lady! Lady!!* (1917).

III   *Pleasures in a Golden Age, 1915–1927*

(opposite)
Marilyn Miller, the young dancing
star who first graced Ziegfeld's
Follies in 1918.

FUN ON THE ROOF

During the early 1900s and until the era of Prohibition, several of New York's theatres used their roofs for gardens and restaurants, some with small stages. When the sumptuous New Amsterdam Theatre was built, the owners, Klaw and Erlanger, turned their roof into what was virtually another theatre, which they called the Aerial Gardens. Ziegfeld, who presented his *Follies* at the New Amsterdam each summer, in 1915 had his gifted architect, Joseph Urban, turn the roof theatre into what was in essence a magnificent supper club. It had a movable stage, a glass balcony-high runway for his glorified girls, a dance floor, and tables for dining and drinking, with telephones that connected with other tables. In this atmosphere, with windows opened wide to the summer air, he presented his *Ziegfeld Midnight Frolic*, often trying out performers who would later go into the *Follies* down below; others from below would come upstairs and perform another routine. The New Amsterdam roof, now known as "Ziegfeld Roof — The Meeting Place of the World," quickly outshone the others, and the thing to do in New York was to crowd into the tiny elevator in the New Amsterdam, which began operating at 11:30 P.M., and ascend to the festivities above. When in 1920 spirits could no longer be served at the roof gardens, the *Frolics* lost their zest, and soon fizzled to a regrettable end.

The architect and designer Joseph Urban.

68

In 1915 a significant new name was added to Ziegfeld's *Follies*, but it was neither that of a glamorous beauty nor a riotous comedian. In this edition of the show the most striking element was the beautifully designed scenery. The settings were the work of Joseph Urban, a Vienna-born architect, illustrator, and stage designer. Ziegfeld, with his librettist, Gene Buck, saw an Edward Sheldon play, *Garden of Paradise*, that had been designed by Urban, and immediately sought him out in a café. Handing him a check for ten thousand dollars, Ziegfeld said, "Consider yourself engaged for the *Follies*." Soon after, he sent Urban a puzzling message that he wanted him to "fix his roof."

The roof in question was the one atop the New Amsterdam Theatre, which Ziegfeld was turning into a supper club with a show called *The Midnight Frolic*, this to follow the evening performances of the *Follies*.

Urban made the roof into a lustrous nightclub with glass balconies and colored lights playing across a movable stage. At first regarded as another of Ziegfeld's follies, in the negative sense, the roof and its elaborate productions became world famous. Young performers were given chances, and regular stars such as Fanny Brice tried out new ideas. The youthful Eddie Cantor appeared there one night, and stayed on for twenty-six performances, eventually entering the *Follies* in 1917. Will Rogers tried out his lariat act, and Lucile, Lady Duff-Gordon, the most fashionable dress designer of the time, showed off her latest creations, which were displayed on her own collection of tall, willowy beauties.

Blue was Urban's favorite color, and he gave the 1915 *Follies* a blue tone. The opening "underwater" sequence rippled with blue light. Ziegfeld liked elephants, and so, for "The Gates of Elysium" sequence, Urban gave him huge reared-up elephants with multicolored water spouting from their trunks. He created a red, white, and blue mélange for "America," a spectacle in which Mae Murray helped represent the army, Ann Pennington the navy, and Olive Thomas the "Dove of Peace."

Ziegfeld's attentions to the fetching Miss Thomas created anything but peace, however. His new wife, actress Billie Burke, who was making a movie on the West Coast, heard disturbing rumors about her husband's cruising Long Island

Pastel drawing by Raphael Kirchner, one of a series the artist created for the Ziegfeld Theatre, designed by Joseph Urban.

Ziegfeld's two wives, Billie Burke (left) and Anna Held.

Olive Thomas, the exquisite beauty who would become very important to Ziegfeld.

Sound on his yacht, with Olive on board. The marriage would have more such strains through the years.

A new star in the 1915 show was W. C. Fields, whose act was a hilarious game of billiards played with a rubber cue stick. Ed Wynn had made his *Follies* debut the previous year, and Fields, apparently outraged by Wynn's attempt to steal his laughs, whacked him over the head with his stick. Ina Claire was in the show that year, as was dancer George White (who would in a few years attempt to rival Ziegfeld with his own *Scandals*).

The Ziegfeld-Urban opulence had already become well established in the 1916 *Follies*, with Lucile's gowns, and a notable assembly of stars: Fanny Brice paying homage to the Russian "belly," by singing "Nijinsky"; Will Rogers twirling his lariat around a chorus girl and interspersing his rope tricks with cogent comments on current affairs; W. C. Fields impersonating Teddy Roosevelt; and Ina Claire mimicking Geraldine Farrar, Jane Cowl, and Irene Castle. Newcomers in 1916 to the traditional beauty parade were Marion Davies and Lilyan Tashman. No wonder ticket prices soared on the scalper's market.

escapism, and now and then an obligatory touch of patriotism. Judging by the titles, one might not have known there was a war on. Hardly reflective of the wartime atmosphere were Sigmund Romberg's popular *Maytime*, or such shows as *Rambler Rose, The Land of Joy, The Rainbow Girl*, and *The Grass Widow*. The always busy Jerome Kern, abetted by Bolton and Wodehouse, gave the Princess another smash with *Oh Lady! Lady!!*, but with hardly a mention of the two million men under arms, of muddy trenches, tanks, poison gas, and deadly submarines. One song, "When the Ships Come Home," did faintly hint at reality. But the main concern of the authors seemed to be to set high standards for

W. C. Fields started his career as a comic juggler, but after his first few *Follies,* he abandoned his juggling in favor of the misanthropic character whom he portrayed with great success on stage and screen for the remainder of his career.

The United States entered the European war on April 7, 1917, and show business responded with a pledge of $100,000,000 to the Liberty Loan drive. Patriotism and, to a degree, chauvinism had seized the country after the sinking of the *Lusitania*. Viennese and German operetta faded into near oblivion. Only a few months before the declaration of war, Woodrow Wilson was elected on a slogan "He Kept Us Out of War." But now the nation was singing "Over There," George M. Cohan's personal contribution to the war effort. Chorus boys were scarce because so many were drafted, and backstage workers were regarded as precious as those up front.

Still, little that happened on the stages of the wartime musicals reflected the grimness of the headlines. If they reflected anything, it was sheer

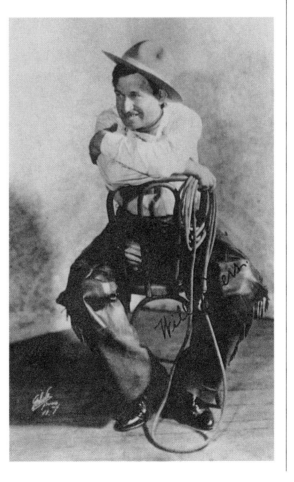

Will Rogers, cowboy humorist and wry commentator on American mores.

William Norris (left), Peggy Wood, and Charles Purcell in *Maytime* (1917).

Sigmund Romberg, composer of *Maytime*.

the American musical: "Every line, funny or serious," Bolton proclaimed in an interview, "is supposed to help the plot continue to hold." As for the songs, "The plot has to build more or less around, or at least with them." The plot in this case again dealt with that staple, a would-be marriage encountering varied obstacles. But the lines were witty, the lyrics urbane, and Kern's score lively, romantic, and jazzy by turns. The *New York Times* even found novel elements in the plot.

Ziegfeld, at least, responded to the wartime mood in his 1917 *Follies* when an actor portraying President Woodrow Wilson reviewed a parade of girls decked out in red, white, and blue. The orchestra broke into a spirited rendition of the "Star-Spangled Banner," the audience rose, and a tremendous flag was unfurled from the theatre ceiling. In 1918, one of Ziegfeld's tableaux showed ragged little French orphans, Red Cross

volunteers attending a wounded soldier, and even a trench scene in which American doughboys charged the enemy amidst ear-splitting gunfire sound effects. A bare-bosomed Ziegfeld girl, Kay Laurell, represented the "Spirit of Victory."

Composers, too, had to face the draft. Irving Berlin was assigned to Camp Upton in upstate New York, where he soon sat down at a piano and wrote the score for an army show, *Yip, Yip, Yaphank*. It came to Broadway and the Century Theatre with its all-doughboy cast in August 1918, and played 32 performances before going on to other cities. One imperishable number was "Oh, How I Hate to Get Up in the Morning," in which Berlin told what he was going to do to the bugler. The audience went wild. But also memorable was Sergeant Berlin himself, when he appeared alone and forlorn on stage, a slight figure wearing a large apron, carrying a mop and bucket, for a number called "Poor Little Me, I'm a KP."

"I scrub the dishes against my wishes," he sang, "to make the world safe for democracy." Hardened critic Robert Benchley recalled it as a moment that gave him one of his greatest thrills in the theatre.

In 1918, Ziegfeld presented a winsome young woman who became one of his and Broadway's greatest stars. First, though, he had to steal her away from Lee Shubert, who in 1914 had found her in London dancing and doing impersonations at the Four Hundred Club. Marilyn Miller was then sixteen, and had been touring with her theatrical

Program for *Yip, Yip, Yaphank* (1918).

BROADWAY BLACKS OUT

Late in 1917, the government ordered a 10:45 P.M. blackout of Broadway in order to conserve fuel, and in 1918 a 10:00 P.M. curfew was declared on all theatre performances. To make the deadline, many theatre managers eliminated intermissions in their shows. A further restriction came when all theatres were ordered closed on Tuesdays — "Garfield holidays," as they were called in honor of President Wilson's fuel administrator. One patriotic theatre manager offered to donate specially trained sea lions to the government to spot lurking enemy submarines. Burlesque theatres fared the worst during this stringent time. With two million males called to military duty, and others working overtime, a great many seats remained unfilled.

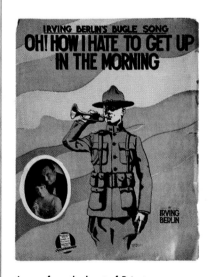

A song from the heart of Private Berlin.

family, the Five Columbians, ever since she was five. For the act she was called Miss Sugarplum. Her delicate beauty was such that critics compared her to a Dresden doll. She was a superb dancer, and she could sing in a small, but sweet voice. Shubert brought her to the States and put her at once into his *Passing Show of 1914* at the Winter Garden.

The *Passing Shows* were revues not unlike the *Follies*, but closer to burlesque and not as resplendent, particularly after Joseph Urban began designing for Ziegfeld. Marilyn Miller stayed with the Shuberts through the 1917 season and then decamped. The Shuberts furiously claimed they had a five-year contract with Marilyn, but since she was a minor at the time of signing, they had no legal claim on her.

She made her first appearance in the 1918 *Follies*, dressed in a minstrel costume, merely walking down a flight of stairs, but revealing legs that, in Billie Burke's words, "have never been matched for slim, provocative beauty." She was more prominently featured in the 1919 edition, appearing as "Sweet Sixteen" in an Urban setting of flowers and urns, singing Irving Berlin's "Mandy" in a minstrel routine reminiscent of the past.

Billie Burke also described her as "a confection of a girl, an elfin creature who presents a most enchanting effect. A delightful thing happens when she comes on stage." The assessment is generous in view of the special interest Ziegfeld took in the young lady. He was possessive of her, so much so that when she fell in love with Frank Carter, another performer in the *Follies*, he attempted in true musical-comedy style to frustrate the match. Nevertheless, she married Carter during rehearsals for the 1919 *Follies*. Ziegfeld promptly fired Carter, upon which Marilyn threatened to quit. She stayed, however. She was on tour with the show when word came to her in her dressing room of her husband's death in an automobile accident. He had been on his way to see her. Trouper that she was, she did not miss her cue and went on stage to sing "Sweet Sixteen" amidst flowers more suited to a funeral. Soon after, Ziegfeld gave her a leave of absence and sent her on a tour of Europe with her mother.

It was that edition of the *Follies* that brought out more superlatives from reviewers than any other. Those privy to performances through the years usually selected 1919 as the greatest vintage. The press that year certainly agreed, with encomiums such as "surpasses all others," and "Ziegfeld out-Ziegfeld's Ziegfeld." It was the year in which Berlin's "A Pretty Girl Is Like a Melody" was first heard. Eddie Cantor made an enormous hit with "You'd Be Surprised." It was the last *Follies* for Bert Williams. With Prohibition looming, he sang "You Cannot Make Your Shimmy Shake on Tea."

Less than two months after the 1919 opening, the members of Actors' Equity went on strike, and almost every theatre in New York was soon closed. (An exception was the nonprofit shows; the teetering new Theatre Guild had one of these, and reaped a welcome box-office bonanza.) Ziegfeld, faced by a

Irving Berlin's tribute to Ziegfeld's showgirls.

(*left*)
Ed Wynn.

(*right*)
Eddie Cantor.

recalcitrant company, obtained temporary injunctions, but two days later a group that included Eddie Cantor refused to appear, and the *Follies* was forced to close. However, in the fall, the tour went on as scheduled.

When Ziegfeld took a Florida vacation early in 1920, he entertained as lavishly as he produced. He rented a millionaire's Palm Beach mansion, leased a yacht, invited several friends and a bevy of his glorified girls, and combined business with pleasure by having Bolton, Wodehouse, and Kern down to talk about a new musical for Marilyn Miller. During the round of cocktail parties, sumptuous dinners, cruises through the Everglades, and (with Prohibition about to take effect) storied imbibing, enough time was salvaged to get some work done.

The musical-comedy team mentioned to Ziegfeld a piece they had abandoned during their Princess Theatre

Caricature of Bert Williams by Antonio Frasconi. Acknowledged as one of this country's greatest stars, Williams worked at a time of crushing racial prejudice, yet his comic genius remained supremely engaging. His friend W. C. Fields said of him, "Bert Williams is the funniest man I ever saw and the saddest man I ever knew."

(*overleaf*) **Three costume dolls dressed by the *Follies* seamstresses after the designer's sketches. Ziegfeld liked to inspect the designs before the actual costumes were constructed. In addition to the magnificent gowns, they wore, as did the actual ladies of the ensemble, exquisite lingerie and French-heeled velvet shoes.**

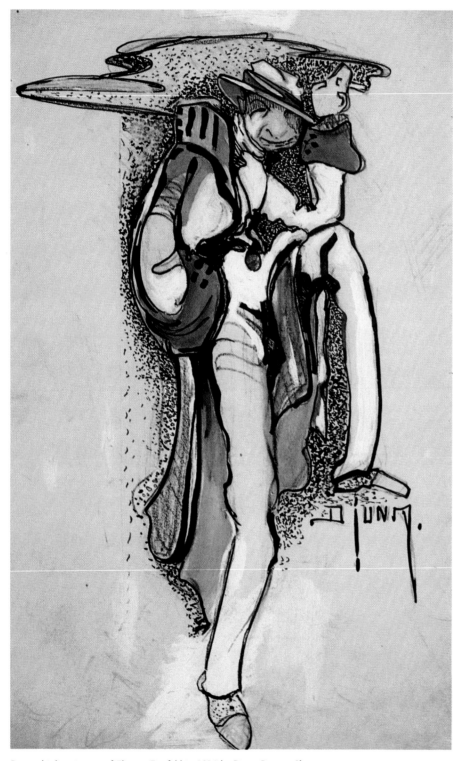

Pen-and-ink caricature of Florenz Ziegfeld in 1914 by Djuna Barnes. She was a young newspaper reporter at the time, and went on to become a noted writer of avant-garde fiction and plays.

days; it had to do with an orphan, Sally Rhinelander (named for the telephone exchange of the booth in which she was found), who washed dishes in an actor's boardinghouse while dreaming of becoming a great dancer. Ziegfeld was taken with the possibilities in the story, perhaps because it resembled *Irene*, a current hit that told of a poor shop girl who meets and marries a rich heir to a Long Island estate. One of its songs, "Alice Blue Gown," was sweeping the country.

Ziegfeld suggested a change: the dishwasher should want to become a great dancer for the *Follies*. Several other changes in the story occurred on the way to its late December 1920 opening at the New Amsterdam. Sally's dishwashing chores take place at the Elm Tree Alley Inn, in Greenwich Village, where she also dances. Her ability is noticed by an agent who has lost his star Russian ballerina and needs a quick replacement for a gala garden party at a posh Long Island estate. Sally fills in, after which she winds up not only dancing a star turn in the *Follies* but at the Little Church Around the Corner with the heir to the estate.

Kern's score for *Sally* included one of his most beautiful songs, "Look for the Silver Lining"; it was so identified with Marilyn Miller that it later became the title for her screen biography. Other audience-pleasing Kern songs were "Wild Rose" and "Whip-Poor-Will." Victor Herbert was commissioned to provide a Butterfly Ballet for Sally's star turn in the *Follies*. *Sally*, with its Long Island garden and backstage settings by Joseph Urban, its brilliant music, its appealing book, comedy provided by Leon Errol and Walter Catlett, and, perhaps most important, the captivating Marilyn Miller, outdid *Irene* as the biggest hit of its day.

Reviewers were ecstatic: They found everything about the lighthearted show sheer delight. "Nothing less than idealized musical comedy," the *World* raved, and one and all acknowledged Marilyn Miller to be Broadway's quintessential musical star. The show ran for 570 performances on Broadway, then toured through 1922 and 1923. Long after *Sally* left the boards, the critic John Mason Brown provided this remembrance: "For me Miss Miller has never stopped dancing. She haunts me as a vision of spangles and sunshine, beautiful of body, empty of face, and supreme in grace, eternally pirouetting as Broadway's Pavlova."

This lovely song, like much of the score of *Sally,* was rescued from a failed musical, in this case something called *Zip Goes a Million.*

Something quite different came to the farther reaches of Broadway in May of 1921 — an all-black show, *Shuffle Along.* It opened at the 63rd Street Theatre, which had been unused for some time, and though considerably uptown from the Great White Way, it soon attracted such large audiences that 63rd Street was clogged with traffic.

The show's book was reminiscent of the Williams and Walker, Cole and Johnson shows of more than a decade earlier, dealing as it did with two grocery-store partners who vie to be mayor of lackadaisical Jimtown, each promising the other the chief of police job if he loses. But the plot was merely an excuse for some of the most energetic and exhilarating dancing yet to be seen in Broadway precincts, allied with music that created several song hits.

To produce the show, four men combined their talents and limited financial resources: Flournoy Miller and

Marilyn Miller in the title role of *Sally* (1920).

Aubrey Lyles (left) and Flournoy Miller in *Shuffle Along* (1921).

Aubrey Lyles, a comedy team, wrote the libretto; the team of Noble Sissle and Eubie Blake the lyrics and music. Costumes were bought secondhand from a show that had closed, and scenery was kept to a minimum. When the company assembled at New York's Pennsylvania Station for a booking at the Howard, a black theatre in Washington, there was not enough money for train tickets, and the producers scurried to find an angel. After the needed funds were scrounged, several cast members, dubious about prospects and fearful of being stranded far from home, had to be coaxed onto the train.

Two weeks at the Howard were successful, and the show moved on to Philadelphia's Dunbar Theatre, another

The chorus of *Shuffle Along*. Broadway was astounded by their beauty and talent.

all-black house. The managers, with their eyes now on opening in New York, attempted to persuade the Dunbar's owner to take a half interest in the show for a thousand dollars, but he thought it a bad bet. Two weeks in Philadelphia brought in just enough money to move the show ninety miles to New York's slightly dilapidated 63rd Street Theatre. Critics were slow to realize it, but on May 21, when the show had its New York premiere, history was being made. Three weeks later, as word got around, it was hard to get a ticket.

Flimsy as the book might have seemed, Miller and Lyles used it to hilarious effect in their burlesque of two ignorant blacks doing "big business" in their grocery-store enterprise, and then competing for mayor. Sissle sang, and Blake played his jazz piano. A quartet, the Harmony Kings, sang in barbershop style, and a group of pretty girls (Josephine Baker was one!) and chorus men did the amazing dancing, which ranged through tap, soft shoe, buck-and-wing, and precision ensembles. "The *élan vital* is inexhaustible and unbridled," Gilbert Seldes wrote in his *The Seven Lively Arts*, a book of the period in which he decided that musical comedy could now be elevated to the status of art. He also singled out the delightful dancer and mime Florence Mills among the performers: "Merely to watch her walk out upon the stage, with her long, free stride and her superb shameless swing, is an aesthetic pleasure."

The outstanding song was "I'm Just Wild About Harry," one of the great hits of its day, but also popular were "Love Will Find a Way," "In Honeysuckle

Time," and "Shuffle Along." The show ran for a year, and its success went a long way toward breaking down Broadway's barrier to shows originated by black producers and performers. The combination that had produced it broke up, with Miller and Lyles coming out two years later with *Runnin' Wild*, and Sissle and Blake with *Chocolate Dandies*, in which chorus girl Josephine Baker demonstrated her flair for comedy.

Drawing of Josephine Baker by Richard Ely.

(opposite) **Florence Mills.**

History was also made in *Runnin' Wild* when it introduced a dance number, the Charleston, the high-stepping dance that became a craze, and a symbol of the so-called Jazz Age. It had come straight from Negro sources, and Miller and Lyles played this up by having the chorus supplement the show's jazz band with hand-clapping and foot-patting. "The effect was electrical," said James Weldon Johnson. "Such a demonstration of beating out complex dance rhythms had never before been seen on a stage in New York."

Florence Mills, born in Washington in 1895, had been a performer since childhood, but had played only in road vaudeville and Harlem nightclubs until she was hired as a replacement in *Shuffle Along*, after which she became Harlem's pride and joy. After a year in the show, she went into Lew Leslie's *Plantation Revue*, expanded for Broadway from a Harlem nightclub floor show. Later, in London, in *From Dover to Dixie*, she won the admiration of St. John Ervine, who called her success "something unequalled by any American playing here in the last decade. She is by far the most artistic person London has had the good fortune to see."

Broadway saw her again in 1924 when the London revue was retitled *Dixie to Broadway*, and once again she stopped the show with her pantomime, singing, and dancing. The upper range of her voice was described variously as bubbling, bell-like, and bird-like. In 1926 Leslie took her to Paris, then London, in a new revue called *Blackbirds*, where she again triumphed. All Harlem eagerly

awaited her return for the planned New York opening of *Blackbirds*.

She came back in October of 1927 for an appendectomy, which she had delayed, unfortunately for too long. Her appendix burst and she died on November 1, 1927. Never before had a funeral like hers been seen in Harlem. More than a hundred thousand people jammed the streets outside the Mother Zion Church. As her cortege moved through the Harlem streets, an airplane circled low and released a flock of blackbirds. Her favorite song, and that of her audiences, too, had been: "I'm a Little Blackbird Looking for a Bluebird."

As the twenties progressed, the nation underwent profound social change. Jazz was now the favored musical mode. Victorian morals were abandoned, emancipated women shed an overabundance of garments, skirts moved ever higher, and flappers danced the Charleston and the black bottom, smoked cigarettes, and drank bootleg gin out of pocket flasks. Disillusioned young men happily regarded themselves as members of "a lost generation," while women, having gained the vote, went in increasing numbers to colleges. Slick-haired Rudolph Valentino worried about this new state of affairs: "I do not like women who know too much," he announced.

The smart and popular magazine *Vanity Fair* took note of the emergence of the flapper in 1922 and defined her thus: "She will never knit you a neck tie, but she'll go skiing with you. . . . She may quote poetry to you, not Indian love lyrics but something about the peace

To
mary with
love

conference or theology." It might have seemed, then, that *Rose-Marie*, a melodious operetta that came to Broadway in September of 1924, would have little appeal to the new woman, or, for that matter, to the new man. Its heroine was part Indian, and her first line was "I am take sleigh ride with Jeem." One of its numbers was "Totem Tom-Tom," and its most haunting and popular song was "Indian Love Call," which sounded sort of Indian.

What happened, naturally, was that *Rose-Marie* was a triumphant hit, not only in New York but on the road in every city or town of fair size, an even greater hit in London, and a record-setter in Paris. If anything was proven it was that new tastes did not necessarily supplant old ones. As if to further prove the point, only a couple of months later *The Student Prince*, set in old Heidelberg, was another smash hit. Viennese operetta was supposed to be moribund, but its reported demise was clearly premature.

Rudolf Friml's score for *Rose-Marie* was one prime reason for its success (as was that of Sigmund Romberg for *The Student Prince*). Another was the unusual Canadian Rockies setting for the romantic and melodramatic libretto by Otto Harbach and Oscar Hammerstein II, which recounted the love of Rose-Marie La Flamme for the robust fur trapper Jim Kenyon. Harbach was a veteran, but for the much younger Hammerstein it marked his emergence into the upper echelons of Broadway fame.

In *The Student Prince*, a romance about a youthful prince and a beer-garden waitress in the Heidelberg of the 1860s, Romberg's melodies were both tender and rousing. Of the former, there was "Deep in My Heart, Dear" and of the latter, "To the Inn We're Marching," and the "Drinking Song." In view of Prohibition, could it have been the sight of all those foaming beer steins, or was it simply nostalgia for the old in the face of

Oscar Hammerstein II felt that the score was so integral to the show that he refused to allow the songs to be listed separately in the program.

The dancing ladies of *Rose-Marie* (1924) dressed appropriately for the "Totem Tom-Tom" number.

rapid and unsettling change? In any case, after more than 600 performances on Broadway, nine touring companies crisscrossed the country, and some twenty-five years later it was still around.

If the above-mentioned operettas were Old World stuff in Americanized form, one 1924 show was right in tune with the spirit of the new age. The rhythms were basically jazz, and the lyrics were clever and colloquial. The book, about a brother-and-sister dance team down on their luck, was perhaps wittier than the usual, and kept the show moving along in spirited fashion. The importance of *Lady, Be Good!* was its score and lyrics by the brothers Gershwin, George and Ira. It also happened to have a captivating brother-and-sister dance team, Fred and Adele Astaire.

At age twenty-six, George Gershwin was already famous. He had done scores for *George White's Scandals*, and a few musical comedies, he had written the smash song "Swanee," and

he had stunned the music world earlier in the same year with "Rhapsody in Blue," written for Paul Whiteman's historic "serious" jazz concert in Town Hall. But *Lady, Be Good!* was his first real hit, and it was also the first time the brothers had collaborated on a complete score. They would be a dominating force in the golden age of musical comedy that lay ahead.

As for the Astaires, Adele Austerlitz arrived first in Omaha, Nebraska, in 1898, and Fred followed her a year later. When they worked in vaudeville they changed their names, and by the time they went into musical comedy in 1917 they had already established themselves as stylish, graceful dancers able to create their own routines. Their voices had no great range, but they managed to get by with charm and personality. Both knew George Gershwin from their vaudeville days, when he was a teenage song plugger, and Fred had confided to him that he

Rudolf Friml, composer of *Rose-Marie*.

Cast of *The Student Prince* (1924), with Howard Marsh, the prince himself, center.

Fred and Adele Astaire, the Nebraska-born brother and sister who brought a shimmering elegance and wit to the Broadway stage.

and his sister wanted to get into musical comedy. George promised to write one for them someday. It took nine years, but *Lady, Be Good!* finally did happen.

Fred told of trying, during rehearsals, to find an exit step for a dance routine. "George happened to drop by," he recalled, "and I asked him to look at the routine. He went to the piano. When we were reaching the last step before the exit, George said, 'Now travel with it.' He jumped up and demonstrated what he visualized. He wanted us to sustain a complicated precision rhythm as we traveled to the side, continuing until we were out of sight off stage. It was the perfect answer to our problem, and it turned out to be a knockout applause puller." So did the song, "Fascinating Rhythm."

Broadway had musicals galore to choose from during the autumn of 1925. Just one week in September brought four noteworthy shows: *No, No, Nanette*, *Dearest Enemy*, *The Vagabond King*, and *Sunny*. Movies were still silent and had not yet made serious inroads on the theatre audience; nor was radio much of a threat to the legitimate theatre. Fifty — count 'em, fifty — musicals played during that year. The first of the four mentioned above had a flapper heroine, stylish settings, and, in a pleasant score, two songs — "I Want to Be Happy" and "Tea for Two" — that kept the nation's Victrolas wound up and playing for months on end. Revived in 1971, it surprisingly ran more than twice as long as in its original outing!

Dearest Enemy, set in New York during the American Revolution, had the slyly witty lyrics of Lorenz Hart and the nicely matched music of Richard Rodgers. Robert Benchley referred to them as a "God-given team," and another critic predicted that one day they would be the counterparts of Bolton, Wodehouse, and Kern. In *The Vagabond*

King, the appropriately named Dennis King made official the star status that had come to him as the stalwart Jim Kenyon in *Rose-Marie*. This, too, was operetta, but unusually interesting in that its hero (King) was the swashbuckling poet François Villon. Rudolf Friml's score was lush and romantic, and the medieval Paris setting was wondrous in itself.

Sunny found Jerome Kern and Oscar Hammerstein II in collaboration, with a valuable assist from Otto Harbach on the libretto. In fact, the show had a plethora of "names." Marilyn Miller was the main attraction as the girl of the title, a circus rider in England. But the cast also featured Clifton Webb, Jack

An advertisement for the 1924 show. The gentleman on the left is comedian Walter Catlett, who sang the title song.

Donahue, and Cliff Edwards. Out of the hugely popular show came another hugely popular Kern hit: "Who?"

Quite a week, considering it featured the music of Kern, Youmans, Friml, and Rodgers, not to mention librettos by Oscar Hammerstein, Larry Hart, Otto Harbach, and Herbert Fields — all resounding names in the American musical theatre. First-nighters who attended all four must have felt as if they had overdosed on banana splits and chocolate sundaes. And every one a hit.

The Gershwins also had a hit later that season with *Tip-Toes*, its story loosely influenced (very loosely) by the great Florida land boom, which had thousands of Americans buying dubious property in the hope of making a killing. No one thought the plot of much consequence, but the influential critic Alexander Woollcott said: "It was of course Gershwin's evening, so sweet and sassy are the melodies he has poured, so fresh and unstinted the gay, young blood of his invention." Fellow lyricist Lorenz Hart was so impressed by Ira Gershwin's lyrics that he felt called upon to send him a letter of congratulation:

It is a great pleasure to live in a time when light amusement in this country is at last losing its brutally cretin aspect. Such delicacies as your jingles prove that songs can be both popular and intelligent.

Certainly, Hart was doing his part in proving the same thing. He was twenty-three, and Richard Rodgers a talented sixteen, when they were introduced by a mutual friend. Rodgers remembered it as a kind of love at first sight. "I acquired in one afternoon," he

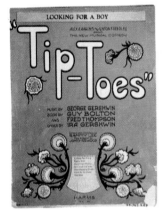

An early Gershwin classic.

(opposite)
Still in their twenties, the Gershwins (George is on the left) had their second hit with *Tip-Toes* in 1925.

remembered long after, "a partner, a best friend, and a source of permanent irritation."

Born in New York in 1895, Hart attended private schools and Columbia College, where, though he was a brilliant student, he found that his main interest was the annual Varsity Show, for which he wrote skits and song lyrics. He did not bother to get a degree; instead he went to work for the Shubert brothers, translating German operettas and, during summers, putting on shows at a boys' camp.

Richard Rodgers's father was a Long Island physician and his mother an amateur pianist. By age four Richard was playing the piano by ear. His father had an excellent voice, and at home would team up with his wife at the piano to sing songs from Broadway operettas. Victor Herbert was Rodgers's first musical love, but when he heard Jerome Kern's melodies for *Very Good Eddie* at the Princess Theatre, he was immediately unfaithful to Herbert. He would go back to see and hear Kern's shows several times. He was only fifteen when he was asked to write a score for a musical being put on by a New York boys' club at the Plaza Hotel.

Hart and Rodgers began writing songs together in 1919, some of which Rodgers brought to Lew Fields, of the old Weber and Fields comedy combination, and by now a producer. Fields put one of the songs into his production *A Lonely Romeo*, and a year later seven more of the young team's songs into *Poor Little Ritz Girl*, which had a modest run. Their progress was slow after that, though, and Rodgers almost gave up attempting to

Richard Rodgers (left) and Lorenz Hart.

write for Broadway. But just in time he and Hart were given the opportunity to write the score for a modest revue being put on by several young people attached to the Theatre Guild.

The lively twenties were the heyday of the revue. Few were able to rival the gloss and prestige of Ziegfeld's continuing *Follies*, but audiences flocked to them nevertheless. Ziegfeld's closest rival was George White, whose *Scandals* began its series in 1919 and continued, yearly at first and then sporadically, through 1939.

George Gershwin wrote for several of the *Scandals* and, in 1922, was bold and experimental enough to write for it a one-act jazz opera called *Blue Monday* — quickly dropped by White when it became more of a critical scandal than one befitting his show. Much more lasting, however, was Gershwin's song "I'll Build a Stairway to Paradise." While it was being sung to Paul Whiteman's orchestral accompaniment, a battalion of girls dressed in black patent leather marched up a shining white staircase. Very *moderne* for those days.

A dozen revues played during 1925, one of them a holdover of Ziegfeld's long-running 1924 *Follies* that had caused him to "skip" a year. Revues were so common that some took to satirizing other revues. A good many featured numbers built around the Charleston, in line with the nation's dance craze. Among the titles of the shows were *Artists and Models*, *The Music Box Revue*, *Puzzles of 1925*, *Charlot's Revue*, *Greenwich Village Follies*, *The Grand Street Follies*, and *Earl Carroll's Vanities*. Carroll, a songwriter-turned-producer, had begun displaying his *Vanities* in 1923. One of his important objects, he proclaimed, was to exalt the human form, by which, from the examples displayed on his stage, he clearly meant the female form. An honored tradition from Victorian times was that the nude form onstage must remain immobile. Carroll, who believed in very little costuming, if any, on his girls, solved this problem by having one of them, unclothed, swing back and forth on a giant pendulum: *it* moved, she didn't.

In 1925 the Theatre Guild was building a handsome new theatre, with room for an acting school. Its younger players, most often used in bit parts, put together a revue to raise money for tapestries for the new theatre. The plan was to stage it on two successive Sunday nights at the Garrick Theatre, where *The Guardsman*, with Lunt and Fontanne, was having a long run. The revue was thus given the title *Garrick Gaieties*. Richard Rodgers was approached to provide the music, but since it was a benefit he was not offered any pay. He had been about to go into business, but the sheer prestige of writing for the Theatre Guild made him change his mind. He insisted, however, that Larry Hart write the lyrics.

Biting the hand that fed it, *Garrick Gaieties* (1925) parodied two George Bernard Shaw dramas being presented by the Theatre Guild at the time.

An intimate show of necessity, with only three thousand dollars for costumes, sets, and lighting, some of its sketches satirized the Guild's own productions, and its need for subscribers. Another, aimed at the stuffier Guild donors, had Saint Peter passing on the moral acceptability of heroines in Guild plays. There was also a bit of political satire: it had Mrs. Calvin Coolidge berating her husband for spending a wild evening with Herbert Hoover listening to the radio and arriving home at the ungodly hour of 10:00 P.M. Libby Holman was in the cast and sang a ballad, "Black and Blue," but it was only when Sterling Holloway and June Cochrane sang "Manhattan," to enthusiastic applause, that both Rodgers and Hart felt they had, after all, a future in the theatre.

Next day the critics made it official, with accolades such as: "Full of youth, energy and fine flashes of wit." The problem then arose: what to do with the revue, since the Guild had no theatre for it? First it was allowed to play matinees at the Garrick, until it became apparent that it was likely to draw more box-office business than *The Guardsman* itself. Rodgers and Hart had the satisfaction of knowing their show took Lunt and Fontanne off the boards; and after the tapestries were purchased, they received royalties of fifty dollars a week. More important, it established their Broadway careers.

In 1924 an import from London, *Charlot's Revue*, introduced three major personalities to American audiences: the dancer and comedian Jack Buchanan; the incomparable comedienne and singer Beatrice Lillie; and Gertrude Lawrence,

(opposite)
Gertrude Lawrence at the time of *Oh, Kay!* (1926)

who, it seemed, was difficult to categorize. Noël Coward said of her that she was "capable of anything and everything. She can be gay, sad, witty, tragic, funny, and touching." Guy Bolton and P. G. Wodehouse had seen her in London, and had been so impressed that they notified her they planned to write a musical expressly for her. George Gershwin had also been impressed by her when he saw her in *Charlot's Revue*. Subsequently they met and became good friends. She was equally admiring of Gershwin's music, and when Bolton and Wodehouse wrote the libretto for the musical they had in mind for her, and when Gershwin said he would be providing the score, she had no problem in accepting the leading role.

Bolton and Wodehouse did their writing in London, but set the show on Long Island, which was a favored setting for a good many musicals, probably because it was regarded as the haunt of the rich and socially prominent. Many of the wealthy built their estates on the Island, with its combination of country air and easy access to the big city. And, during Prohibition, Long Island, with its countless coves and lonely beaches, provided an ideal place for rum-runners to sneak their cargoes ashore.

Lawrence's role was that of Lady Kay Durham, a member of the British peerage, whose brother has run out of funds and turned to rum-running, or, rather, Scotch-running. The two of them use as their port of entry the beachfront of a mansion belonging to a millionaire playboy, who soon falls in love with Kay and helps her avoid the revenue agents who are after her and her brother. The

show, right up to its first tryout in October 1926 in Philadelphia, was variously called *Mayfair, Miss Mayfair,* and *Cheerio!,* but was changed to *Oh, Kay!* by the time it reached New York. Largely because of its superb score, it has become a benchmark Gershwin musical. Seldom has a musical engendered so many long-lasting hit songs. Nor were they all of a piece. There was the joyous "Do, Do, Do," the lyrical "Maybe," the infectious "Clap Yo' Hands," and the plaintive "Someone to Watch Over Me," the last sung by Lawrence, at Gershwin's suggestion, to a doll. They all still sound wonderful.

The critic for the *New York Times* declared *Oh, Kay!* to be an "excellent blending of all the creative arts of musical entertainment." Yet, it has to be said that,

Oscar Hammerstein II (left) and Jerome Kern, who teamed up for *Show Boat*.

despite Lawrence's glowing performance and Gershwin's captivating music, the show did not break much new ground, certainly not with its easygoing story, which stressed the comedy as much as the music. It simply did very well what had been done before. The golden twenties had yet to produce a masterpiece. It would not be long in coming.

In 1926 Edna Ferber published a novel called *Show Boat*. Jerome Kern read it and, before he was halfway through, excitedly telephoned Oscar Hammerstein to tell him he was going to make it into a musical. "It's a million-dollar title," he told him. Kern then asked Alexander Woollcott, a friend of Miss Ferber's, to write him a letter of introduction, so that he could present his idea to her. She thought preposterous the notion of her bestselling book adapted as a musical, with fifty scantily clad showgirls prancing on the deck of the *Cotton Blossom*, the Mississippi showboat of her story. The story was complex as it followed three generations of a showboat family for half a century and took its many characters from New Orleans to Chicago, to New York, and eventually back to the Mississippi. Its main thread was the romance and marriage of the showboat's captain's daughter, Magnolia, to Gaylord Ravenal, a handsome riverboat gambler who eventually deserts her. It dealt, too, with the touchy subject of miscegenation, and the resulting prejudice that came from the marriage of the showboat's singer, Julie La Verne, who is part Negro, to Steve, a white man.

Kern, though, was confident that a workable libretto could be made from the material, and that thirty-one-year-old Oscar Hammerstein II was the man to do it.

Hammerstein had the advantage of being born into an important theatrical family. His grandfather was the Oscar Hammerstein who had challenged the Metropolitan with his Manhattan Opera House; his uncle Arthur was a Broadway producer, and his father ran the Victoria, a leading vaudeville house at the corner of 42nd Street and Seventh Avenue. Oscar's first choice of study was law, but at Columbia he found himself among a group of theatre-infatuated classmates, among them Lorenz Hart. Like Hart, he wrote skits and lyrics for Columbia's Varsity Show. Although he took his law degree, the theatre proved too great a lure, and soon he was writing book and lyrics for a show produced by his uncle Arthur. Around the time of his first major hit, *Rose-Marie*, he encountered Kern at Victor Herbert's funeral, a meeting that led to their collaboration on *Sunny*.

Hammerstein and Kern went immediately to work on *Show Boat*, even though Ferber was still dubious about the project. Kern would visit her and play the music he was writing and sing Hammerstein's lyrics. One day he brought her "Ol' Man River," to be sung by the black stevedore, Joe. "The music mounted, mounted," Ferber wrote in her memoirs, "and I give you my word my hair stood on end, the tears came to my eyes. I breathed like a heroine in a melodrama. That was music that would outlast Jerome Kern's day and mine."

THE POWER AND THE PAPER

While Brooks Atkinson presided over the drama desk of the *New York Times* from 1926 to 1959, he was regarded as the dean of American theatre critics. His measured judgments were tempered by his own awareness of his power (derived largely from the importance of the newspaper that employed him) to affect the financial health of the Broadway theatre. Massachusetts born and a Harvard graduate, he taught briefly at Dartmouth before becoming assistant drama critic for the *Boston Evening Transcript*. He joined the *New York Times* in 1922 as its literary editor, and four years later succeeded Stark Young as its first-string drama critic. His devotion to the artistic health of the theatre was recognized shortly before his retirement, when several hundred leading figures of the theatrical world — many of whom had felt his critical lash — gave him a surprise testimonial dinner, a clear-cut case of feeding the hand that bites one.

Hammerstein and Kern felt that Ziegfeld was the impresario to produce *Show Boat*; they wanted the richness he would bring to a production. Ziegfeld agreed to take it on, but wanted it finished in time to open his handsome new theatre, the Ziegfeld, designed by Joseph Urban, which was nearing completion. Ziegfeld gave the team only a few weeks to finish their work. "We worked fast," Hammerstein recalled, "but the writers of *Rio Rita* worked faster, and it was their show that opened the Ziegfeld."

Rio Rita became a prosperous hit. It was a dazzling show, with a south-of-the-border theme, richly cast, its dancing hot-blooded. Ziegfeld's interest in *Show Boat* became lukewarm, and he kept putting off a definite production date. This, however, as Hammerstein later noted, turned out for the best. "The blessing was time," he said. "That year's delay made *Show Boat* a much better play than it would have been if we had produced a first draft. We kept rewriting and improving our adaptation. We had fallen in love with it. We acted out scenes together and planned the direction. We sang to each other."

Both were aware they were breaking a good many musical-comedy traditions, and they were warned of this by well-meaning friends, but, said Hammerstein, "this was the very thing that endeared it to us." They tried to encompass as much of the novel's drama as possible, although inevitably some characters had to be dropped and incidents eliminated. They worked toward tight dramatic continuity, to make every song pertinent to the story. The

Joseph Urban's three-dimensional set model of the interior of the showboat.

showboat setting allowed for liveliness and color, but its unconventional story (for a musical) had much in it that was dark and anguished. Magnolia is first met at seventeen, but matures through trouble and travail into a woman past middle age. Its chorus was revolutionary for Broadway, in that it joined white and black singers and dancers together on the stage. And it had no line-up of fifty high-kicking chorus girls.

When it was time for its out-of-town opening in Washington, the show, with its multigenerational story, was an hour and a half too long, and was kept on the road for eight weeks, paring it down to a reasonable playing time, and, said Hammerstein, "waiting for that infernal *Rio Rita* to drop off in business so that we could at last get into the Ziegfeld Theatre." Kern begged Hammerstein to cut out words; Hammerstein begged Kern to cut out music, and Ziegfeld to cut out dances. And *Rio Rita* played on. Ziegfeld decided to open *Show Boat* at a smaller theatre, the Lyric, but Joseph Urban had by this time designed sets that were too large for that theatre. Ziegfeld made the decision to transfer *Rio Rita* to the Lyric, and *Show Boat* opened at the Ziegfeld on Tuesday, December 27, 1927.

Paul Robeson was to play the stevedore, Joe, but the long delay made him unavailable, and the robust-voiced Jules Bledsoe was tapped instead. The cast was not of large-star caliber. It had comedian Charles Winninger as Cap'n Andy, stern-faced Edna May Oliver as Parthy Ann, Norma Terris as Magnolia, and Howard Marsh as Ravenal. All were first rate, but it was Helen Morgan, in a

heartbreaking performance as Julie, who was catapulted into greater stardom.

Kern first saw her sitting atop a piano in a revue, singing a teary song. Ziegfeld saw her, too, and signed her, without realizing he had signed her for the chorus of *Sally* several years before. Later she appeared in *George White's Scandals*, then opened her own nightclub, the Helen Morgan Club. There she sang her songs on a white baby grand piano.

Drawing of Helen Morgan by Martha Sawyers.

Charles Winninger, the captain in *Show Boat* (1927).

Ring Lardner gave her a literal boost when she was appearing at a Billy Rose nightclub. She was so small that few could see her when she sang; so he lifted her onto the piano. Two of *Show Boat*'s great songs made her a celebrity and kept her sitting on the piano for a long time: they were "Bill" and "Can't Help Lovin' Dat Man."

In Washington at the National Theatre, prior to its opening in New York, Ziegfeld was convinced that the

Edna May Oliver, as Parthy Ann.

Norma Terris and Howard Marsh, *Show Boat*'s Magnolia and Ravenal.

show would be a flop. He sat on a staircase at the back of the theatre and began crying when important numbers failed to draw much applause. He was used to hearing cheers, not this unusual quiet. It was only when enthusiastic reviews came out the next day, and long lines formed around the National, that he began to take heart. By the time the show reached New York, tickets were being snatched up at higher than usual prices.

Ziegfeld's heart sank again in New York, when at the end of the second act there were several seconds of silence. But then came a thunderous burst of applause. It had taken the people of the audience a few moments to realize they had witnessed a show far from the ordinary, they had seen the first true American musical drama. Critics were unsure of how to describe it; they kept referring to it as light opera or operetta. As such, the consensus was that it was the "most distinguished of its generation." Brooks Atkinson wrote: "*Show Boat* becomes one of those epochal works about which garrulous old men gabble for twenty-five years after the scenery has rattled off to the storehouse." He was not far wrong; it has only grown in esteem through several revivals and three film versions.

A sidelight on the perils of producing in the twenties: an incident occurred that threatened to kill the show four days after the opening. After her nightly performances, Helen Morgan had continued to sing in the late hours at her nightclub. On New Year's Eve a phalanx of FBI agents burst in and smashed all the liquor bottles in the place and, for good measure, shot out the lights of the chandeliers. Helen herself was hustled to the FBI's offices in a police van and charged with violations of the Prohibition laws. Ziegfeld, fearful of losing his star just as the show was a clear smash at the box office, called the FBI official in charge of the raid, and demanded to know if he had had a warrant. When it turned out he had not, Ziegfeld asked for Morgan's immediate release, and she was allowed to return to the show.

No less than six of *Show Boat*'s songs became part of America's musical heritage. "Ol' Man River" will seemingly roll on forever. "Make Believe" and "Why Do I Love You?" are still heard on concert stages, in recordings, and in revivals of the films. So respected has the work become that archivists have resurrected song numbers cut (even by Kern and Hammerstein) on its way to its premiere. A full score containing every treasured note has been recorded, and it goes on for a Wagnerian length of nearly four hours. Perhaps most important, though, is *Show Boat*'s lasting influence as a breakthrough that led our musicals into fascinating new territories.

Sammy White and Eva Puck, who sang and danced the roles of Frank and Ellie.

Show Boat employed a chorus of forty black singers and dancers, and another of thirty-one whites.

(*overleaf*) Costumes, from left to right: Suit worn by the character "Gabriel" in *Evangeline* (1874). This was a "trouser role," always played by a woman. Gown worn by Norma Terris in the original production of *Show Boat* (1927). Embroidered tailcoat worn by Victor Moore in *Of Thee I Sing* (1931). Annie Oakley's frontier dress worn by Ethel Merman in *Annie Get Your Gun* (1946). Coat worn by Alice Nielsen in *The Fortune Teller* (1898).

George Gershwin
Dec. 18, 1931.

Pencil sketch of George S. Kaufman by George Gershwin.

IV *Depression, but the Band Plays On, 1927–1940*

STRIKE UP THE BAND	**ANYTHING GOES**
BLACKBIRDS OF 1928	**PORGY AND BESS**
WHOOPEE	**ON YOUR TOES**
GIRL CRAZY	**PINS AND NEEDLES**
THE BAND WAGON	**THE CRADLE WILL ROCK**
OF THEE I SING	**PAL JOEY**
AS THOUSANDS CHEER	**LADY IN THE DARK**

Bobby Clark (left) and Paul McCullough, a partnership of zany clowns that endured for thirty-one years.

Depression, But the Band Plays On, 1927–1940

Satire in the theatre, in the estimation of George S. Kaufman, was something likely to close on Saturday night, and the foreboding proved accurate in the case of his satirical libretto for a 1927 antiwar musical, *Strike Up the Band*. In spite of lyrics and music by Ira and George Gershwin, it got only as far as Philadelphia before expiring on Saturday night. However, it turned out that there was life after Philadelphia, although resurrection would require a few more years.

Kaufman, a former newspaperman turned playwright, aimed barbs at militarism, jingoistic patriotism, and blunt diplomacy — not exactly the kind of light and charming material to match the mood of the affluent audiences for musicals. Just about everything during that time seemed to be booming. The Dow-Jones average was reaching new levels, Babe Ruth was on his way to hitting sixty home runs, and a record two thousand tons of ticker tape and shredded newspaper were showered on a parade for Charles Lindbergh after his solo flight across the Atlantic.

Kaufman's way of ridiculing warmongers was to use little Switzerland as the target for the animosity of American cheese interests. When Switzerland understandably protests a fifty percent tariff on its cheese, sanctions are applied against the recalcitrant country. The wearing of Swiss watches becomes un-American; libraries remove *William Tell* and *The Swiss Family Robinson* from the shelves; Switzerland is ultimately invaded — all of which is assumed to demonstrate the folly of making war. Behind it lies the notion that wars are instigated by commercially motivated interests.

Neither the humor nor the Gershwins' lyrics and music were enough to save the show. In Philadelphia the producers gloomily watched as each evening more and more seats remained empty. It was plain that the show needed a reworking, but it also needed a different time, and a different national mood.

The latter would not be long in coming. Broadway, meanwhile, welcomed *Blackbirds of 1928*, in which Lew Leslie, its producer, had planned to feature Florence Mills. Unlike earlier all-black reviews, *Blackbirds'* score was the work of a white songwriting team, Jimmy McHugh and Dorothy Fields, who also wrote for Harlem's famed Cotton Club. They came up with "I Can't Give You Anything But Love," "Diga Diga Do," and "Doin' the New Low-Down," the last introduced by Bill "Bojangles" Robinson in his first Broadway appearance. Adelaide Hall's career was launched when she substituted for the sadly departed Florence Mills.

After his success with *Show Boat*, Ziegfeld teamed up with pop-eyed Eddie Cantor in a new spectacle, *Whoopee*, which became one of the longest-running hits of the late twenties. It was the kind of Ziegfeld show that audiences were more accustomed to: a Joseph Urban Grand Canyon setting, a plentiful number of nearly nude girls, who, appropriately for a story (from Owen Davis's comedy, *The Nervous Wreck*) set in the Wild West, came in on horseback. Cantor played a hypochondriac in

HOLLYWOOD WHOOPEE

Eddie Cantor, who had previously made two silent films, was called into Ziegfeld's office one day in 1930 to meet a Hollywood producer, Samuel Goldwyn, who was trying to talk Ziegfeld into letting him do a sound film of *Whoopee*, then a huge hit on Broadway. Paramount was also after the picture rights, and planned to film in its studios in Astoria, Long Island. Goldwyn argued that Hollywood had more experience, the best technical staffs, and natural scenery for the horses and Indians that the story featured. Though Goldwyn had never made a musical, Cantor was impressed with his confidence and know-how; Goldwyn was the first man he'd met who was the equal of Ziegfeld. "I made up my mind," Cantor said later, "that if I was going into talkies, this man was for me."

Arizona for a health cure. One of his Gus Kahn songs, "Makin' Whoopee," became virtually his trademark. Ruth Etting, too, was associated ever after with her song, "Love Me or Leave Me," which also became the title of her fine film biography many years later.

The show played through 1929, and would have run much longer if Ziegfeld had not been financially wounded by the stock market crash. As it was, he was forced to sell the movie rights to Sam Goldwyn, who removed it from Broadway to use Eddie Cantor for the film version.

In October 1927, long lines around the Warner Theatre sent a premonitory chill through Broadway's theatrical community. The people in line were waiting to see a movie called *The Jazz Singer*, in which the popular Al Jolson sang three songs and spoke a few lines of dialogue. Within six months,

talking pictures were a cataclysmic fact of life for both the silent film industry and the live theatre. Worse for the Broadway musical scene was the advent in 1929 of the "all talking, all singing, all dancing" movie. Stars of the musical stage went westward, as in Eddie Cantor's case, seeking new and more profitable careers, and the songwriting industry found it necessary to establish a new headquarters in Hollywood. The combined onslaught of the movie musical and the Great Depression that followed the crash drastically reduced the number of musicals on Broadway: only thirty-two opened during the 1929–1930 season, compared to the fifty or more in previous years, and the number would continue to decline.

Nevertheless, the general mood of discontent fostered by the deepening depression and the loss of faith in the hollow words of politicians made it a propitious moment to bring a refurbished *Strike Up the Band* to Broadway.

The cynical tone of George S. Kaufman's libretto was lightened considerably in a rewriting by Morrie Ryskind. He turned Kaufman's war into a dream fantasy that took place all in the mind of a manufacturer and fanatic militarist, Horace J. Fletcher. During his dream he, too, comes under suspicion when he is found wearing a Swiss watch. Ryskind decided that cheese was too strong a commodity to fight over, and sweetened the plot by substituting chocolate. The war manages to please everyone. Swiss hotel owners make fortunes by overcharging American soldiers for their room and board, and the war ends when the secret Swiss

(opposite)
Ethel Merman, only twenty-two years old, in *Girl Crazy* (1930). She became a star the night it opened, and never looked back.

Guy Bolton (center) with the Gershwins, George (left) and Ira.

yodeling code is broken. About half of Gershwin's songs for the former production were scrapped, and replaced by new ones. For the important martial title number, which opened and ended the show, George wrote five different versions before he was satisfied.

Just as *Show Boat* had benefited from a longer-than-normal gestation period, so did *Strike Up the Band*. And, like the former, it broke new ground with its pertinence to social issues, its willingness to pillory self-important politicians, diplomats, and military hawks. It was a tighter show, too, with a stronger integration between the story elements and the music, a musical with a bite but also funny enough for audiences to enjoy. Opening in January 1930, it ran nearly 200 performances — a very good showing for the straitened times. It also solidified the relationship between the Gershwins and Kaufman and Ryskind: more satirical musicals would be coming.

Before that happened, though, and only eight months later, the always-busy Gershwins were back with another musical, entitled *Girl Crazy*. Its book by Guy Bolton and John McGowan had a wealthy young New Yorker sent to a supposedly soporific western town of Custerville by a father worried about his son's fondness for girls. Not only was it "a big and breathless musical show," in the words of one reviewer, but it had the distinction of introducing an electrifying twenty-two-year-old singer, Ethel Merman (who had changed her name from Zimmerman because she feared it had too many letters to fit on a

marquee). She was an untaught singer who worked as a stenographer by day and sang in nightclubs by night. When she moved into vaudeville, the producers of the upcoming Gershwin show heard her at the Brooklyn Paramount and signed her for the role of Frisco Kate, a brassy bar girl with a soft heart.

During rehearsals she was given more to do than first planned for the part. "When I delivered my lines I got a response," she remembered. She was

"Post office" set design for *Girl Crazy* (1930) by Donald Oenslager.

THE BIG C NOTE

Ethel Merman made her Broadway debut in 1930 in the Gershwins' *Girl Crazy*. Toward the end of the first act she roused the opening night audience when, in the second chorus of "I've Got Rhythm," as she remembered it, "I held a high C note for 14 bars while the orchestra played the melodic line — a big, tooty thing — against the note. By the time I'd held that note for four bars the audience was applauding. They applauded through the whole chorus, and I did several encores. It seemed to do something to them. Not because it was sweet and beautiful, but because it was so exciting. When I finished that song, a star had been born. Me."

simply trying for the same sincerity the character would have. New lines were handed to her and additional verses were written for her songs. Ira Gershwin called her one day and gave her new verses for her song "Sam and Delilah." Trained secretary that she was, she took them down in shorthand.

When *Girl Crazy* opened she just about lifted the audience out of its collective seat with her delivery of "I Got Rhythm," during which she held a C note for longer than anyone else in living memory.

Grace Moore once said to her, "Your diction is perfect, your projection effortless, you break all the rules of nature. Where do you breathe from?"

"Necessity," Merman answered.

"But you've taken lessons."

Ethel shook her head. "With me, breathing always seemed to come naturally."

One writer said of Merman that she had somehow developed "the art of belting." This he described as "a gutsy, vibrant sound with little beauty of tone and a sharply curtailed range." Many others have developed the same art, but without the superb clarity and the ability to project to the farthest reaches of a theatre.

The cast of *Girl Crazy* had other notable names: Ginger Rogers, in her second Broadway appearance, as the pretty postmistress of Custerville; Allen Kearns as the fun-loving romantic lead; and the comedian Willie Howard as the taxi driver who becomes the town's sheriff. Ginger Rogers sang two

memorable Gershwin songs, "Embraceable You," and "But Not for Me," but was present more for her dancing than her voice. With Merman, it was the exact opposite.

During the intermission, when all the audience was talking about was Merman, George Gershwin climbed the stairs to her dressing room in the Alvin Theatre. "Ethel, do you know what you're doing?" he asked.

She shook her head.

"Well," he advised her, "never go near a singing teacher — and never forget your shorthand."

Depression or no, Broadway continued to furnish the nation with a full quota of fine songs, as new

Ginger Rogers introduced two Gershwin classics in *Girl Crazy*— "Embraceable You" and "But Not for Me."

Design for the show portal by Donald Oenslager.

composers and lyricists developed their talents. A standout song in 1931 was the unusual and dark-toned "Dancing in the Dark," from a clever revue, *The Band Wagon*, still regarded as an epitome of the genre, largely because of its brilliant score by Howard Dietz and Arthur Schwartz. Dietz was a publicist for a film company, and Schwartz a virtually self-taught composer who had taken a law degree at Columbia and practiced law for several years. Columbia was apparently the seedbed for a generation of musical comedy luminaries. Schwartz wrote his first songs, for camp shows, in collaboration with Lorenz Hart of the same college, when both were counselors at a boys' camp in the Adirondacks.

The easier way for song writers to gain admission into the ranks of Broadway musicals was to write for revues. Schwartz lacked the confidence to devote all his time to composing and settled for contributing individual songs to revues, but was persuaded to give up his law practice and join with Dietz in a partnership. For *The Band Wagon*, they were commissioned to do the entire score: it had such noteworthy songs as "New Sun in the Sky," "I Love Louisa," and "High and Low." Of the composition of "Dancing in the Dark," Schwartz recalled that he was asked during a rehearsal to compose "a dark song, somewhat mystical, yet in slow, even rhythm." The following morning he

Howard Dietz (left) and Arthur Schwartz, librettist and composer for *The Band Wagon..*

The elegant and witty *Band Wagon* (1931) made a fitting farewell to the stage for Adele Astaire. She would soon be followed by her brother, who heeded Horace Greeley's advice, went west, and never returned to Broadway.

awoke with the feeling that he somehow already knew the song, as though it had formed itself while he slept. He went immediately to the piano and, with no hesitation, played its melody from beginning to end.

The revue's sketches, written by Dietz and George S. Kaufman, were built primarily around the stars, Fred and Adele Astaire. It had an inventive opening. When members of the audience arrived, the curtain was already up, and they saw, like a reflection of themselves, the show's entire company seated on the stage, even to ushers costumed exactly as the ushers in the aisles. As the lights dimmed, the company set the mood by singing "It Better Be Good."

(*overleaf*) The original prompt script for *Of Thee I Sing,* the first musical to win the Pulitzer Prize.

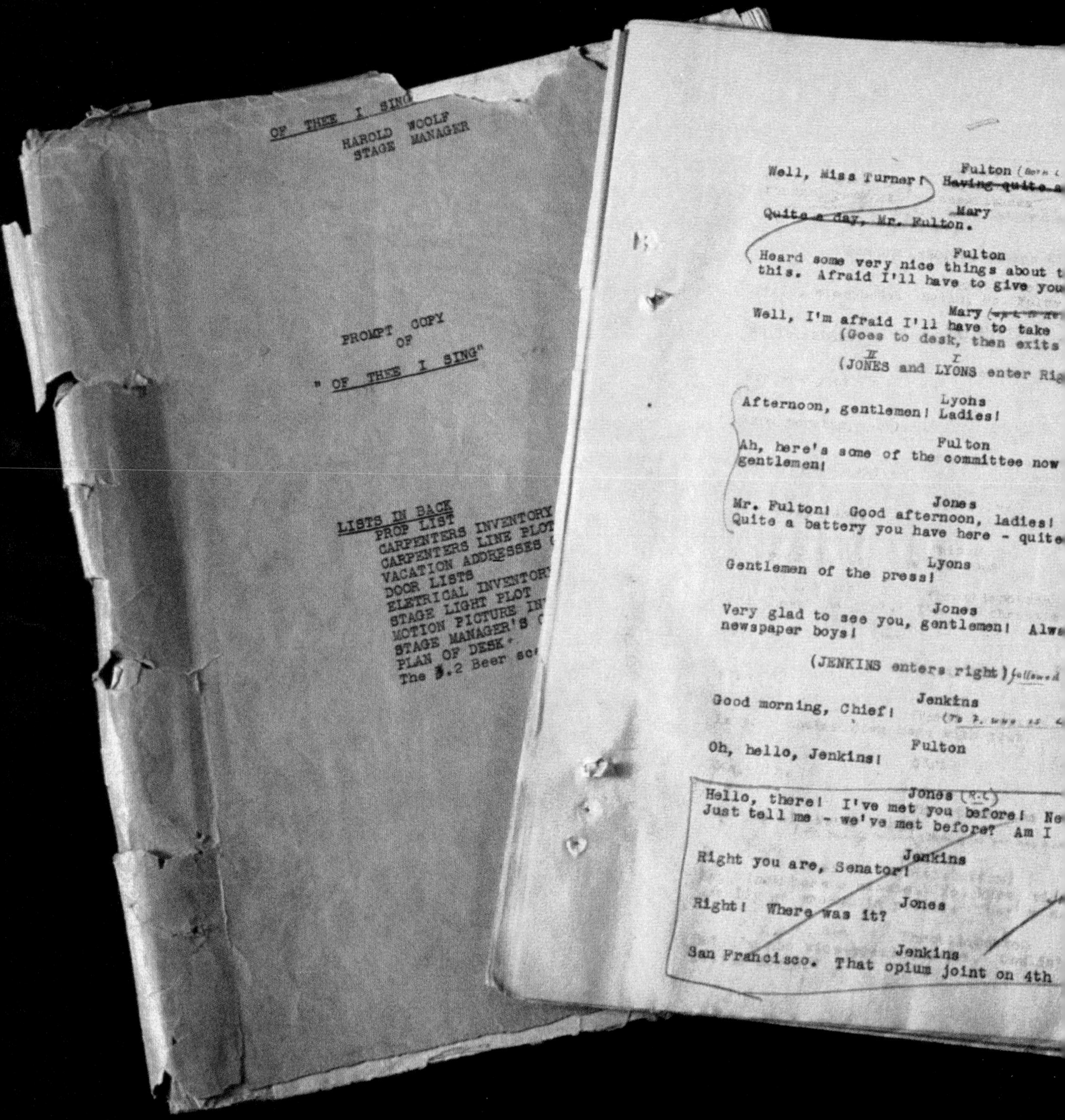

OF THEE I SING
HAROLD WOOLF
STAGE MANAGER
PROMPT COPY
OF
" OF THEE I SING"
LISTS IN BACK
PROP LIST
CARPENTERS INVENTORY
CARPENTERS LINE PLOT
VACATION ADDRESSES
DOOR LISTS
ELETRICAL INVENTORY
STAGE LIGHT PLOT
MOTION PICTURE IN
STAGE MANAGER'S
PLAN OF DESK.
The $.2 Beer sc
Fulton
Well, Miss Turner! Having quite a
Mary
Quite a day, Mr. Fulton.
Fulton
Heard some very nice things about t
this. Afraid I'll have to give you
Mary
Well, I'm afraid I'll have to take
(Goes to desk, then exits
(JONES and LYONS enter Rig
Lyons
Afternoon, gentlemen! Ladies!
Fulton
Ah, here's some of the committee now
gentlemen!
Jones
Mr. Fulton! Good afternoon, ladies!
Quite a battery you have here - quite
Lyons
Gentlemen of the press!
Jones
Very glad to see you, gentlemen! Alwa
newspaper boys!
(JENKINS enters right)
Jenkins
Good morning, Chief!
Fulton
Oh, hello, Jenkins!
Jones
Hello, there! I've met you before! Ne
Just tell me - we've met before? Am I
Jenkins
Right you are, Senator!
Jones
Right! Where was it?
Jenkins
San Francisco. That opium joint on 4th

                    Wintergreen
Take a memo to the Secretary of State: Referring to last
Tuesday night's poker game, please note that the Liberian
minister's check for twelve dollars and forty-five cents has
been returned for lack of funds. Kindly get a new minister
for next Tuesday night's game, and add $12.45 to the Liberian
National Debt."

                    Jenkins
Yes, sir.

                    Wintergreen
          (Takes Jenkins downstage out of earshot
Get the Governor of Maryland on the phone and ask him what
horse he likes in the fourth race at Pimlico.

                    Jenkins   WARN
Yes, sir.   PHONE

                    Wintergreen
          (Brandishing a telephone bill)
And tell the telephone company that this is not my bill.
          (Hands it to secretary)
That long distance call was March 3rd.

                    Jenkins
Yes, sir.

                    Wintergreen
          (As JENKINS starts to go)
Oh, anybody in the ante-room?

                    Jenkins
Yes, sir. Secretary of the Navy, Secretary of Agriculture,
and four zebras.

                    Wintergreen
Zebras?

                    Jenkins
There's a man who wants to give them to you.

                    Wintergreen
Well, I could use two.

          (A SECRETARY enters, with a wooden board,
          about two feet square, covered with elec-
          tric buttons. A long wire is attached to
          the board, and stretches across the stage
          as the SECRETARY advances to Jenkins.)

                    Jenkins
All ready, Mr. President.
          (Takes the board. The SECRETARY exits)
Time to press a button.

PULITZER PRIZED

The first musical to be awarded a Pulitzer Prize was a political satire, *Of Thee I Sing*; the second was *South Pacific* (1949); and the third was a political biography, *Fiorello!* (1959), based on the life and career of La Guardia, New York's colorful mayor. The book, which stayed reasonably close to the facts, was by Jerome Weidman and George Abbott; the lyrics and music were by the new (to hit status) team of Jerry Bock and Sheldon Harnick. The sentimental fondness for the mayor who fought Tammany Hall and read comics on the radio to kids may have contributed to its successful run of nearly 800 performances, for it had hardly the bite or wit of its Pulitzer predecessor.

The Pulitzer Prize people apparently prized satire, for, only two years later (1961), they gave their award for drama to *How to Succeed in Business Without Really Trying*, based more or less on Shepherd Mead's comic treatise on getting ahead in the corporate world without benefit of a Harvard MBA. The talents responsible for the slyly entertaining musical were formidable: Frank Loesser for the music and lyrics, Abe Burrows for the book and direction, and Bob Fosse as choreographer and co-director. But the show was firmly stolen by its pint-sized star, Robert Morse, first seen on a window washer's platform. Soon he is on his guileful way to the chairmanship of the board. *Time* magazine said he was the only Broadway actor "who could turn this despicable crud into the most lovable monster since Barrie's crocodile."

Another interesting, more technical aspect to the show was its double revolving stage, which was kept moving throughout the evening. When "Dancing in the Dark" was sung, Tilly Losch danced to changing lighting on a stage that was tilted and mirrored. In the "I Love Louisa" number, the performers were spun around on what appeared to be a Bavarian carousel. This was also the show that marked the end of Adele Astaire's stage career: she went to England to marry, leaving her brother to perform alone. As it turned out, he did not do badly.

"It's funnier than the government and not half so serious," wrote the *New York Times* critic of the irreverent musical satire on American politics, *Of Thee I Sing*, that came to the Music Box Theatre during the last week of 1931. The same critic felt, also, that the spirit of fun with which it took on presidential electioneering, the White House, the Senate, and the Supreme Court, gave proof that the nation could laugh at its own foibles and was still safe for democracy.

The musical's instigators, as might have been expected, were George S. Kaufman and Morrie Ryskind. Working in close collaboration with them were George and Ira Gershwin, and it was George's involvement with the show from its inception that produced a marked change in his style of composition. Instead of a conventional series of song inserts that were more likely to interrupt a story flow than carry it along, here the scoring was more complex, the songs firmly interwoven and necessary to the scenes of the play. George's musical

accomplishments were deepening, too: new concert pieces, such as "An American in Paris," were performed in concert halls, and he was already thinking seriously of composing a grand opera.

For the first time in a modern musical, rhymed recitative replaced dialogue, and the title song, first sung individually, swelled into a remarkable chorale. Understandably, critics began referring to the brothers as the jazz counterparts of Gilbert and Sullivan.

Just as *Show Boat* became a landmark of the twenties, so did *Of Thee I Sing* in the thirties. While the Gershwins deserved the praise showered on them, the libretto by Kaufman and Ryskind was a delight in itself — this attested to by its publication (a first for a musical) in book form. With its adult and joyfully jaundiced view of American politics, its inspired kidding of back-room bargaining, the rallies, speeches, and parades attending the election of a

The "Nine Old Men" of the Supreme Court.

president, its satire was both well aimed and hilarious.

The candidate who is the focus of all the commotion is John P. (for Peppermint) Wintergreen, a man with little but good looks and a hearty personality to qualify him for high public office. With few convictions, if any, he badly needs a plank to run on. There is a vice-presidential candidate, too, although none of the party bosses are able to remember his name. In any case, Alexander Throttlebottom tries to resign, because he doesn't think his mother would approve of his being vice-president.

The banners with their slogans appear: "A Vote for Wintergreen Is a Vote for Wintergreen!" "Vote for Prosperity and See What You Get!" and "Wintergreen — the Flavor Lasts!"

A platform issue is found. Wintergreen will run on — love! A beauty contest will be held in Atlantic City, the winner of which will become his wife. However, Wintergreen prefers his secretary, Mary Turner (Lois Moran), who makes wonderful corn muffins, over the contest winner, Diana Devereaux. The election results are flashed on a jittery screen: voting heavy in the South for Jefferson Davis; many write-in votes in California for Mickey Mouse; scattered votes for light wine, beer, and straight whiskey.

When Wintergreen, elected president, jilts the contest winner and marries his secretary, he precipitates a national and international furor. The French ambassador sees it as an insult to the honor of the entire French nation, on the grounds that Miss Devereaux is "the

Victor Moore in the midst of an apparently difficult campaign in *Of Thee I Sing* (1931).

illegitimate daughter of an illegitimate son of an illegitimate nephew of Napoleon." War is narrowly averted.

William Gaxton's performance as Wintergreen was thought by many to be a take-off on New York Mayor Jimmy Walker, although Kaufman, the director, denied this was his intent; Victor Moore was warmly applauded for the bewildered innocence of his Throttlebottom, a man so shy and inconspicuous that to enter the White House he has to join a guided tour. "They have fitted the dunce's cap to politics," wrote Brooks Atkinson, "and crowded an evening with laughter." The songs "Wintergreen for President" and "Of Thee I Sing, Baby" soon were at the top of the year's list and since have earned high places in the Broadway musical treasury.

Such political figures as Mayor Jimmy Walker and Al Smith, the 1928 presidential candidate, were in the first-night audience and were seen laughing heartily. The only ones not amused, apparently, were members of the Franco-American Society. They protested some lines in the show about France's unpaid war debts to America, and the ludicrous portrayal of a French ambassador. Kaufman offered to make changes, if the society could come up with lines just as funny. And there the matter rested.

The Pulitzer Prize committee awarded *Of Thee I Sing* the 1932 prize for

The pro-love candidate (William Gaxton) and the next First Lady (Lois Moran), in the glare of the political spotlight.

drama, a first for a musical show. "The play is unusual," the citation read. "Its effect on the stage promises to be very considerable." The rules, however, did not allow for an award to a show's composer. Thus, the names of Kaufman, Ryskind, and Ira Gershwin were cited for the award, but not George's.

The year 1933 was neither good for the nation nor for Broadway's musicals; only an unlucky thirteen opened, and most of them closed. One exception was *As Thousands Cheer*, a revue that carried a definite chip on its shoulder toward the events of the time. The nation was deep in the depression, with one out of every four workers unemployed. Bank holidays were declared, relief lines grew, apples were sold on corners, and the new president, Franklin Delano Roosevelt, felt it necessary to take to the airwaves with the calming message that "The only thing we have to fear is fear itself."

The Pulitzer Prize committee's remark about the potential effect that *Of Thee I Sing* might have on the public could also have applied to *As Thousands Cheer*. In fact, it went its predecessor one better, and named names. The targets on this occasion were not farcical reflections, but a bunch of real people: of the power elite, the Roosevelts, the Hoovers, the Rockefellers; of names in the news, the Prince of Wales, Queen Mary, Gandhi, rich girl Barbara Hutton, effete Noël Coward, censorious movie czar Will Hays, and the divorcing pair, Joan Crawford and Douglas Fairbanks, Jr.

Irving Berlin was in top form with the songs "Not for All the Rice in China,"

"Harlem on My Mind" and "Easter Parade"; while Moss Hart, a New York public school–educated playwright, provided the acid-tipped sketches. Critics were now noticing that the musical show could be much more than fluffy nonsense and moon-June type romance, that it could be a funnel for sharp American humor and clever satire, yet still have the visual beauty of the kind customarily provided by Ziegfeld and others.

In its presentation as a kind of living newspaper, *As Thousands Cheer* was clever, too. Columns of type streamed up and down on the curtains, with headlines introducing the various numbers. The headline, FRANKLIN D. ROOSEVELT INAUGURATED TOMORROW introduced a sketch that had Mr. and Mrs. Hoover packing up in the White House, and saying what they really thought of people in the cabinet. A weather report brought on "Heat Wave," sung by Ethel Waters.

While much of the show was given over to rather deadly impersonations of the targets by Clifton Webb, Marilyn Miller, Ethel Waters, and Helen Broderick, it did not stint on the customary girls. The dances, though, were unusual enough to draw mixed critical reaction. One of these, headlined REVOLT IN CUBA, was a frenetic, sexy rumba in a darkened cellar accompanied by the flash and booming of guns from the outside. The *Commonweal* critic called it "elaborately disgusting," but the *World-Telegram* thought it "sophisticated."

Not all of the show was sheer nose-thumbing fun. One headline produced a unique and searing theatre

Ethel Waters ran an emotional gamut in *As Thousands Cheer* (1933), ranging from a hilarious parody of Josephine Baker to the searing "Supper Time."

moment: NEGRO LYNCHED BY FRENZIED MOB led to Ethel Waters's singing of "Supper Time," a black woman's lament for her lynched husband. On the other hand, a lavender-scented segment had Marilyn Miller and Clifton Webb emerging from a photo in the rotogravure section to join a long-ago Easter parade on Fifth Avenue — to the Irving Berlin song, of course.

Among the distressing series of flops that year was *Pardon My English*, a show that a score by the Gershwins was unable to save. One of its producers, Vinton Freedley, was determined not to fail the next time out. He was on holiday, fishing in the Pacific Ocean, when he evolved what he thought would be a sure-fire formula: three hot stars, the best book-writers in the business, and the brightest new songwriter and lyricist.

On land again, though as yet lacking words and music, he got commitments from Ethel Merman, who had lighted up *Girl Crazy*; William Gaxton and Victor Moore, the delightfully mad pair in *Of Thee I Sing*; the veterans Bolton and Wodehouse for the book; and for lyrics and music, Cole Porter, whose song "Night and Day," from his recent show, *Gay Divorce*, was the nation's number one hit.

An idea was needed, of course. Freedley, fresh from the ocean, suggested to Bolton and Wodehouse a comic story about some zany characters on a Europe-bound ocean liner, its climax to be a shipwreck.

This slapdash way of assembling a show was hardly unique then on Broadway. Vinton, though, faced more than ordinary difficulties in pulling together his several strings. Bolton had tax problems and was living in England, while Wodehouse refused to go there. Their collaboration on the script was by transatlantic telephone. Meanwhile Cole was drifting down the Rhine on a faltboat and was difficult to reach. When he came back to the States with his songs, Ethel Merman insisted he play and sing them for her parents before she would sign her

contract. Then, when the book for the musical arrived, Freedley found it disappointing — lacking in humor, and, since Merman was not the romantic lead, with not much of a part for her. Worse, though, was a recent tragic news event: the steamship *Morro Castle* had caught fire and more than a hundred passengers had perished. The story's comic shipwreck would seem in bad taste and had to go, but Bolt and Wodehouse were unavailable for the indicated major surgery.

The director, Howard Lindsay, had already been hired, and, with rehearsals about to begin, he was prevailed upon to rewrite the script with a collaborator, the Theatre Guild's press agent, Russel Crouse.

The basic idea was that William Gaxton, in love with an heiress about to marry (as usual for Bolton and Wodehouse) the wrong man, follows her aboard ship, but fails to debark before sailing. Beyond that, as Freedley told Lindsay and Crouse in the course of making changes, "Anything goes." Since they also lacked a good title, they forthwith adopted it for the show.

In freshening the plot, Lindsay and Crouse decided to make Victor Moore Public Enemy Number Thirteen and put him aboard ship disguised as the Reverend Dr. Moon with a machine gun hidden in the saxophone case he carries with him at all times. William Gaxton has no passport, and to keep from being caught and put in the brig, adopts several disguises: a sailor, a cook, John Dillinger, and a bearded Spanish grandee. To fashion the beard he shaves off hair from a dog. "Are you Spanish?"

(*opposite*)
Like Fred Astaire, Clifton Webb, who appeared in *As Thousands Cheer* (1933), was a midwesterner who brought urbane glamour and sophistication to Broadway.

Watercolor of Cole Porter by
Ben Hur Baz.

(opposite)
Ethel Merman, William Gaxton in
sailor disguise, and Victor Moore, an
unlikely Public Enemy Number
Thirteen in *Anything Goes* (1934).

a woman asks him. "No," he replies, "Pomeranian."

Creating a role for Ethel Merman was more difficult. Lindsay and Crouse were lunching when they noticed a woman they took for a well-known evangelist. It turned out she was an equally well-known nightclub hostess. Merman was to meet the two for lunch, and when she arrived they promptly told her she would be playing a reformed evangelist who was now a nightclub singer in love with William Gaxton. She took the information down in her customary shorthand.

One might have assumed from the desperation with which the changes were made, many in the midst of rehearsals, that a disastrous fate loomed when the show opened at the Alvin Theatre in late November 1934. Instead, with Merman belting out "You're the Top," "I Get a Kick Out of You," and

"Blow, Gabriel, Blow," and with critics saying *Anything Goes* was "as light as air, as bright as sunshine, and as joyous as laughter" (John Mason Brown), it was a triumph, and ever after regarded as the "quintessential musical comedy of the thirties."

Admittedly, it followed well-worn conventions of musical comedy, but with its sprightly inventiveness, madcap humor, topicality, and naughty spirit, it made the conventions serve a worthwhile purpose: top-notch entertainment. Five of Cole Porter's songs became great hits. Simultaneously, his "Night and Day" from *Gay Divorce* was being heard in a movie version, retitled *The Gay Divorcee*. All this was more than enough to lift him to elite status among Broadway's lyricists and composers.

He had been composing for many years, and was forty-three at the time of *Anything Goes*, but a major hit had been eluding him until *Gay Divorce* of two years earlier. Born into a wealthy Indiana family, he went to Yale, where he composed for college shows, and from there to Harvard Law School. Over his family's objections, he shifted to the Graduate School of Arts and Sciences and studied music composition.

Talented as he was, he was as intent on a pleasurable social life and travel as on his songwriting, and while contributing to several shows through the twenties, he also evoked media interest because of his high style of living. He was talked and written about as a playboy, a sophisticate, a snob partial to socialites, a highbrow, and an expatriate. His success seemed to come easy to him, achieved apparently between partying

120

and visits to exotic places, but the more accurate case was that wherever he worked, whether in Paris, in a palazzo in Venice, or in the Waldorf Towers in New York, he toiled mightily to master a difficult craft.

George Gershwin was on a quite different course during the months that *Anything Goes* was selling out at the Alvin Theatre. He was completing his full-length "folk opera," *Porgy and Bess*, a project that had been on his mind since

1926 when he had first read a novel, *Porgy*, written by the Southern author DuBose Heyward. He informed Heyward by letter that he would be interested in using the book as a basis for an opera.

Heyward was elated by the prospect, until his wife, Dorothy, told him she had been secretly working on a play version of the story. Heyward loyally chose his wife. Gershwin was not put off by this news. No reason his opera could not be done from the play and, anyway, he wanted time to broaden his compositional skills. The play, *Porgy*, now a collaboration between husband and wife, was successfully mounted by the Theatre Guild in 1927, and ran more than a year.

Gershwin's fame grew apace, but it wasn't until 1933 that Gershwin decided it might be time to take up the *Porgy* opera idea. Even so, he was somewhat chastened when Heyward informed him that the Theatre Guild was considering a musical version of the story to be done by Oscar Hammerstein and Jerome Kern — Al Jolson to play in blackface the crippled hero who gets around with a goat cart. Not that Heyward approved of the choice of Jolson — indeed, he wanted an all-black cast to inhabit the setting of the story, a Charleston slum called Catfish Row.

Gershwin got down to work, with Heyward supplying the libretto and lyrics of what was eventually described as "An American Folk Opera." The collaboration was unusual in that most of it was done by letter — Heyward did not enjoy traveling from his Charleston abode — and, after a time, when necessary, Ira Gershwin pitched in for

Al Jolson, in blackface makeup. He was the Theatre Guild's choice to play the title character in their proposed musical version of the play *Porgy*.

THE THEATRE GUILD PRESENTS
PORGY
BY DUBOIS & DOROTHY HEYWARD

GUILD THEATRE 🕮
52 STREET WEST of BROADWAY

Window card from the original production of the play *Porgy* (1927), from which the opera *Porgy and Bess* was adapted.

some of the lyrics, one of his happiest inspirations being "It Ain't Necessarily So," sung by the rascally dope peddler, Sportin' Life.

There was a question at one point about where the opera would be performed, with the Metropolitan Opera under consideration. That, though, would have necessitated at best a mixed white and black cast, for the Metropolitan had no black singers on its roster. George Gershwin felt he owed a decided debt to the jazz and blues of the great black musicians, the music that had so inspired and informed his own during his youthful years. He agreed with Heyward that the opera should be performed by blacks. Also, he felt, the salary requirements of the huge cast needed the kind of long run Broadway

AGREEMENT made this 28th day of June 1935, by and between THE THEATRE GUILD, INC., of the City of New York, hereinafter designated "Manager", and GEORGE GERSHWIN, Composer, IRA GERSHWIN, Lyricist, and DuBOSE and DOROTHY HEYWARD, Authors of the book, hereinafter designated "Authors".

WITNESSETH:

WHEREAS, the Authors respectively have composed and written the music, lyrics and book of a dramatico-musical composition which the Manager intends to produce, at present entitled "PORGY" (title subject to change), hereinafter referred to as the "Opera", and

WHEREAS, the said Manager has signed the Minimum Basic Agreement and is in good standing with the Dramatists' Guild of the Authors' League of America, Inc., of which Guild the Authors are members, and

WHEREAS, the Manager desires to obtain an exclusive lease to produce and present the Opera in the United States of America and the Dominion of Canada as provided for in and subject to said Minimum Basic Agreement, and the Authors wish to grant such lease,

NOW, THEREFORE, in consideration of the premises and the sum of One Dollar and other good and valuable con-

—7—

at the cost and expense of the Manager, but and title of the original score shall with George Gershwin and the title of all shall at all times be vested in George shall be entitled to the possession there-ination of the Manager's rights of presen-ited States and Canada hereunder.

agreed by the parties hereto that the said omed a collaboration but that after the of presentation herein shall terminate, y mutual consent arrange for the separate ics and libretto.

agreement is binding upon the Manager and their personal representatives.

WHEREOF, the Manager has caused these by its duly authorized officer and nto set their hands and seals the e written.

THE THEATRE GUILD, INC.
By

George Gershwin (L.S.)
Ira Gershwin (L.S.)
DuBose Heyward (L.S.)
Dorothy Heyward (L.S.)

Contract for the opera *Porgy and Bess* (1935) between DuBose and Dorothy Heyward and the Gershwins.

could provide. The Theatre Guild became the producer, its first musical outing other than the *Garrick Gaities* revues of the mid-twenties.

A widespread search was made for the best-trained black singers and performers. Many hundreds were sought out and interviewed. For his Porgy, Gershwin enlisted Todd Duncan, a fine baritone and music professor, who needed train fare from Washington to New York, so that Gershwin could hear him sing. Young Anne Wiggins Brown wrote him a letter applying for an audition. She was chosen for Bess, the somewhat sullied woman who becomes the object of Porgy's love and devotion. John W. Bubbles, a delightful song-and-dance vaudevillian, had problems reading music, but was championed by Gershwin as ideal for the villainous and comic role of Sportin' Life.

To distinguish it from the play version, the opera was named *Porgy and Bess*. It premiered at the Alvin Theatre on October 10, 1935, already the object of

Ira and George Gershwin share a work session.

Opening-night curtain bows. George Gershwin and DuBose Heyward join the cast of *Porgy and Bess*.

CAN THIS BE OPERA?

After the premiere of *Porgy and Bess* in 1935, critics seemed uncertain as to just what it was. Lawrence Gilman, for instance, wrote: "Whether *Porgy and Bess* is or is not a blown-in-the-bottle opera seemed of no concern to anyone at all last evening. But that is little reason why one should not call it that. Mr. Gershwin thinks it is, and the music critics present will surely agree with him."

One of those critics, Olin Downes of the *New York Times*, however, felt that Gershwin "has not completely formed his style as an operatic composer. The style is at one moment of opera and another of operetta or sheer Broadway entertainment." His colleague, Brooks Atkinson, admired the dramatic values, but turned grumpy over the recitatives: "Why commonplace remarks that carry no emotion have to be made in a chanting monotone is a problem that this reviewer cannot fathom." Composer Virgil Thomson called the work "crooked folklore and halfway opera," and decided that it came from "impure musical sources . . . at best a piquant but highly unsavory stirring up-together of Israel, Africa, and the Gaelic Isles."

much anticipation from the periodic announcements about the progress Gershwin was making while he composed and orchestrated the score. In the midst of the depression, the opening attracted probably the most distinguished and the best- and most expensively dressed patronage of the decade. The audience was made up of stars of opera, stage, and films; of financiers and society leaders; and of two kinds of critics, for the newspapers had sent representatives of both the music and drama desks.

Although given a long standing ovation that first night, *Porgy and Bess* drew a curiously mixed response from the critics. The theatre critics mostly lauded it; the music critics wondered whether it was truly an opera — or was it some kind of hybrid? A dramatic musical, or a music drama, perhaps. Most everyone agreed that there was genius in the work, that it brought something new and original to American music, that it contained several superlative arias and songs: the haunting "Summertime," the soaring "Bess, You Is My Woman Now," and the catchy "I Got Plenty o' Nuttin'." But it took many more years before it reached its present-day status as an operatic masterwork.

In 1942, *Porgy and Bess* was brought back to Broadway by Cheryl Crawford and became an instantaneous hit. Critics took back their earlier reservations. After World War II it was performed frequently in European opera houses to much acclaim, but mostly in blackface. Then, in 1952, director Robert Breen and producer Blevins Davis, idealistically motivated, mounted a production that began in Dallas, moved on to Washington, after which it embarked on a series of tours — some with State Department assistance — that took it to Europe, the Middle East, and South America. It became the first American opera to play at the prestigious La Scala in Milan. In Leningrad and

Moscow, it was the first American theatre company to play in the Soviet Union since its Revolution.

Oddly, not everyone was happy about this breach of the Iron Curtain. Some thought that by showing blacks living in the slum quarters of Catfish Row, the opera could be used as propaganda about conditions for blacks in the United States. Some black critics, while admitting the opportunities given

Poster advertising *Porgy and Bess* when it came to Milan's La Scala opera house in 1954.

Silver tray signed by 143 theatre notables, and given to George Gershwin on the opening night of *Porgy and Bess.*

125

BEHIND THE CURTAIN

When *Porgy and Bess* broke through the Iron Curtain in late 1955 and early 1956, the American theatre troupe was the first to visit Russia since the Revolution. Tickets were so scarce that some were awarded as prizes to workers who exceeded their quotas. Gala openings were held in Leningrad and in Moscow; at the latter, in the famed Stanislavsky Theatre, several in the audience wept at the end, some were silent, still hypnotized by the melodies, while others shouted and stamped their feet. The interest in the opera and its remarkable black cast was so high among the Russians that, to the amazement of everyone, the top brass of the Soviet Union — Khrushchev, Bulganin, and Molotov — attended the second performance. One Russian minister remarked that they came so soon because they were afraid they couldn't get tickets later.

Sumptuous parties were given, at which the members of the cast mingled with ambassadors, Soviet officials, and important "People's Artists." United States Ambassador Bohlen reciprocated with a party at which ham, turkey, fresh fruit, and Coca-Cola were served. Russian guests were seen stuffing their pockets with oranges, apples, and bananas, rare commodities at the time. The rubles paid the cast by the Russians did them little good. There was little to buy, and some of the money was simply placed in a Moscow bank and left there.

Todd Duncan, the opera's Porgy.

Anne Wiggins Brown, who sang Bess.

to many black singers to advance their careers, thought the opera's story derogatory, in that it portrayed the poverty-stricken denizens of Catfish Row as superstitious, shooting craps, selling drugs, and engaging in violence. Others defended the opera, saying that its more melodramatic aspects had to do with a certain time and a certain place, and that its human values far outweighed the less savory aspects. Meanwhile, arguments continued as to whether *Porgy and Bess* was an opera or something else.

Most of the controversy had ended when, in 1985, the Metropolitan Opera, fifty years after the premiere of *Porgy and Bess*, added it to its repertory. But there still remained one last question

Catfish Row on stage.

to be resolved. Many of those with long memories of the early productions still thought it had played better on Broadway.

The canvas was widening. Broadway's musical theatre, having accommodated an operatic work, next achieved a breakthrough in dance. It was only a few months after *Porgy and Bess* closed that a Rodgers and Hart musical, *On Your Toes*, with choreography by the talented Russian-born ballet-master George Balanchine, came to the Imperial Theatre. But it had taken a roundabout way to get there.

Richard Rodgers and Lorenz Hart were working in Hollywood, riding out the depression, when they heard that RKO was looking for a vehicle for its smashingly successful dance team of Ginger Rogers and Fred Astaire. They promptly concocted a story about a vaudeville song-and-dance man with higher cultural aspirations, who rescues a struggling Russian ballet company from its financial difficulties by staging a jazz ballet. They presented their idea to Fred Astaire, but he decided against it because he felt his movie image now made it necessary for him to wear his trademark top hat, white tie, and tails.

On their return to New York, Rodgers happened to bump into Harry Kaufman, a producer for the Shubert brothers' musicals, who asked if maybe he and Hart had something in mind for a musical. Rodgers mentioned the idea that Astaire had turned down but said it would need a dancer of commensurate ability. "How about Ray Bolger?" Kaufman asked. Bolger had recently appeared to advantage in the revue *Life Begins at 8:40.*

Rodgers thought Bolger would be perfect; more, that he was sure to become a star, and contracts soon were signed with the Shuberts. However, the Shuberts, dubious about the prospects of a show larded with so much ballet, allowed their option to lapse, and another producer, Dwight Deere Wiman, took it up. The Rodgers and Hart book needed more work, so the veteran director and playwright George Abbott was brought in as co-author. He also subsequently took over the direction

Tamara Geva and Ray Bolger in the "Slaughter on Tenth Avenue" ballet from *On Your Toes* (1936).

when the show had to be rescued out of town.

Two important sequences were full-fashioned ballets choreographed by Balanchine, the second, "Slaughter on Tenth Avenue," serving as the show's climax. The hero of the story, the target of gangsters, has to keep on dancing to keep from being killed. Before matters are resolved in his favor, he dances to the point of collapse.

Rodgers and Hart had picked Balanchine because of his fresh and inventive work with his own dance company, then resident with the Metropolitan Opera, but they had trouble communicating — at least in English. Rodgers asked him how best to coordinate the music with the choreography. "You write, I put on," Balanchine told Rodgers.

"He used the music just the way I had written it," Rodgers said later, "and created his dance patterns to conform."

The first of Balanchine's tasks was to create a wild satire on classical ballet called "The Princess Zenobia." Bolger, as the vaudevillian Phil Dolan, is smitten with ballet and, in particular, with the lovely Vera Baranova of the Russian Ballet. To be near her he joins her company and participates in the Scheherazade-like ballet as a black-skinned native. Unfortunately, he paints his face, but forgets the rest of his body, thereby precipitating a fiasco. Later, though, he fashions "Slaughter on Tenth Avenue," a jazzy ballet takeoff on a gangster movie, which turns "real" when the gangsters enter. Rodgers's music for the ballet was his most accomplished composition yet. More standard was the fetching, much-sung ballad "There's a Small Hotel."

The first-rate cast had Tamara Geva as the Russian ballerina, Monty Woolley as the ballet company's impresario, and Luella Gear as his cynical adviser. The critics, without exception, praised the innovative use of ballet, but saved their loudest cheers for Ray Bolger, with one of them voicing the virtually unthinkable: that he was better than Astaire!

The long run of *On Your Toes* gave a needed boost to the careers of Rodgers and Hart. Never again, said Rodgers, would they have to retreat to the limbo of Hollywood; they now had the professional and financial security to do the kind of creative work they had always had in mind. "Slaughter on Tenth Avenue," by the way, became a modern ballet classic on its own.

When Franklin D. Roosevelt was inaugurated for his second term in 1937, he faced widespread unemployment, labor unrest, and a tragic migration from the Midwest caused by the prairies that had become vast dust bowls. In his echoing inaugural words he said: "I see one third of a nation ill-housed, ill-clad, ill-nourished." Storm clouds abroad were increasingly heavy. Spain was in deadly conflict, Mussolini was bombing Ethiopia into submission, and Hitler in Germany was making menacing moves in the directions of Czechoslovakia and Austria. How was the theatre reacting to all this?

Note the stage hits of 1937: *Golden Boy, Having a Wonderful Time, Susan and God, French Without Tears.* In a time when two of the most prevalent buzzwords

were "social significance," very little of it could be found on Broadway, either in straight plays or in musicals. Rodgers and Hart turned out another hit, *Babes in Arms,* which was full of youthful fun and spirits and had the memorable songs "Where or When" and "The Lady Is a Tramp," but it addressed no basic social problems of the day. In their *I'd Rather Be Right,* George S. Kaufman and Moss Hart aimed some gentle satire at Roosevelt (portrayed by the anti-Roosevelt George M. Cohan), but hardly a word about that "one-third of a nation" mentioned by the real president.

It remained for an unpretentious revue, *Pins and Needles,* performed by amateurs, to say something in musical terms relevant to the contemporary scene. It is not inaccurate to say that the show sneaked up on the somewhat patronizing critics. It was produced by the International Ladies Garment Workers Union with the aim of attracting new members and entertaining old ones. The union had put Louis Schaffer, a former labor reporter, in charge of its new Labor Stage, which sponsored various performing arts activities for its members. For a headquarters, Schaffer acquired the old Princess Theatre (of Jerome Kern fame) and then looked around for something for the union's drama group to do.

He searched through dozens of scripts for one with a labor theme that would say something about the cause and do so entertainingly. Most of the submissions were cut from a solemnly proletarian pattern, and usually ended with a group of people yelling "Strike!" He decided that a musical review was a

Drawing of George Balanchine by William Auerbach-Levy.

Cast of *Babes in Arms* (1937). Mitzi Green (left), Wynn Murray, and Ray Heatherton (center).

OH, FOR A PLACE TO PLAY

When *The Cradle Will Rock* was abandoned by the Federal Theatre Project, the managers, John Houseman and Orson Welles, decided to put it on anyway at the Maxine Elliott Theatre. But Actors Equity enjoined the cast from performing there because of its contract with the Project, and the opening night had to be canceled. A hurried search was made for another theatre, even a ballroom or a nightclub, but an hour before performance time, with the cast and composer Marc Blitzstein waiting to play the score on piano without benefit of orchestra, nothing had turned up. John Houseman, in his autobiography *Run-Through*, describes what happened:

"It was then that the miracle occurred. The down-at-heel theatrical agent rose and moved toward the stair. In the doorway he paused, turned, and spoke. It was an exit speech, uttered in a weak, despondent tone. The gist of it seemed to be that since there was nothing more he could do, he might as well go home. Only he couldn't understand what was wrong with the Venice Theatre (twenty blocks uptown). He turned and started up the stairs. He was already halfway up when he was seized, dragged down, shaken and howled at. *What* Venice Theatre? He then explained that for three hours he had been offering us a theatre that was open, empty, available, unpicketed and suitable to our requirements — but that no one had listened to him. . . .

"Our curtain time was changed to 9 P.M. Everyone was urged to invite one or more friends. There was cheering as the voyage began — by bus, subway, taxi and (it being a fine June evening) on foot."

more palatable way of sending a labor message, and, providentially, found Harold Rome, a young composer-lyricist who had done shows on the active summer circuit in the Catskills. Skits for the show came from several sources.

Schaffer presented the material to the members of the union's drama group, made up of dressmakers, garment cutters, buttonhole makers, and the like, anyone, in fact, interested in singing, acting, and dancing in the off hours. The group thought the revue form too frivolous; they wanted something more substantial. Schaffer took another tack; he gave the same material to a professional group, which put it on for one performance so successfully at the Princess (renamed the Labor Stage) that several Broadway producers wanted to stage it in a larger house. Instead, Schaffer returned the revue material to the drama group, which had now reversed its collective mind about it. "I couldn't believe it," Rome said later. "Here was a chance to go to Broadway and Schaffer, the lunatic, stood pat!"

For the next year and a half a cast of forty-five garment workers worked at their jobs all day and rehearsed three and four hours several nights of the week. Several learned to tap dance. A group of dress cutters and knitwear men were trained by Rome as a harmonizing quartet. When *Pins and Needles* opened in late November 1937, it gave only Friday and Saturday performances; during the week the performers needed all their energies for their jobs.

The *New York Times* sent a second-string reviewer to the opening night performance (initials J.G.) who reported it to be "a witty and tuneful morsel considerably enhanced by the infectious enthusiasm of the cast." He mentioned, too, that they didn't miss "many plugs for the anti-fascism cause and for the working man in general." Not all the critics attended the premiere, but when word got around that something bright, funny, and clever was going on at the Labor Stage, they belatedly sang the show's praises.

One of the show's virtues was the rapport established between the performers and the audience. In place of an orchestra, two pianists (one of them Harold Rome himself) strolled down the aisle and took their places. When the curtain went up, cast members described their work, and then broke into the witty "Sing Me a Song With Social Significance." In another number the "Four Little Angels of Peace" were Mussolini, Hitler, an unnamed Japanese, and Neville Chamberlain. When war broke out in 1939, Chamberlain was dropped and the four angels became three. A dance number, "Doin' the Reactionary," pilloried the supposedly complacent upper classes.

Ticket demand was such that soon the show was playing every day, and then had to be moved from the 300-seat theatre to a larger house. As new events occurred, the numbers underwent change. In response to the refusal of the Daughters of the American Revolution to allow Marian Anderson to sing in their Washington auditorium, a Gilbert and Sullivan parody was added, "Three Little DAR's Are We." The DAR, in turn, claimed that the show would "make any adult ashamed to be in the audience."

Mrs. Eleanor Roosevelt was not ashamed. She saw the show four times, and invited it to the White House. Her husband loved it, and was much taken with the song "Call It Un-American," about certain patriots wont to attack his New Deal policies by terming them "un-American."

The ILGWU's benefit fund was augmented by more than a million dollars during the run of some 1,100 performances, and the subsequent tours. Few in the cast were seduced into theatre careers by their success, and most of them went back to their regular jobs, satisfied at having said something.

A much more savage attack on the status quo was Marc Blitzstein's *The Cradle Will Rock*, which took a rocky road to reach Broadway in January 1938. It, too, had its say, but in the very pamphleteering way that *Pins and Needles* had avoided. Trading on the satiric opera-bouffe style of Bertolt Brecht and Kurt Weill in their *Threepenny Opera* of the Berlin twenties, Blitzstein used cardboard stereotypes to get his pro-labor message across, with the implication that unless things changed drastically the "cradle" would not only rock but fall.

The action took place in "Steeltown, USA," and just in case anyone missed the point, the lordly mill owner was named Mr. Mister, while Larry Foreman was the name of the heroic union organizer who succeeds in rallying the proletarian workers to strike for their salvation. The accompanying atonal score, with its percussive effects, was as bleak as the harsh agit-prop libretto. If the work retains a certain significance, it is as an artifact of the

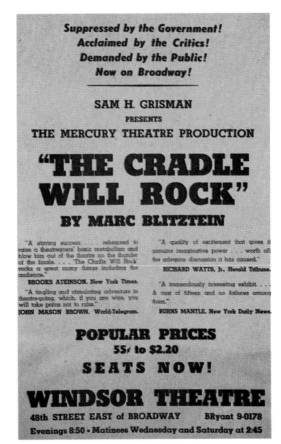

Special program issued for *The Cradle Will Rock*, when it found a home at a commercial theatre.

Marc Blitzstein, who wrote *The Cradle Will Rock* (1937).

labor struggle of the thirties, and it is more remembered as a cause célèbre than for its inherent musical qualities.

It was first scheduled to be produced by the Federal Theatre Project of the Works Progress Administration, a program designed to provide work for theatre professionals. When John Houseman, the supervisor for the New York branch of the project, decided to put on an Orson Welles staging of *The Cradle Will Rock*, Congress was already rumbling with rumors of fund cuts and cut-offs of the many arts projects, the Federal Theatre being a particular target because of what was regarded as a too-liberal slant of some of its productions. At the same time, labor strife, accompanied by violence, was racking the industrial cities of the Midwest.

The WPA administrators in Washington, without using that inflammatory word "censorship," placed an injunction against the show just before it was scheduled to open. This precipitated a parade twenty blocks up Broadway, led by Houseman and Welles, to a theatre where an unusual performance was put on. Neither musicians nor actors were allowed to perform by their unions, so the actors bought their own tickets and performed from their seats in the audience, while Blitzstein played his score from a piano onstage. Newspaper headlines the next day proclaimed it "The Runaway Opera." Some six months later, the show was given a Sunday-evening performance at the Mercury Theatre (run by Houseman and Welles), where it won praise from several reviewers, after which it ran for three months at the Windsor Theatre.

The Federal Theatre Project, for all its good and innovative productions, had constant trouble with local and state censorship. Because of *The Cradle Will Rock* rebellion, Houseman was dismissed from his supervisory post, but he and Welles responded by forming their own Mercury Theatre repertory company. Eventually, in his autobiography, Houseman admitted that the work was a "time bomb" that had threatened to wreck the entire theatre program. Undoubtedly it had its influence on the Congress when, in 1939, it did indeed end all funding for the Federal Theatre.

In October 1939, Richard Rodgers received a letter from the writer John O'Hara suggesting a musical show be made from a series of short stories he had published in *The New Yorker* magazine. The stories, written in the form of letters, concerned a small-time nightclub dancer who signed himself "Pal Joey," and who revealed himself as something of a heel. He lied, bragged, preyed on women, and was, in general, an embodiment of the sleazier side of show business. On the surface he was anything but the kind of romantic lead usual to musical comedy.

Rodgers, though, saw in Joey an opportunity to do something different, to portray a character close to real life, and a way of enlarging Broadway's musical boundaries. Hart also saw possibilities in the stories, and O'Hara went to work on a book for the show, developing the plot from several incidents and characters in the series.

Meanwhile, Rodgers found his ideal Pal Joey in an engaging young actor and dancer, Gene Kelly, whom he had seen recently in William Saroyan's play *The Time of Your Life*. For Vera, an

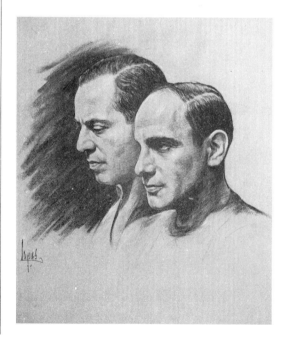

Drawing of Richard Rodgers (left) and Lorenz Hart by Louis Lupas.

experienced older woman who temporarily loses her heart and some of her pocketbook to Joey, Vivienne Segal was chosen.

George Abbott took on the production and direction, though dubious about the chances of a show with a stage full of unsavory characters. An exception is Joey's innocent young girlfriend, Linda, met early on. She is quickly ditched for Vera, who finds Joey attractive enough to keep him in an expensive apartment and to underwrite his nightclub, Chez Joey, where several of the production numbers take place. Vera, at one point, tries to account for her unseemly choice of a lover by singing the quite wonderful Rodgers song "Bewitched," with inventive words by Hart that captured her rueful mood.

Broadway was unused to a musical that took a cynical view of life, that had a most unlikable hero, that had a pretentious stripper (in Joey's nightclub) singing "Zip," with lines that reveal her highbrow literary tastes, and unzipping herself at the same time. A supposed love ballad, "I Could Write a Book," is actually a smooth line with which Joey charms Linda. However, when Linda learns that Joey is even more rotten than she had realized, she sings a duet with Vera, "Take Him," in which each offers Joey to the other while itemizing his odious characteristics. Is Joey disturbed? Hardly. Last seen he is propositioning another young lady.

The unconventional musical found enough adherents to last on Broadway for eleven months, but without a great deal of help from the reviewers. Brooks Atkinson, for one, found himself unwillingly entertained by the bright and expert production, but asked "Can you draw sweet water from a foul well?" The answer, eventually, was yes, because *Pal Joey* returned to Broadway some twelve years later, with hardy Vivienne Segal still playing Vera, and the critics, this time, lauding it as a landmark musical. Atkinson decided that the well was not so foul, after all, and John Mason Brown humbly confessed that on the first occasion he had missed the point of a brilliant and distinguished contribution to our theatre.

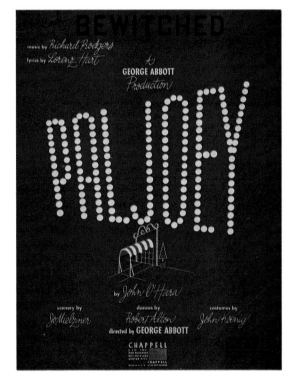

Bittersweet lyrics of the song "Bewitched" in *Pal Joey* (1940) reflect the feelings of a woman in love with a younger man.

Just a month after *Pal Joey* opened, the musical entered further unfamiliar territory — this time, the realm of psychoanalysis. Musicals often seemed to be born out of happenstance, and *Lady in the Dark* was no exception. Moss Hart, the show's principal author, had been undergoing psychoanalysis for several

Joey (Gene Kelly) and the girls polish a Robert Alton tap routine for *Pal Joey* (1940).

years, part of his therapy involving the recital and analysis of his dreams. He wanted to work on his own, and he also wanted to break away from conventional musical-comedy formulas. Which posed a problem, since he was morally bound to his longtime collaborator, George S. Kaufman.

The composer Kurt Weill, who had been in the country for four years after fleeing Nazi Germany, was also anxious to do something less formalized in musical theatre. He had written the music for Maxwell Anderson's *Knickerbocker Holiday*, which had achieved little success, but out of it had come Weill's great "September Song," sung by

Walter Huston. When he and Moss Hart met, they found a common ground in their mutual desire to do a different kind of musical.

Hart, as it turned out, had something in mind — a drama with music, first called "I Am Listening," about an unhappy career woman who visits a psychoanalyst to resolve her problems, and whose fantastic dreams would provide the main musical sequences. Weill took to the idea at once, and Hart traveled to the West Coast to enlist Ira Gershwin for the lyrics. George Gershwin had tragically died of a brain tumor at age thirty-eight two years earlier, and the grieving Ira had done little since. Now he was ready to go to work again.

Gertrude Lawrence was the star of choice to play the emotionally muddled fashion-editor-heroine, Liza Elliott, although Hart had earlier thought of Katharine Cornell. For Lawrence, the show was a major challenge. She had to act, sing, dance, and hold the stage for virtually the musical's entire length. Instead of consulting an analyst, she asked her friend Noël Coward what she ought to do, and he advised her by telegram that if she didn't do it, he would never speak to her again.

Four men play a part in Liza's life. One is her married lover, who is about to divorce his wife and wants Liza to marry him. Others are a handsome movie star (played by Victor Mature), her foppish photographer (Danny Kaye), and her plain, unassuming advertising manager

Oil painting of Gertrude Lawrence by Simon Elwes.

135

(Macdonald Carey). Her dreams provide the elaborate musical interludes: a "glamour" dream, a wedding dream, a circus dream, and a childhood dream. A kind of leitmotiv, the haunting song "My Ship," floats through Liza's reveries and the show.

During rehearsals a problem developed when it became clear that Danny Kaye's hilarious tongue-twisting rendition of the patter song "Tschaikowsky," in which he reeled off the names of fifty-seven Russian composers, would put a damper on the following song given to Lawrence. A new song, "Jenny," about a woman who couldn't make up her mind, was added for her, and she sang it with such gusto, vocal and physical, that she, too, stopped the show.

Lady in the Dark was hailed for its remarkable performances — notably those of Lawrence and Kaye — and for its artistry and style, and, with its long run, raised expectations that an era was looming of a more literate and sophisticated American musical.

It was all the more surprising, then, that instead of forging ahead into new uncharted musical waters, the Broadway musical reversed course and went back to the folksy past.

The circus dream in *Lady in the Dark* (1941). Victor Mature (left) and Danny Kaye (right). Both would soon leave the stage for Hollywood careers.

Silver cigarette case given to Ira Gershwin by Moss Hart. The date probably marks the beginning of their collaborative work on the show, since it opened a year later.

OKLAHOMA!

ST. JAMES THEATRE
44th ST. W. of BROADWAY   **MATINEES THURS. & SAT.**

V *In the American Grain, 1941–1949*

OKLAHOMA!

ON THE TOWN

CAROUSEL

ANNIE GET YOUR GUN

FINIAN'S RAINBOW

BRIGADOON

KISS ME, KATE

SOUTH PACIFIC

(opposite)
Poster design for the original production (1943).

Through the last half of the thirties and into the forties, Richard Rodgers and Lorenz Hart, in spite of an unparalleled string of successes, faced a difficulty, related to Hart's personal problems, that threatened their collaboration. A lonely, sensitive man, a homosexual, he drank to such excess that his health began to fail and his behavior became erratic and unpredictable. Rodgers bore with him through their years together, but there were times when he would finish an entire score before Hart got himself together enough to write a single lyric. Luckily, when Hart wrote, he did so at lightning speed. Amazingly, from *On Your Toes*, through *Babes in Arms, The Boys from Syracuse, Pal Joey*, to *By Jupiter* in 1942, the pair turned out year after year a string of hits that took them to the summit of musical comedy.

Meanwhile, Oscar Hammerstein II, after the great success with his libretto and lyrics for *Show Boat*, had a long, lean period. His witty and romantic period piece, *Sweet Adeline*, with charming music by Jerome Kern, seemed headed for a lengthy run, when the 1929 market crash scared off ticket buyers. After that, only one of his efforts, *Music in the Air*, lasted on Broadway for more than six months. Then one day in 1942 Richard Rodgers called him and suggested they talk about collaborating on a musical suggested by Theresa Helburn and Lawrence Langner, the directors of the Theatre Guild.

It was not that Rodgers had a falling out with Hart. They had simply disagreed about the merits of the proposed musical, which would be based on the Lynn Riggs 1931 play, *Green Grow the Lilacs*. Rodgers had liked the play and was enthusiastic about its possibilities for a musical. Hart, pleading exhaustion and his need for a vacation in Mexico, told Rodgers that he, Hart, would not mind if Rodgers found another lyricist. But, he added, "I think you're making a mistake."

Over lunch, Rodgers, who had great admiration for Hammerstein as a lyricist, discovered that he not only knew and liked the play, but had recently gone to the West Coast in an attempt to interest Jerome Kern in collaborating with him on a musical version. Kern had simply remarked that there was no third act in it, and the matter was dropped. So the new pairing became Rodgers and Hammerstein.

The Theatre Guild was also having a distressing time. Its preceding season had resulted in so many failures that it was facing bankruptcy. The hope was that a successful musical would help restore its fortunes, which was why Helburn and Langner turned first to Rodgers and Hart. Even though they had Rodgers to "sell" to the needed investors, Hammerstein's recent track record was not reassuring. Nor was the "property" — the Lynn Riggs folk play in its original form had lasted only a few weeks. Much of its bucolic tale had to do with the romantic tribulations of a cowboy, Curly, and a farm girl, Laurey, the complications arising out of the girl's innocent flirtation with a malevolent farmhand. These quite unearthshaking events take place against the larger frame of the impending statehood of Oklahoma.

In its early stages the musical became known as "Helburn's folly," as

141

HER OWN THING

When Agnes de Mille heard that Rodgers and Hammerstein were preparing a musical based on Lynn Riggs's play *Green Grow the Lilacs,* she felt it would be perfectly suited to the kind of native American traditional material she used for her own ballets — in particular, her recent *Rodeo* for the Ballets Russes de Monte Carlo at the Metropolitan Opera. They failed to respond, though, to her expression of interest. One day she met Oscar Hammerstein on the street and said, "This is my thing, how about it?" Hammerstein checked with Rodgers, who checked with master choreographer George Balanchine, who provided the needed recommendation.

De Mille found that Rodgers hadn't composed any ballet music for what became *Oklahoma!,* a real problem when it came to choreographing a seventeen-minute dream ballet. The orchestrator, Robert Russell Bennett, tided her over until Rodgers got around to the task. It was de Mille who changed Hammerstein's vague idea of a circus ballet into a dream ballet that would dramatize the anxieties and emotional dilemma of the heroine, Laurey, while turning the dream image of the oafish Jud into a nasty villain. Thus, the first act, through the story-telling ballet, ended on a menacing and suspenseful note. No musical, until then, had integrated dance with plot and music to so complete a degree. Americana and dream ballets infected musicals for quite a while thereafter. De Mille, now Broadway's most sought-after choreographer, found steady employment with such shows as *Carousel, Allegro, Brigadoon,* and *Paint Your Wagon,* at a higher fee, by the way, than the $1,500 salary for her work on *Oklahoma!*

she attempted, with little success, to raise money for what was initially titled *Away We Go!* Nevertheless, Rodgers and Hammerstein proceeded with their work. Rouben Mamoulian, who had directed *Porgy and Bess* for the Guild in 1935, was brought from Hollywood for the direction, and Rodgers hired Agnes de Mille for the dances after he saw her brilliant ballet choreography for Aaron Copland's *Rodeo.* Helburn and Langner felt "names" would help attract investors, and suggested Shirley Temple for the youthful heroine, and Groucho Marx for a country peddler. Rodgers and Hammerstein talked them out of these dubious choices, and through a series of auditions Joan Roberts was chosen for the youthful Laurey, and Alfred Drake as Curly. For an important subsidiary role — the comic Ado Annie — Celeste Holm, until then a dramatic actress, revealed a pleasing singing voice and won the part.

Hammerstein preferred to work on his own while writing lyrics, then give them to Rodgers to put to music, the reverse of the way Rodgers had worked with Hart. The idea for the opening came directly from Riggs's play: a woman seated on the stage churning butter. Riggs in his stage directions had described the scene as "a radiant summer morning several years ago," with cattle in a meadow, the young corn, the streams, "the kind of morning which . . . makes them seem to exist now for the first time."

From that evocative description, Hammerstein developed the verses for the show's opening song, "Oh, What a Beautiful Mornin'." He labored on them

for three weeks before giving the completed song to Rodgers.

"I was a little sick with joy," Rodgers recalled afterward, "because it was so lovely and so right. When you get words like that you're given words to say musically."

Inevitably, working with Hammerstein changed the music of Rodgers. Hart's words were brittle, knowing, sophisticated. Hammerstein's style was more direct, more lyrical, and verged on the sentimental. Both Rodgers and Hammerstein thought it essential that the story's open-air spirit be maintained, that its first scene tell the audience they were going to be seeing a different kind of musical. When the curtain goes up against a wide-open backdrop, a woman, Laurey's aunt, is seated on a porch in a rocking chair churning butter, while listening to someone offstage singing about the beautiful morning. Then the fellow, Curly, appears, leans on a rail fence, and keeps singing the song until he's finished it.

The songs carry the story forward, as when Curly tries to get Laurey to go to a box social with him by describing the imaginary surrey that will carry them there. Hammerstein found the mention of the surrey in the play, and used it to fashion the "Surrey with the Fringe on Top," to which Rodgers gave a kind of clip-clop rhythm.

They wanted a different kind of love song, too. Songwriters had labored for generations over the all-but-impossible task of saying "I love you" in a new way. Hammerstein's new way was to come up with a song in which Laurey and Curly warn each other not to give away their budding romance — otherwise "People Will Say We're in Love."

Raising money was the most difficult task of all. Rodgers, Hammerstein, Alfred Drake, and Joan Roberts helped out by resorting to the method known as "the penthouse tour." They held backer auditions in rich homes, with Rodgers at the piano, Hammerstein relating the story, Drake and Roberts performing. Still, the money dribbled in

Costume design for Ado Annie by Miles White.

so slowly that Theresa Helburn invited potential backers to rehearsals. Some were impressed, others justified their refusal by saying "No legs, no jokes, no chance."

By the time the show, still shy of its production cost of $75,000, got to the Shubert Theatre in New Haven for its tryout, temperaments and tempers were flaring, with de Mille raging about interruptions to her dance rehearsals and Mamoulian complaining he had not been consulted in advance about costume and set designs. Hammerstein and Rodgers managed to keep cool heads. At one point Hammerstein addressed an anxiety-ridden group and calmed them by simply saying: "Do you know what I think is wrong? Almost nothing."

The rousing reception the first night in New Haven, March 11, 1943, bore him out. While there, a new ensemble number, "Oklahoma!," was added, and it was decided to give this title to the show. After another enthusiastic reception in Boston, the show moved to New York. Hammerstein began to feel that his long dry period was coming to an end. He wrote to his son in the navy that though he doubted he would have as great a success as with *Show Boat*, he felt the new show was comparable in quality. "All this," he added, "is said in the hope that a handful of beer-stupefied critics may not decide that we have tried to write a musical comedy and failed."

The first-night Guild subscription performance in New York was not a sellout, but those who were there loved *Oklahoma!* from the first offstage notes that told of a bright, golden haze on the meadow. If the critics were stupefied it was because of a show that was "a jubilant and enchanting musical" (Howard Barnes, *Herald Tribune*); "completely enchanting" (Wolcott Gibbs, *The New Yorker*). From the others there was a virtual thesaurus of praise: "fresh, diverting, lively, colorful, imaginative, stylish . . ."

Mention should be made of a minority report, because it was the only one, by Wilella Waldorf of the *New York Post*, whose faint praise was dampened by what she thought was a "mild, monotonous opening," and "songs pleasant enough," but sounding "quite a bit alike." In addition to those mentioned earlier there were "Kansas City," "I Cain't Say No," "All er Nothin'," and "Out of My Dreams," twelve in all that millions have been able to differentiate easily ever since.

Despite Wilella Waldorf's mild reservations, *Oklahoma!* went on to shatter the record for a continuous run of a musical, and by the time it left the St. James Theatre on May 29, 1948, it had played 2,212 performances. Those who had been brave enough to back its production were rewarded with an enormous return on their investments — some 3,000 percent. The Theatre Guild was brought back to fiscal health, and investors began regarding musical theatre with the same hopes of a bonanza as with the drilling of a promising oil well.

All of *Oklahoma!*'s dancers were classically trained, many being recruited from ballet companies.

Set drawing by Lemuel Ayres for the smokehouse scene in *Oklahoma!*

The show was showered with awards, including a special Pulitzer citation. Celeste Holm and Alfred Drake went on to more and greater fame, and Agnes de Mille took a leading place as a choreographer on Broadway.

In retrospect, we can now see that *Oklahoma!* was a Broadway milestone, marking the end of one era in musical theatre and ushering in another. Brooks Atkinson thought the historic moment of change occurred with the show's first song, as it likened the sound of the earth to music. "After a verse like that," he said, "sung to a buoyant melody, the banalities of the old musical stage became intolerable."

Oklahoma! could hardly have come at a more propitious moment. Nearly ten million Americans were under arms. The need for defense and war workers had ended the depression. Those at home felt a solidarity as never before, and rallied with clear purpose to the great challenge of defeating the Axis powers. This "last good war" was fought against manifest evil. Here was a show that exalted the American spirit. It provided a vision of a simpler, more golden time, and it spoke, too, of wide open spaces, their dangers and freedoms. In its lively, folksy way it stressed traditional American values of individualism, family, and religious faith.

Yet the musical's charm persisted after the war was over and won. Credit, then, Rodgers and Hammerstein, and their co-workers, director Mamoulian and choreographer de Mille, for blending and meshing together words, music, dance — expertise all around, everyone at his or her best. Their celebration of so American a theme, and its fervent acceptance, inevitably begat emulators.

Soon came more Americana:

Bloomer Girl, adapted from a comedy about Evelina Applegate, the niece of Dolly Bloomer, whose bloomers supplanted the hoop skirt, was set to music by Harold Arlen, with lyrics by E. Y. Harburg. The resemblance to *Oklahoma!* was hardly accidental. It starred Celeste Holm from that show's original cast, along with dancer Joan McCracken. The dances were staged by Agnes de Mille, whose "Civil War" ballet had relevance to the story because it showed the effect of war on women left behind. *Bloomer Girl* was quickly followed by *Up in Central Park*, with a flimsy plot

about a courageous reporter's exposé of the corrupt Boss Tweed political ring. Its Sigmund Romberg tunes were not distinctive, but it did have a pretty Currier and Ives ballet.

Thoroughly American, too, was the contemporary *On the Town*, about three sailors on a day's leave in New York. Derived from the Jerome Robbins ballet *Fancy Free*, it had the distinction of introducing to the musical stage composer Leonard Bernstein, Jerome Robbins for the show's dances, and the writing team of Betty Comden and Adolph Green.

Left to right: Leonard Bernstein, Adolph Green, Betty Comden, and Jerome Robbins, the talented young creators of *On the Town* (1943).

Costume designs for *On the Town* by Alvin Colt.

147

On the subway in *On the Town.*

Original souvenir book cover design for *On the Town* (1943).

No resting on their laurels for Rodgers and Hammerstein, though. They would have liked to collaborate again, but Rodgers still retained his sense of loyalty to Lorenz Hart. Hammerstein understood, and went to work on his pet project of updating Bizet's *Carmen* for Broadway, with an all-black cast. He had not the slightest problem in getting *Carmen Jones* underwritten by producer Billy Rose. Rodgers, meanwhile, looked around for something to do with Hart. In view of his friend and collaborator's unfortunate condition, he was reluctant to undertake a new project, and instead thought of reviving an old show, *A Connecticut Yankee,* which he had done with Hart in 1927 and which had produced two memorable songs, "Thou Swell," and "My Heart Stood Still."

Hart was agreeable. More than that, he managed to stay away from the bottle during the time it took to revise and prepare the show. But the moment the rehearsals were over he lost his resolve. On opening night in New York, he was so drunk that he began talking to the actors on stage and had to be hustled out of the theatre and taken home. Then he disappeared for two days. When he was found, he was taken to the hospital with double pneumonia. He died on November 22, 1943, just nineteen days after the show opened.

About a year later Rodgers and Hammerstein met with Helburn and Langner for one of their weekly lunches at Sardi's to discuss ongoing matters relating to *Oklahoma!* "Gloating lunches," Rodgers called them. In a conspiratorial whisper, Langner asked: "How would you like to do a musical play based on Ferenc Molnár's *Liliom*?"

"No," the composer and lyricist whispered back.

Their refusal was based both on the fact they did not know the play itself and on the wartime fact that Hungary, where the play was set, was allied with Nazi Germany. Helburn then suggested that the play's story about a tough carnival barker could be transferred to a Louisiana setting, and that the servant girl, Julie, who falls in love with him, could be Creole or Cajun. The answer was still no, until Rodgers came up with the notion of changing the setting to a New England coastal village.

Hammerstein, as he said later, began "to see an attractive ensemble, sailors, whalers, girls from the mills upriver, clambakes on nearby islands, an amusement park on the seaboard, people who were strong and alive and lusty, people who had always been depicted on the stage as thin-lipped Puritans, a libel I was eager to refute."

The play was a mixture of tragedy and fantasy, its "hero," Liliom — whom the authors renamed Billy Bigelow — likable but wayward. After marrying Julie, he neglects her, and eventually, while bungling a robbery to get money for the child they are expecting, commits suicide rather than be caught. Sentenced to Purgatory, he is allowed to return to earth for one day to atone for his transgressions with one good deed. His by now teenage daughter is an outcast because of her father's lingering bad reputation, and, when Billy attempts to give her a stolen star, she rebuffs him. He slaps her in anger and frustration and is then led away to, presumably, his eternal punishment.

Neither Hammerstein nor Rodgers could see how they could end a musical on so dismal a note, so they decided — though worried about

offending Molnár — to provide a more hopeful ending. They didn't mind moving the audience to tears, but they wanted it to be a nice cry. Thus, Billy is allowed to stay on earth long enough to witness his daughter's high-school graduation and convince both her and Julie that they will have his eternal love. Curiously, Molnár, who had refused Puccini the right to make an opera of the play, approved of the new ending. Because the title *Liliom* no longer had meaning, it was changed to *Carousel*.

There was of necessity more sentiment than comedy in this musical, and a delicate balance was needed to keep the basically melancholy tale (enlivened though the original was by Molnár's wit) from collapsing of emotional overweight. Hammerstein's treatment made Billy pathetic and touching beneath his swagger, and he gave Julie an appealing sweetness and a survivor's strength. The 1873 setting allowed for Jo Mielziner's picturesque New England fishing village. Rodgers's score told the story as much as did the words, with the show's first half hour almost all music, both orchestral and vocal. He decided to dispense with the customary overture, more often accompanied by coughing and the audience's settling in seats, and instead opened with an ingratiating "Carousel Waltz." Agnes de Mille's pantomime ballet to the music depicted the meeting of Billy and Julie.

How to avoid that inevitable "I love you" ballad? Again Hammerstein found an answer by having Billy, who is uncomfortable about committing himself to Julie, sing, "If I Loved You," with the

Miles White costume design for the character of Mrs. Mullin in *Carousel* (1945).

Julie Jordan's first sight in *Carousel* (1945) of the man she will love for the rest of her life.

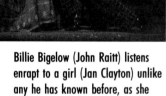

Billie Bigelow (John Raitt) listens enrapt to a girl (Jan Clayton) unlike any he has known before, as she ponders the possibility of loving him.

stress on the "if." Other songs helped the plot along — the authors were now firmly committed to an integration of words, music, lyrics, and dance. When Julie expresses uncertainty about her feelings for Billy, her friend sings "You're a Queer One, Julie Jordan." When the pair are ready for marriage, "June Is Bustin' Out All Over." Billy, contemplating fatherhood, is given a remarkable seven-minute "Soliloquy" about his new joys and responsibilities. And, after Billy's suicide, Julie is comforted by the song "You'll Never Walk Alone." Rodgers said of the richly melodious score that it was the most satisfying to him of any that he had written.

Rodgers and Hammerstein had no need of big-name stars: excellence, rightness, were the casting criterions. Starring relatively unknown John Raitt as Billy, and little-known Jan Clayton as Julie, *Carousel*, directed by Mamoulian, was greeted on April 19, 1945, with fully as much enthusiasm as *Oklahoma!*, and it ran side by side with it for more than two years. The drama critics voted it the season's best musical, although one of the critics withheld full approval: Wilella Waldorf, of the *New York Post*, the same lady who had not much liked *Oklahoma!* She wrote, bravely, "The *Oklahoma!* formula is becoming a bit monotonous, and so are Agnes de Mille's ballets. All

Jo Mielziner's scene design for a backdrop of carnival girls in *Carousel*.

right, go ahead and shoot." In view of the show's many adherents, it seems strange that no one did.

Rodgers and Hammerstein became a formidable force on Broadway when they added producing to their battery of skills. Apparently they could do no wrong, for their next production, the play *I Remember Mama*, became a hit, too. Rodgers liked to say that he could smell a success or failure as soon as someone said, "Let's do a show about . . ." One day, late in 1945, the brother-and-sister writing team of Herbert and Dorothy Fields (who had provided libretto and lyrics for *Up in Central Park*) asked them what they

thought of Ethel Merman in a show about the legendary sharpshooter Annie Oakley. "Go home and write it and we'll produce it," they said.

"The idea of our writing the score was never brought up," Rodgers related in his autobiography, "because neither Oscar nor I thought we were the right ones for it."

What they did recognize was a subject well in line with the prevalent interest in Americana. The war had ended, America had triumphed, evil had been put to rout, and the mood was hopeful and optimistic. Dorothy Field had conceived the idea for *Annie Get Your Gun* when her husband, home from late-

The song that became Broadway's anthem.

night volunteer war work, told her about a soldier whose sharpshooting had won him a batch of prizes in a Coney Island shooting gallery. "Annie," she said, came to her "as if out of the sky, from heaven."

Jerome Kern, the longtime friend and collaborator of Oscar Hammerstein, was asked to write the music, and

accepted. But, shockingly, the legendary composer died of a cerebral hemorrhage shortly after arriving in New York from Hollywood, where he had been living.

However, shows must go on, even before they are staged. Finding another composer of equivalent stature would not be easy. As the two producing partners went down an alphabetical list, they came across the name Irving Berlin, who had not done a show since his 1942 *This Is the Army*, which he had taken around much of the world as his much-praised contribution to the war effort.

They would be aiming high, they knew, and since Berlin normally wrote both lyrics and music, there was the problem that Dorothy Fields was already contracted for the lyrics. Berlin found the partially completed libretto, with its folkish humor, to his liking, and Dorothy stepped down and concentrated with her brother on the libretto. In hardly any time at all, Berlin came up with "You Can't Get a Man with a Gun," "Doin' What Comes Natur'lly," and "There's No Business Like Show Business."

The choice of Ethel Merman for Annie was a bull's-eye in itself. She had the confidence, presence, and voice to portray Annie Oakley, known as the world's greatest markswoman and, in her time, as one of show business's great personalities. Starting out as a backwoods Ohio girl, the real Annie developed an uncanny skill with a muzzle-loader, and bested all the area's expert riflemen in shooting matches. When braggart sharpshooter Frank Butler came to Cincinnati, she took him for a hundred dollars, too, fell in love with him, and the two soon married. They became headliner partners in Buffalo Bill's Original Wild West Show, which traveled the country and a good part of the world. Annie, deadly in her aim but feminine in her yellow buckskin costume, was idolized by many American males of her generation. When the Indian chief Sitting Bull came into the Buffalo Bill

show, he made Annie, through the urging of a publicist, "a full Indian princess," and the story hit the newspapers straight. This much of verifiable history was skimmed in the libretto concocted by the Fields.

Much of the conflict they posited had to do with Annie's infringing the precincts of the male world. "Anything You Can Do, I Can Do Better," she boasts. Frank Butler (Ray Middleton) puts her down by singing, "The Girl That I Marry," who, he asserts, will have qualities quite different from those of the brash, capable Annie. "They Say It's Wonderful," she opines about falling in love, but ruefully realizes that "You Can't Get a Man with a Gun." She has her career to fall back on, though, and praises it loudly, helped by a chorus, in "There's No Business Like Show Business." And, after a drum-thumping ceremony of induction into Sitting Bull's

Annie Get Your Gun (1945): Ethel Merman as the sharpshooter Annie, and Ray Middleton as Frank Butler, who thought he was looking for a girl "as soft and pink as a nursery."

tribe, during which the gods are invoked fiercely, she sings "I'm an Indian, too." The chief is also instrumental in reuniting her with Butler, when he counsels her to lose a shooting match to him.

The musical came to Broadway in May of 1946, and, with its fun-filled libretto, several of Berlin's best songs, brightly colored Jo Mielziner settings, direction by the talented Joshua Logan, it was a delight and a runaway hit. As for Ethel Merman's "romp through show business, love, and Indian affairs," the *New York Times* critic said: "She is not only Forty-Fifth Street's nightingale, but a comedienne with a knowledge of tactics."

New York's drama critics, who more often had to contend with embarrassing flops (to which they made their own modest contributions) than the excitingly new, who night after night were treated to hopeful variations on familiar themes, were heartened by two arrivals in 1947, so much so that their faith in the artistic potential of the American musical was renewed and strengthened.

The objects of their affections were *Finian's Rainbow* and *Brigadoon*, each refreshingly different. They left the mundane world entirely and placed their stories, in the first instance, in a mythical valley in a mythical state called Missitucky, and, in the second, a nonexistent Scottish village called Brigadoon. For the time being, the enchantments of magic spells, lovesick leprechauns, and moonlit folklore dispersed the wave of musical Americana that had dominated Broadway since *Oklahoma!* had set the fashion.

Of the two, *Finian's Rainbow* was the more gaily comic, concerned as it was with a daffy old Irishman named Finian, his pretty daughter, Sharon, and a crock of gold stolen from a leprechaun who will lose his immortality if he doesn't retrieve his magic treasure. *Brigadoon* had to do with two young Americans who, while shooting in Scotland, suddenly find themselves in a village that comes to life only once every hundred years — in this way slowing the inevitable and distressing march of time and progress. Love, of course, importantly entered both stories, and both had points to make, on the one hand social, and on the other, gently philosophic.

Finian's Rainbow also had more than a touch of satire as it blended its pixie Irish whimsy with an unveiled attack on racial prejudice, as though something of the socially conscious thirties was left over in the minds of the authors of the libretto and lyrics, E. Y. Harburg and Fred Saidy. The story, in fact, came from two unrelated notions. As Harburg relates it, he had tentative ideas for two nonmusical plays: one dealt with a bigoted southern senator who would learn what prejudice was like for those affected by it, and the other was about a leprechaun with three magic wishes to spend. Harburg's flash of inspiration was to combine the two, simply by having one of those three wishes turn the senator black, and to have the idea serve as the basis for a musical.

Having written the libretto while he was still employed in Hollywood, Harburg asked Burton Lane, a film composer and occasional contributor of songs to Broadway revues, to work on the score with the more politically motivated Earl Robinson, but Lane felt their compositional styles would clash and took on the whole task. The combination of Lane's melodies and Harburg's witty and intelligent lyrics turned out to be a wholly winning one.

The authors had the good sense to keep the social satire light rather than heavy, and they ingeniously explained how Finian and daughter Sharon, the gold, and the leprechaun, got near enough to Senator Rawkins to work a spell on him. Without going too deeply into the twists and turns of the plot, Finian, from Glocca Morra in Ireland, is impressed with the American way of burying gold at Fort Knox, where presumably it multiplies. He therefore sets out for Missitucky with his stolen treasure, followed by Og the leprechaun. After Finian has buried the gold not far from fertile Fort Knox, rumors about it bring prosperity to a valley inhabited by previously poor sharecroppers, and cause the senator, who is as avaricious as he is bigoted, to try to get his hands on it.

About those three wishes: the first turns the senator black, and acquaints him hilariously (for the audience) firsthand with racial prejudice; the second turns him white again, and blessedly rids him of his social and racial affliction; a third gives the power of speech to a formerly mute valley girl, who has hitherto only been able to express herself through dance, much to the delight of the choreographer, Michael Kidd, who achieved a first by mixing black and white dancers in his chorus. As for the love element, it had its own

twists and subtwists involving Sharon, a young man of the valley, and the leprechaun, who finds himself much too humanly attracted to Sharon — and just about every other girl in sight.

In the end, it's not riches that bring happiness to the valley's people, but trust in one another, a point Harburg was anxious to make. Lane went to Irish and native mountain music sources for inspiration, and turned out some of the loveliest melodies ever heard on Broadway. Ella Logan sang the everlasting "How Are Things in Glocca Morra?" and David Wayne, as the romantically uncertain Og, sang "When I'm Not Near the Girl I Love, I Love the Girl I'm Near." Richly melodic, too, were

David Wayne, as Og, the leprechaun in *Finian's Rainbow* (1947), and Anita Alvarez as Susan, the mute girl he hungers for.

Frederick Loewe (left) and Alan Jay Lerner, the creators of *Brigadoon*. A few years later, they would write a brilliant musical about another pair of unlikely lovers—*My Fair Lady*.

"Look to the Rainbow," "Old Devil Moon," and "If This Isn't Love," and the amusing "Something Sort of Grandish." The show ran triumphantly for two years.

Just as gorgeously melodic was *Brigadoon*, the third collaboration between composer Frederick Loewe and writer Alan Jay Lerner. Their two earlier Broadway entries, *What's Up?* and *The Day Before Spring*, had not lasted long, although critics commented favorably on several of the songs of the latter, and called it a very near miss. Loewe, born in Berlin of Viennese parents (1904), was a child prodigy on the piano. He came to this country in 1924, began a concert career, and unaccountably abandoned it to become, in succession, a prizefighter, a riding instructor, and an organist for silent movies, before turning to songwriting. Lerner, fourteen years younger, came from a well-to-do family, and took to theatre at Harvard, where he wrote for the Hasty Pudding revues. In

Agnes de Mille's dramatic dances in *Brigadoon* underscored the dark side of this fairy-tale romance.

New York, he joined an advertising agency as a radio scriptwriter, and contributed in his spare time to the *Gambols*, the shows put on annually at the Lambs Club, an organization for theatre people.

"One day," as Lerner recalled, "I was sitting in the Lambs when a man came to my table and said, 'I hear you write lyrics.' I said, 'I try.' He said, 'I write good music. I don't have a lyric writer. Why don't we try it together?' "

It wasn't until their third attempt that they found success. The key came with a casual remark dropped by Loewe, something about faith moving mountains. Lerner began thinking about a play on the theme, something that would deal with a miracle, until the two thought of a miracle of faith moving a town clear out of time. Lerner was a devotee of the works of the whimsical James M. Barrie, and this led to the Scottish setting of the town he named Brigadoon.

His libretto was essentially a fairy tale, requiring a mood of legend and magic to sustain its tale of love, death, and timelessness. Two hundred years before the story begins, the minister of the town had decided that outside influences were corrupting his people, and he therefore asked God to make Brigadoon and its inhabitants vanish into the highland mists, allowing it to return once every hundred years. During that day of return, should one of the villagers leave, the spell would be broken, and Brigadoon would disappear forever. It is, of course, on that very day in 1947 that the two American vacationers, Tommy and Jeff, happen on the village, where

Tommy falls in love with Fiona, who had not yet found the right man, and Jeff flirts with the village wench, a comic character.

The plot has Tommy leaving Brigadoon to return to New York, but he is now so unhappy in the brittle and sophisticated city that, with Jeff, he returns to the Scottish woods in the hope that the town will somehow reappear. And here is where that earlier-mentioned faith comes in: Tommy hears the people of Brigadoon singing in the distance, and is off to join them, presumably forever.

If this truncated synopsis seems mawkish, it wasn't so onstage. Lerner's libretto was literate and sensitive, and it fused with charming lyrics and music, and dancing of an extraordinarily high order, choreographed by Agnes de Mille. Billy Rose had been slated to produce the show, but he gave up his option to Cheryl Crawford, who had had recent successes with a revival of *Porgy and Bess* and with *One Touch of Venus*. With *Brigadoon*, she moved high into the ranks of Broadway's producers. David Brooks and Marion Bell played the two timeless lovers, and the direction of Robert Lewis had the required felicity of touch the fanciful material required.

Loewe's score relied less on Scottish sources than on giving it a Scottish feel here and there, as in the captivating "The Heather on the Hill." On the other hand, an equally instantaneous hit was "Almost Like Being in Love," which could have been transferred to almost any musical of the period. Miss de Mille managed to avoid returning to the style she had set in *Oklahoma!* and *Carousel*, and this time injected the

Original poster design for *Brigadoon* (1947).

157

vivacity of Scottish folk dancing into her ballets, thereby extending her range. Among the many critical accolades was that of Brooks Atkinson, who decided that *Brigadoon* had helped prove that "the musical stage is the most creative branch of the American commercial theatre."

It took almost two years before those words were fully justified, although the period highjinks of *High Button Shoes*, with Phil Silvers and its Jule Styne and Sammy Cahn songs, kept audiences well entertained. So did *Where's Charley?*, with Ray Bolger singing and dancing to "Once in Love with Amy." But it was not until *Kiss Me, Kate* came along on December 30, 1948, that critics dared toss around the word "masterpiece."

Cole Porter, who wrote the lyrics and music, had not exactly fallen on hard times, but few of the songs he had furnished for his recent shows, *Mexican Hayride* and *Around the World in 80 Days*, came close in wit, sophistication, or melody to those of earlier days. Among the most memorable had been "I Get a Kick Out of You," and "You're the Top" from the exuberant *Anything Goes*; "Begin the Beguine" from *Jubilee*; and "My Heart Belongs to Daddy" from *Leave It to Me*.

Porter's problems were partly physical. In 1937, while a guest at a Long Island estate, he was out riding horseback with a group. Against the advice of a groom, he had chosen a mettlesome and nervous horse. Only a few minutes out, the horse reared and fell back on Porter, crushing both his legs. He was in and out of hospitals for several years, undergoing in all thirty-five operations, and there were very few days when he was free of pain. Eventually, one of his legs had to be amputated. Yet he managed to carry on, always in search of the second "perfect show." His first, in his estimation, was *Anything Goes*.

The idea for a play-within-a-play musical that would deal with actors performing the *Taming of the Shrew* came to a young would-be producer, Arnold Saint Subber, when he was backstage in 1935 watching a Theatre Guild production of the play with Lynn Fontanne and Alfred Lunt in the leading roles. What struck him and put the idea in his head was an offstage scene: the two famous stars, dressed as Kate and Petruchio, vehemently arguing while waiting to make their entrances. The rowdy, raucous Guild revival was a great success. Eventually, Saint Subber interested the talented set designer Lemuel Ayers in producing a musical *Shrew* with him, and their first step was to convince a clever writing team, Bella and Samuel Spewack, to work up a libretto. Bella took the more convincing, because she didn't much care for that Shakespeare play.

The story they evolved echoed what Saint Subber had witnessed when he was backstage at the Theatre Guild. Two famous actors, formerly married, are in Baltimore for a pre-Broadway engagement of a musical version of *The Taming of the Shrew*. The two stars, Fred Graham and his ex-wife, Lilli Vanessi (the latter, by the way, not coincidentally echoing Fontanne's real name, Lillie Louise), are feuding, and the feud carries from offstage to on. Matters are exacerbated by Graham's dalliance with an ex-chorine in the cast, Lois Lane,

while she has romantic problems with another member of the troupe, the gambling-addicted Bill Calhoun. Kate is finally mollified and gentled both offstage and on, and Lois and Bill resolve their differences, too, through their Shakespearean roles.

When the Spewacks came to Cole Porter to ask him to do the lyrics and music, he strongly doubted that musicalizing Shakespeare could be done in any satisfactory manner. He said he was the wrong lyricist to tinker with Shakespeare. In any case, the show was

bound to fail. The Spewacks showed him a completed scene, he liked it, and tested himself by writing a song to it: "Another Op'nin', Another Show." He was off and running. "So the second great perfect hit was born," he said later.

Bella Sewack recalled: "I wrote out suggestions for song titles to stimulate him and it just came like an avalanche once the initial strivings were over."

The songs also had a way of mirroring the story line, seeming to come right out of it — the always looked for integration of elements that distinguished the more artistic musicals. When Lois berates Bill about his gambling, she sings "Why Can't You Behave?" When Fred and Lilli reminisce about a travesty of an operetta they were in during their early days, they sing and dance a schmaltzy waltz from it, "Wunderbar." Incidentally, the same song had been dropped from several previous Porter shows before it had ever gotten to be heard publicly. Porter, for all his worldly wit, could come up when needed with a superlative love song, as here with "So in Love," which could have graced many a musical. In spite of his reluctance to tinker with the Bard's words, he borrowed Petruchio's boastful song, "I've Come to Wive It Wealthily in Padua," from Shakespeare's:

I come to wive it wealthily in Padua;
If wealthily then happily in Padua.

And he made lyrical use of several lines and speeches from the play. Others, such as the strident "I Hate Men," were pure *Kiss Me, Kate*, and pure Porter.

In spite of seventeen songs with lyrics that had more than a touch of genius, backers for the show were hard to find. Porter's recent lackluster record caused some of the reluctance, along with the lack of experience of the two would-be producers. Tax laws for theatrical investment had changed in a way to lessen the incentive to take risks on anything that was not sure-fire. Nor was there a big-name star for the all-important role of Kate.

The finale of *Kiss Me, Kate* (1948), in which the bickering duo come to a happy agreement about a woman's place in marriage.

To buttress their forces, Porter brought in his close friend, John C. Wilson, to co-produce and direct. Wilson tried to interest Lily Pons in taking on Kate, but she felt she wasn't up to the rigors of a Broadway run, not to say the strain on the vocal cords when singing "I Hate Men" night after night. Mary Martin was interested, but she sensed a lack of real commitment in Porter, and did not pursue the opportunity.

Alfred Drake, everyone agreed, was an ideal Petruchio, but Porter's selection of a little-known Hollywood actress, Patricia Morison, for Kate worried everyone, including her own agent. Morison made the most of an audition for the Spewacks, and they sided with Porter about her suitability. Porter was also stubborn about the role of Lisa. Most everyone wanted Ann Miller from films, but Porter insisted on the lively Lisa Kirk. The lithe ballet dancer Harold Lang was chosen for Bill Calhoun.

It took a year before the money was raised. Porter helped out by entertaining nightly at his home, playing the score and recruiting some young performers to sing for the potential angels, who numbered seventy-two by the time the show opened in Philadelphia. It was clear almost from the first number, sung and danced (to Hanya Holm's appropriate choreography) in rehearsal clothes in a backstage setting, that *Kiss Me, Kate* was headed for Broadway glory.

So certain was Porter of success this time out that on opening night at Broadway's New Century Theatre, he bought seats for a hundred friends and dressed according to his well-known image in white tie and tails. No opening-night jitters for him. He enjoyed himself hugely, forgetting the pain in his legs, laughing and applauding along with everyone else. The next morning's reviews justified his enthusiasm, among them one that reported that "by some baffling miracle," everything in the show had dropped "gracefully into its appointed place." Howard Barnes in the *Herald Tribune* seconded the judgment, calling it "a bewitching entertainment."

Unlike *Kiss Me, Kate*, Rodgers and Hammerstein and their associates had no difficulty raising the needed financing for *South Pacific*. They simply formed a corporation, with the show as its basis, and limited participation to ten — as it turned out, very fortunate — investors. Yet this great mountain of a Broadway hit began as a hardly discernible anthill of a suggestion made to director Joshua Logan, who was not at the time looking to do a musical. He was rehearsing the play *Mr. Roberts* when a story editor for a film company mentioned a book laid in the Pacific during wartime that had the kind of atmosphere that could apply to the play he was working on. The book, by an obscure writer, James Michener, was called *Tales of the South Pacific*.

Logan read it, and was caught most by one of the stories, "Fo' Dolla," about a doomed romance on a South Sea island between a young marine lieutenant and a pretty Tonganese girl, whose disreputable old mother, known as Bloody Mary, wanted to marry her to an American. The story's title has to do with the grass skirts she sells for four dollars as take-home souvenirs.

Logan's co-producer on *Mr. Roberts*, Leland Hayward, was intrigued by the story, too, and both thought it could serve for a musical that would be perfect for Rodgers and Hammerstein. The two were looking for a subject after the fairly lackluster reception of their *Allegro*, which ran for less than a year. Hayward cautioned Logan that they ought to tie up the rights first. "Otherwise," Hayward said of the powerful composer and lyricist, "they'll want all of it. They'd gobble us up for breakfast."

Logan couldn't wait. After making only an informal agreement with Michener, he ran into Rodgers and gave him a note, advising him to read the story. Logan mentioned it to Hammerstein, too, who read the entire book of tales, got Rodgers's agreement, and soon the project was under way. As Hayward had predicted, Rodgers and Hammerstein asked for fifty-one percent of the production as a means of controlling both the business and creative ends of the show. Neither he nor Logan was happy about the arrangement, but they went along with it. Relations between Logan and the powerful pair were never very happy afterward.

Hammerstein, in reading through the nineteen loosely related tales, preferred one called "Our Heroine," about a romance between a young navy nurse, Nellie Forbush, from Arkansas, and a middle-aged French planter, Emile de Becque. He was worried about "Fo' Dolla" because it seemed to him too closely related to *Madame Butterfly*, dealing as it did with an ill-fated love between an oriental and an American

officer. Both stories touched on racial prejudice: in "Fo' Dolla," Marine Lieutenant Joseph Cable, though in love with Liat, the Tonganese girl, is saddled by the prejudices instilled in him by his wealthy suburban Philadelphia background; Nellie Forbush finds it difficult to accept Emile de Becque, who has children from a liaison with a dark-skinned native islander. Hammerstein decided to make the Nellie Forbush story dominant, but to include the other as a subplot. This would be a break with tradition, in that romantic subplots in musicals were generally of a comic kind. To provide comic relief, he brought in a tattooed sailor, Luther Billis, from another of the stories.

Providentially, Rodgers learned that the opera singer Ezio Pinza wanted to appear in a musical. He was quickly signed for the role of de Becque. Next a call was put in to Mary Martin for Nellie, but she was worried that her voice could hardly match that of the great Pinza, and how could she possibly sing duets with him? Rodgers assured her that the score would be written without a duet for her, and played some of it for her. What sold her was hearing "Some Enchanted Evening."

"It wasn't my song," she wrote later, "it was Ezio's, but that didn't matter. I was convinced it would be one of the memorable songs of the musical stage."

Then Rodgers and Hammerstein put on their producer hats and realized they had committed themselves to two star salaries far beyond budget limitations. The problem was solved when both Pinza and Martin agreed to take half their usual salaries.

Ezio Pinza, Barbara Luna, Michael DeLeon, and Mary Martin in *South Pacific* (1949).

Hammerstein ran into something of a writer's block with the book for the show. Not having been in the war, he knew nothing about military behavior, and he was forced to call on Logan, a former army air-force officer, for help. They worked together for ten days straight, talking into a Dictaphone, with a secretary transcribing as they went along, and their wives collating pages. Michener felt it was the clear vision of Logan that saved the show. Logan felt similarly, and wanted credit as co-author of the libretto, and the royalties that went with the credit, but lawyers intervened. He was threatened with dismissal unless he adhered to his director's contract, and more bitterness on his part ensued.

In view of the discord between partners, it might have been expected that the fate of *South Pacific* would not be a happy one. But that would have been to overlook the talents of Rodgers and Hammerstein, and their accumulated know-how and wisdom about what made musicals work. They made sure Mary Martin would hold her own with a love song, "I'm in Love with a Wonderful Guy," which contained the famous line, "I'm as corny as Kansas in August." Kansas was chosen instead of Martin's place of birth, Texas, or Nellie's Arkansas, because Hammerstein wanted an alliteration for corny.

Mary Martin got an idea while taking a shower one day: a scene in which she would wash her hair right on stage. The suggestion was relayed to Hammerstein and Rodgers, who were trying to come up with a song about

Nellie's wish not to carry any further her romance with de Becque. That led to the song "I'm Gonna Wash That Man Right Outa My Hair." Martin adopted a short haircut, so it would dry quickly, and with a bar of soap in one hand, and a palmful of shampoo in the other (to make bubbles quickly) washed her hair while singing the song. By the time she left the show she had washed her hair on stage 1,886 times — a record that is not expected to be surpassed ever.

Hammerstein did not avoid the racial overtones in the Michener stories he employed, and, in fact, directly attacked ethnic and racial prejudice in Lieutenant Cable's song "You've Got to Be Carefully Taught," which some regarded as too preachy and controversial and thought ought to be eliminated. But the two stuck to their guns, saying the song, with its clear message of tolerance, was what they wanted very much to say in their musical.

Hammerstein was so intrigued by a beautiful small island that Michener had described in one of his *Tales* that he decided it warranted a song of its own. He had the island seen in the distance — a welcome stimulus to Jo Mielziner, the set designer. During a lunch in Logan's apartment, Hammerstein handed the verses of "Bali Ha'i" to Rodgers, who went to a piano in another room and came back a few minutes later with a finished song that not only fitted the voice of Juanita Hall as Bloody Mary, but added a mystical oriental note to the show. Rodgers explained the seeming stroke of genius by saying he'd already had the sound he wanted in his mind for several days.

A show-within-a-show was developed by having the military men and women of the island base put on comic skits of their own, an opportunity for scene-stealing by Myron McCormick as the rowdy Luther Billis, whose gyrations made the tattooed ship on his stomach rock back and forth — the sight further enhanced by the grass skirt and coconut bosom he wore.

It took a full year for the book, lyrics, and music to be completed, and by the time the show went into production expectations about it had mounted to a fever pitch. While the musical was still under preparation, Michener's book was unexpectedly awarded the Pulitzer Prize for fiction. Understandably, and with an R and H musical from it in the offing, the book zoomed onto the bestseller lists and stayed there for months. Then word came filtering down from the tryouts in New

Myron McCormick as Luther Billis. He is Nellie's "Honey Bun," having won her by his fetching ability to make that schooner ripple over the waves of his stomach. From Mary Martin's scrapbook of the show, also shown.

Haven and Boston that Rodgers and Hammerstein had another stupendous hit, and lines formed early and long at the box office of the Majestic Theatre. The advance sale of tickets reached an historic high.

Brooks Atkinson reported: "On the day of the opening [April 7, 1949] business practically stopped all over town, as on the day before Christmas. Everyone was obsessed with one idea. The teller at the bank murmured wistfully, 'I hope *South Pacific* is as good as they say it is.' " The bank manager

promised him he was "going to see a wonderful show." He knew because a friend had seen it at an out-of-town preview.

Atkinson was pleased to sustain the bank manager's promise. Mr. Rodgers and Mr. Hammerstein, he said, had composed "a drama in terms of fable, song and verse, to evoke and sustain a golden mood . . . that it was as lively, warm, fresh, and beautiful as we had all hoped it would be." The rich and colorful Rodgers score was praised in all quarters, and became so popular that one

A gift of love from Mary Martin to Richard Rodgers.

DEAR DICK
"YOU'RE MY HONEYBUN
TONIGHT AND EVERY NIGHT"
LOVE
MARY

Tony Award won by *South Pacific* (1949) as best musical of the year. The award was named for Antoinette Perry, actress-director and chairman of the American Theatre Wing. The show also won ten additional Tonys, the Pulitzer Prize, and the New York Drama Critics' Circle Award.

columnist complained after a time that he'd had a dream in which the entire score, complete with the vocals of Mr. Pinza and Miss Martin, was played.

There was a reason behind the disturbance to his slumbers. *South Pacific* arrived just as the long-playing record made the breakable 78s obsolete, and was the first "blockbuster" recorded musical album, its songs heard day and night over the radio and from phonographs and jukeboxes. Only the profoundly deaf escaped hearing Pinza sing "Some Enchanted Evening."

The scramble for tickets to the show at least equaled that for *Oklahoma!*, and stories abounded about ruses and stratagems employed to get them. One enterprising thief sent a pair to a suburban couple, who, hardly believing their good luck, went to the show. While they were enjoying themselves, their home was meticulously ransacked.

Every conceivable award was showered on the show, which ran for nearly two thousand performances: it garnered a slew of Tonys and Donaldsons, the New York Drama Critics Circle Award, and the Pulitzer Prize for drama. Twenty-five years later, Brooks Atkinson, in his book *Broadway*, still felt that *South Pacific* expressed "the real genius of Rodgers and Hammerstein — their insight into character and their sympathy for the common dilemmas of people. More than any other pair they mastered the technique of the modern musical theatre."

Yul Brynner and Gertrude Lawrence in *The King and I* (1950).

VI *The Changing of the Guard, 1949–1957*

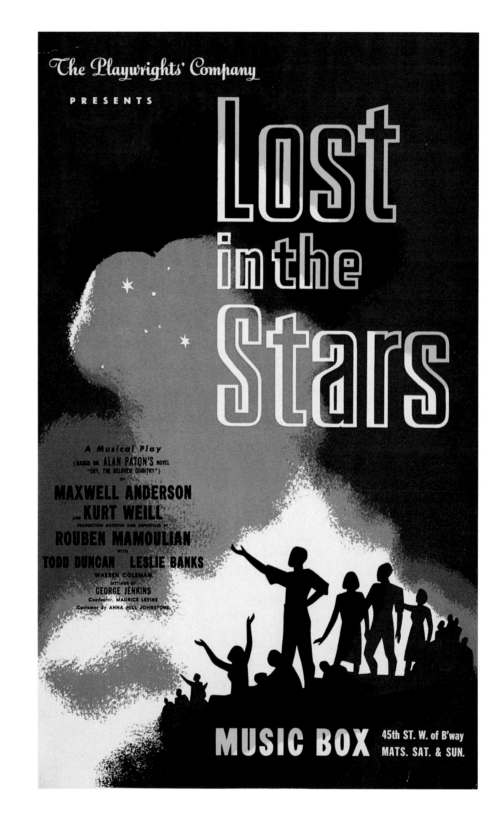

Lost in the Stars (1949): Poster design for a Broadway musical that told the tragedy of South Africa decades before it reached the front pages.

The Changing of the Guard, 1949–1957

It was Maxwell Anderson's contention that producing a play was about ten times as much work as writing one. As a member of the Playwrights' Company, a distinguished group that produced its own plays, he had to struggle through "a maze of auditions, readings, casting interviews, discussions of sets, long and short-distance telephone calls, revisions, re-revisions, a constant balancing of costs, meanings, hopes and beliefs."

When he read Alan Paton's 1948 bestselling novel, *Cry, the Beloved Country*, which reflected the tragic situation of blacks in South Africa, he found it easy enough to get Paton's permission to dramatize the novel into musical terms. Nor was there difficulty in enlisting Kurt Weill, also of the Playwrights' Company, to compose the score. They had worked together previously on Anderson's *Knickerbocker Holiday*, one result of which was the perennial "September Song."

Rouben Mamoulian was quickly persuaded to undertake the direction. The hardest task was finding the right actor and singer for the main role of the preacher Stephen Kumalo. There were many fine black actors, and many fine black singers, but the two seldom came together in one person. After several hundred fruitless auditions, Mamoulian reached the conclusion that there was only one suitable candidate, and he happened to be in South Africa on an extensive concert tour. He was Todd Duncan, who had triumphantly created Porgy in the 1935 and 1942 productions of *Porgy and Bess*, and he was at last reached by telephone. His contract for the tour, he said, would make him unavailable for many months.

Mamoulian and Anderson persisted via long-distance telephone. The concert managers allowed Duncan out of his contract only after he had them read the libretto of the musical. "Now, gentlemen," Duncan said, "do you see why I must give up the concerts and do this play?" The gentlemen agreed that the nature of the project was indeed important to the cause of blacks, and allowed him to go.

Anderson and Weill referred to their work not as a musical comedy, but as "a musical play." Its stark story focused on a humble preacher who leaves his parishioners in the hills to look for his son Absalom in crowded Johannesburg. Absalom has fallen in with bad company and, in a moment of panic during a robbery, shoots and kills a white man who ironically has befriended blacks. The aftermath of the tragedy severely strains the preacher's faith. Mamoulian was as anxious as Anderson to symbolize the plight of millions of oppressed people, and to do this he employed the device of a Greek-like chorus that framed the principal characters and commented on the action.

Weill did his own orchestrations (rare among Broadway composers) for a score that gave melodic richness and significance to the various scenes. Now and then he broke away from the tragic mood of the drama for a lightly humorous song, but in the main the music expressed fear, anguish, and the spiritual burden carried by Kumalo. For Broadwayites seeking their accustomed light entertainment, *Lost in the Stars*, as

WEILL IN AMERICA

German-born Kurt Weill came to the United States in 1935 when he heard he was about to be arrested by the Nazis. The then thirty-five-year-old composer had produced such Berlin theatre hits (with librettist Bertolt Brecht) as *Mahagonny* and *The Threepenny Opera*. His first work in America was for Max Reinhardt's biblical pageant, *The Eternal Road*, but he soon discovered that his new country was "an ideal place for a theatre composer. I found on Broadway an audience as receptive and as sensitive to music as any European audience." During the next fifteen years, until his premature death in 1950, he ranked among the very best of Broadway composers, with a roster of shows that included *Knickerbocker Holiday, Lady in the Dark, One Touch of Venus, Street Scene*, and *Lost in the Stars*. Off-Broadway, his widow, Lotte Lenya, starred for many years in his *Threepenny Opera*.

171

Maxwell Anderson (left) and Kurt Weill, librettist and composer of *Lost in the Stars*.

the musical was named, was highly unusual and serious fare. Critics hailed the show with few reservations, most of them overlooking — because of the play's worthy message — the static quality created by the hovering presence of the chorus. Audiences were less forgiving, presumably, because the show failed to achieve prolonged popularity. Nevertheless, it ran for a respectable nine months, and still holds an honored place in theatre annals. Sadly, on April 3, 1950, in the midst of the run, Kurt Weill died suddenly of a heart attack.

Producers Cy Feuer and Ernest Martin, like just about everyone else in the musical field at that time, were impressed by the sensational success of *South Pacific*, which had replaced *Oklahoma!* as the show to emulate. In 1948 they had revived an old chestnut of

a farce, *Charley's Aunt*, and turned it into a popular musical called *Where's Charley?* Devotees of Damon Runyon, they decided that one of his short stories, "The Idyll of Miss Sarah Brown," possessed *South Pacific*–like possibilities because of its unusual romance between a professional gambler, Sky Masterson, and a Salvation Army worker, Sister Sarah Brown, who tries to save the souls of the dubious characters who hang out around Broadway. Feuer had headed a music department in Hollywood, and Martin had been a television executive, and perhaps because of their connections they turned first to a Hollywood screenwriter, Jo Swerling, to do a libretto.

Runyon, who had begun as a newspaperman in Kansas, did not reach Broadway until he was twenty-six, after which he seldom left the region bounded by 42nd Street on the south and 57th Street on the north. His fiction and fables, based on the types he encountered, were a mixture of the hard-boiled and the sentimental, and for many years they captivated a wide readership across the country. His was a special world where men were guys and women were dolls. His characters employed a kind of Broadway grammar distinctly their own, talked loud, and dressed flashily. Feuer and Martin wanted the raffish atmosphere inhabited by the Runyon types, but felt the romance needed more serious treatment. They settled on *Guys and Dolls* for the title. Getting a workable libretto was another matter altogether.

Swerling's was deemed unsatisfactory. Feuer and Martin tried ten more writers before they turned to Abe

Burrows, who wrote funny stuff for television. By this time, they had reached the conclusion that the Masterson-Brown romance, and another between a nightclub singer, Miss Adelaide, and Nathan Detroit, the organizer of the "oldest established permanent floating crap game in New York," dictated a much more humorous treatment than they had first had in mind. Greatly responsible for the change was Frank Loesser, the lyricist and composer, whose songs captured with stylistic brilliance the characters and situations. Burrows succeeded in injecting humor into the story where others had failed. Michael Kidd's choreography, and George S. Kaufman's direction, added expert polish to the show.

The opening-night performance (November 24, 1950) established the fact that Broadway not only had another sure-fire hit but a musical-comedy masterpiece. Loesser's clever songs were in no way akin to those of Rodgers and Hammerstein; they did not immediately turn everyone in the nation to humming, whistling, and singing. In themselves, though, they added wonderfully funny definition to the types and characters. With "Fugue for Tinhorns," he created a Bach-like fugue for Times Square touts as they sing their tips on the races. Another song, "Adelaide's Lament," explained the psychosomatic cold developed by the nightclub singer: it came from Nathan Detroit's continually postponing their marriage for no less than fourteen years. More dramatic was "Luck Be a Lady," which Sky Masterson and the other gamblers sing during their thousand-dollar-per-bet crap game.

The chorus girl routines were done deliberately as stereotypes in the onstage Hot Box nightclub; the girls managed to modestly display much of themselves while virtuously singing "Take Back Your Mink" (and other valuable and suspicious gifts). When the basically likable miscreants are finally gathered together by Masterson (who has won his bet to that effect) in the Salvation Army mission, Sister Sarah Brown, the least likely of the Runyon dolls, delivers her message to them, but not before her

Set design of the show curtain for *Guys and Dolls* by Jo Mielziner.

Frank Loesser, who wrote both words and music for *Guys and Dolls* (1950). He would go on to create another masterpiece of musical theatre, *The Most Happy Fella.*

Mielziner's design for the underground tunnel used as a meeting place by the gamblers in *Guys and Dolls* (1950).

Costume designed by Alvin Colt for the character Nathan Detroit.

loyalists sing the lively "Sit Down, You're Rockin' the Boat." During an interlude in Havana, Sister Sarah, encouraged by Sky, gets very drunk and sings the tipsy "If I Were a Bell."

Winning performances were given by Vivian Blaine as Miss Adelaide, and Sam Levene as the crap game impresario, neither particularly well known before opening night. Robert Alda played the slick Sky Masterson, and Isabel Bigley was praised for her sweetly innocent Sarah Brown. *Guys and Dolls* stayed exuberantly on Broadway for three years and became one of the American musical theatre's best-loved achievements.

The rift that had occurred between Joshua Logan and Rodgers and Hammerstein deprived the former from participating in the next runaway hit that came to Broadway only a few months after *Guys and Dolls.* The new show was *The King and I*, based on Margaret Landon's novel *Anna and the King of Siam.* Gertrude Lawrence thought the role of Anna ideal for her talents and managed to persuade Rodgers and Hammerstein of the same.

Hammerstein had asked Logan to direct the show, and to collaborate with him on the libretto. Logan, still nursing his grievances over credits and royalties on *South Pacific*, refused. After *The King and I* had played some 1,200 performances, he said that his turning down the offer was "a decision I will regret for the rest of my life."

Rodgers and Hammerstein did not break much new ground, but they made a captivating display of the musical theatre arts, filled it with exotic color,

Hard at work against Mielziner's background. At center is Robert Alda, playing Sky Masterson, for whom everything was going just right until he had the misfortune to fall in love with a girl from the Salvation Army.

sumptuous settings, and an overflow of their by now virtually patented mixture of charm and sentiment.

The Landon novel about an English governess to the children of a semibarbaric monarch of Siam had already been filmed with Irene Dunne and Rex Harrison in the lead roles. Harrison was interested in playing the king in the musical, but could not agree on conditions and terms. The next choice was Alfred Drake, who was shy about committing himself so soon after his triumph in *Kiss Me, Kate*, and this left the door open for vaguely oriental-looking Yul Brynner, who claimed to be part Mongolian and part Gypsy, and was part bald, part folksinger, part acrobat, and at this moment the host of a television variety show. He came to an audition recommended by Mary Martin, and was instantly chosen.

Yul Brynner and Gertrude Lawrence, the stars of *The King and I.*

The King and I (1951): His Majesty teaches Mrs. Anna a woman's place (always lower than the king).

Irene Sharaff, who designed the costumes, advised Brynner to shave his head completely, and so he remained for the rest of his career, much of which was spent playing in *The King and I*. The playwright John van Druten was asked to direct, though he had never done a musical before. The choreographer Jerome Robbins, in charge of the musical sequences, created a show-stopper with a charming ballet pantomime, "The Small House of Uncle Thomas," meant as a demonstration to the King of the arrogant error of his ways. Another highlight was the swirling polka the hoop-skirted Anna danced with the King. Radiant though Lawrence was, her voice was plagued by faulty pitch; Rodgers compensated for its deficiencies by limiting the range of her songs. Even so, "Hello, Young Lovers," "I Whistle a Happy Tune," and "Shall We Dance?" were marvelously melodic and long-lasting. Lawrence's voice became weaker during the lengthy run, and it was finally clear that she was persisting in the role despite increasingly poor health. Midway in the run she left the show and entered a hospital, supposedly to be treated for hepatitis. But it turned out to be cancer and she died on September 7, 1952. She was buried in the ball gown she had worn in the show.

During the 1950s, Broadway's musicals were based increasingly often on preexisting material. Safety tested, it could be said, but a firm structural basis aided librettists, lyricists, composers, set and costume designers to weave their often wondrous elaborations. Back in the 1930s Ruth McKenney had published a series of semi-autobiographical short stories in *The New Yorker*, which became the basis of *My Sister Eileen*, a play by Joseph Fields and Jerome Chodorov. Over the next several years, various producers tried to do a musical version, but were stymied by problems stemming from Columbia Pictures' control of the screen rights.

Success!

Robert Fryer, who had successfully produced a musical version of *A Tree Grows in Brooklyn*, went ahead with the project, but other than landing George Abbott to direct, had a hard time lining up the right people for it. He was hoping to persuade Irving Berlin or Frank Loesser to compose the score, but when they did not pan out he turned to Leroy Anderson. Meanwhile he offered Rosalind Russell, who had appeared in the film version, the role of elder sister Ruth Sherwood, who shepherds her pretty younger sister from Ohio to Greenwich Village in New York. Russell, though worried about taking on a singing role, agreed to fit it into her schedule.

In *Wonderful Town* (1953), Rosalind Russell meets the Brazilian navy for a free-style conga.

Fields and Chodorov worked up a satisfactory libretto, but the lyrics and music were so far off the mark that the desperate Fryer — about to lose Russell if he didn't get a show ready in a hurry — asked Betty Comden and Adolph Green to write the lyrics. They said they would — on condition that their friend

Leonard Bernstein, of their *On the Town* ten years before, composed the music.

All three knew Greenwich Village very well. In their younger days Green and Bernstein had shared a Village apartment. Green was then writing and performing for The Revuers, an act at the Village Vanguard, a small nightclub. With him as performers were Betty Comden and Judy Holliday. Bernstein, headed for a fabulous conducting and composing career, was on hand to laugh and applaud almost every evening. Because of Rosalind Russell's schedule, Comden and Green and Bernstein were allotted only five weeks by Fryer.

The pressure proved to be a stimulus rather than a hindrance. Bernstein rose to the musical challenge provided by the 1930s depression setting of the story. During the five weeks, the three virtually lived together in his studio, and managed not only to meet but beat their deadline.

The musical opened up the stage play's setting of a moldy basement Village apartment to allow for more decorative streets and backyards, and even a jail where the sisters land after a raucous encounter with some Brazilian sailors who desire only to "Conga!" Both Rosalind Russell and Edith (later Edie) Adams, as Eileen, won the plaudits of critics, Russell less for the qualities of her voice than for her comic authority and clowning, and Adams for her daffy innocence and ability to stagger hilariously through a wild "Swing!" ballet. Bernstein's music was acclaimed for its versatility and sophistication, but oddly, none of the songs reached popular hit status, although it had been predicted that one, "Ohio," a drolly doleful ode the homesick girls sing to the state they have left behind, certainly would.

Alan Jay Lerner was curious enough to ask the veteran music publisher Max Dreyfuss why "Ohio" hadn't become a big hit. "The public knows they're kidding," Max sagely explained.

Wonderful Town opened in February 1953, a time when Senator Joseph McCarthy was peering under government rugs for suspected Communists, and when the general aura of suspicion developed around entertainers of every persuasion, whether in movies, television, or on stage. Performers, artists, writers, and academics were called before congressional committees either to confess their past leftish leanings or prove their true-blue Americanism. Jerome Robbins, who had assisted on the choreography of *Wonderful Town*, testified during the run, and among the "names" he mentioned was that of Jerome Chodorov, co-author of the libretto.

Soon after, the producer, Fryer, learned through patriotic Ed Sullivan's *Daily News* column that a left-wing publication, *The National Guardian*, had bought three hundred seats to a performance to sell as a benefit for the paper. It is a sorry commentary on the time that Fryer hastily canceled the performance so that the organization, he said, would not use the tickets "to disseminate ideas thoroughly hostile to the interests of America."

Far less dazzling than *Wonderful Town* was *Can-Can*, which followed it to

Broadway a few months later. It was a slick show, written by Abe Burrows, its main distinction a Cole Porter score that was compared unfavorably, without real reason, to his incomparable *Kiss Me, Kate*. Yet it had several vintage Porter songs, among them "C'est Magnifique," and "I Love Paris," a soaring tribute to the city Porter loved so much. The show also marked the spectacular Broadway emergence of Gwen Verdon.

Musicals continued to decline in number during the 1950s, but that did not prevent new faces and talents from emerging. The old guard of composers and librettists was either slowing down, had retired, or had gone to some musical heaven. Irving Berlin would do one more show, but not until the early 1960s, while Cole Porter had one left, the 1955 *Silk Stockings*, based on the delectable film *Ninotchka*, which had featured Garbo in one of her last performances. The musical version suffered by comparison, and about the best that could be said of it was that it added more fine Porter songs to his already superlative list.

Between the above two shows came a surprising smash hit, *The Pajama Game*, a musical especially noteworthy because it marked the emergence of the youthful Harold Prince as a producer, of dancer Bob Fosse as choreographer, and of the young songwriting team Richard Adler and Jerry Ross.

Prince, who had hoped to become a playwright, entered the theatre by becoming an all-around assistant to director George Abbott. After two years of army service he came back to Abbott and was put to work with his veteran stage manager, Robert E. Griffith. It was

FRAYED LEGEND

One of the least successful but more legendary musicals is *House of Flowers*, the work of Truman Capote (book and lyrics) and Harold Arlen (score). Capote, then thirty, the author of the highly acclaimed novels *Other Voices, Other Rooms* and *The Grass Harp*, had been in Haiti, where he conversed with the girls who inhabited a strip of bordellos, and then wrote the short story which he used as the basis for the musical. Much was expected of *House of Flowers* (1955), a tale of the rivalry between two of the unsavory establishments, but when it arrived, the thud was heard all over Broadway. The critics turned their thumbs downward, Atkinson, for one, saying that "Mr. Capote's feeling for the joint is perfunctory," and Kerr deciding that the author "has run out of inspiration too soon." Credit went, however, to Oliver Messel's evocative sets and costumes, Arlen's score, and to Pearl Bailey for her performing and singing, but the drumbeat dances were regarded as conventional and repetitious.

Then, somehow, word got around that backstage bickering, particularly between Capote and Peter Brook, who staged the show, had caused its miseries. A revival, with the book supposedly improved by Capote, came to the downtown Theater de Lys fourteen years later, and again the critical verdict was sour. As Clive Barnes said, "A legend came face to face with reality." Legends die hard, however; some theatre buffs still claim that *House of Flowers* was a case of critical neglect.

(*left*)

Hal Prince at the time of his first produced show, *The Pajama Game* (1954).

(*right*)

Bob Fosse. *The Pajama Game* was his first show as a Broadway choreographer.

while both were assisting Abbott on *Wonderful Town* that Prince and Griffith decided to join forces as producers and make a musical from Richard Bissell's novel *7½ Cents* about a threatened strike in a pajama factory.

When asked to direct the proposed show, Abbott was not exactly overwhelmed, in those days of McCarthy hysteria, with the idea of a musical about employee-management relations in a garment factory. But one day, while out walking, a title came to him: *The Pajama Game*. He liked it and changed his mind. Prince and Griffith were already seeking, without success, someone to write a libretto when Abbott sensibly suggested getting hold of the author of the novel, saying that he would write it with him.

Bissell had actually worked for several years in the family pajama business in Dubuque, Iowa. He quickly came east and developed a libretto with Abbott that added romantic complications to the story. The new songwriting team of Richard Adler and Jerry Ross came through a recommendation by Frank Loesser. They had written several popular songs, but never a score for a musical. They were asked to write three songs as a sort of audition, after which they were quickly hired. One of the songs became one of the show's best numbers, "Steam Heat." Bob Fosse's helpful wife, Joan McCracken, who had appeared in *Wonderful Town*, suggested him to Abbott for the choreography.

Fosse, a superb and inventive dancer in films and Broadway shows, was unproven enough to cause Prince and Griffith to ask Jerome Robbins to back him up. As a reward, Robbins was made co-director with Abbott.

The cast of the show was good, but not a guarantee of success. Janis Paige came from the movies; John Raitt and comedian Eddie Foy, Jr., though experienced, were not important stars, and dancer Carol Haney was a newcomer to Broadway. It was understandable that a show with so many relatively untried talents would be difficult to capitalize, and it was, until Frederick Brisson, the husband of Rosalind Russell, came on board as co-producer.

Guided by Abbott's experienced hand and staging, the show was fast, funny, and full of sparkle. Fosse's jazzy offbeat dances, replete with caricatured postering and snapping fingers, startled and captivated audiences, as did the catchy love song, "Hey, There," and an exaggerated Latin tango, "Hernando's Hideaway." One critic carped that *The Pajama Game*'s show-stoppers were so frequent he had trouble keeping his concentration. But he saw no way to solve this happy problem.

It was almost exactly a year later, in May of 1955, that the same combination brought another joyous hit, *Damn Yankees*, to Broadway. The subject — a rabid Washington Senators fan who sells his soul to the devil in return for being able to play for the team and help them defeat the detested New York Yankees — came from the Douglass Wallop novel, *The Year the Yankees Lost the Pennant*. Again Abbott wrote the

The cast singing the joys of a unionized life.

SAUCY SIREN

Walter Kerr in his

review of *Damn Yankees* said of
Gwen Verdon, as Lola, the devil's
red-haired temptress, "she is
simply and insanely inspired.
She is everything undesirable
made absolutely and forever
desirable." Two years earlier, Miss
Verdon had danced her way into
better billing and a raise from her
$250-a-week salary in *Can-Can*,
but it was *Damn Yankees* (1955)
that established her stardom.
"Whatever Lola wants, Lola
gets," she sang, while slithering
on a locker-room bench and
beating the floor with whatever
clothing was handy. Much of her
success, she said, she owed to
choreographer Bob Fosse, whom
she later married, crediting him
for "the flirtatious quality, the
accent, minuscule things like
where you push your hair back,
when you breathe, when you
blink your eyes and when you
move your little finger."

Born in Culver City,
California, in 1926, Gwen was
trained by her mother — a dance
instructor. She danced
professionally at age thirteen, but
gave it up for marriage at
seventeen. After her divorce, she
took up dancing again ten years
later, after auditioning for
choreographer Jack Cole. In
several Broadway shows she was
relatively anonymous until the
audience kept calling her back in
Can-Can.

As dancer, singer and
actress she was the *New Girl in
Town*, the redhead in *Redhead*,
and Charity, a dance-hall girl at
the Fandango Ballroom, in *Sweet
Charity*, based on the Fellini film,
Nights of Cabiria. In *Chicago*, Bob
Fosse's 1975 rendering of the 1926
play by Maurine Dallas Watkins,
and the 1942 movie *Roxy Hart*,
Verdon took on the Ginger
Rogers role of the chorus girl
who confesses to the murder of
her lover for the publicity it
brings her. The critics weren't too
happy with the brassy show as a
whole, but for the nearly fifty-
year-old Gwen Verdon it was one
more triumph.

Gwen Verdon in *Damn Yankees* (1955).

libretto with the author; Prince, Griffith, and Brisson produced; and Fosse choreographed.

As the handmaiden to Ray Walston's devil, red-haired Gwen Verdon, with her slithering "Whatever Lola Wants" (she gets), became an immediate star.

Gabriel Pascal, a film producer, who was once described as "a swarthy adventurer from Transylvania," had a dream of making a musical from George Bernard Shaw's *Pygmalion.* When he approached Alan Jay Lerner and Frederick Loewe in 1952 to do the conversion, he told them they were the

only people who could possibly realize his dream. This, Lerner and Loewe knew, was a Transylvanian exaggeration. Word was about that he had told much the same thing to Noël Coward, Cole Porter, E. Y. Harburg, and Rodgers and Hammerstein, all of whom turned down the "unique" opportunity.

Lerner and Loewe were interested enough to work on an adaptation for three months before giving up, because, they realized, the play was basically drawing-room comedy, and turning it to musical form would entail doing violence to Shaw's structure. Two years later they tried again, but Pascal died, creating a confused legal situation. Lerner and

Original poster design for *My Fair Lady.*

My Fair Lady (1956): Robert Coote (left) as Colonel Pickering, bemused friend to Henry Higgins, played brilliantly by the nonsinging Rex Harrison (right). Seated between them is the redoubtable Doolittle, played by Stanley Holloway, who appears to be exploring the possibility of dental work.

MUSIC TO THEIR EARS

My Fair Lady, with its way of reaping unsolicited publicity, was a press agent's bonanza. When President Eisenhower dashed in to see the second act on a speechmaking visit to New York City, it made every newspaper in the country because it was the first show he had seen since occupying the White House. Others whose presence was noted were Harry Truman, Richard Nixon, Nehru, Prince Rainier and Princess Grace, Princess Soraya of Iran, and King Mahendra Bir Bikram Shah of Nepal.

During half-time at the 1957 Army–Notre Dame game in Philadelphia, the Notre Dame band played the show's entire score, which was thus seen and heard by the hundred thousand at the game, and twenty million on TV. During the Democratic convention at Chicago in 1956, the delegates and TV watchers heard a rendition of "I Could Have Danced All Night." Not to be outdone, the Republicans in San Francisco's Cow Palace a week later heard "On the Street Where You Live." Meanwhile, hundreds of department store window-display designers clamored for posters and copies of Cecil Beaton's costume design sketches for use in their window displays.

Loewe went on working, hoping the rights' difficulties would be clarified. By then they had decided it would do no great harm to Bernard Shaw (also gone from this earth) if the audience was told what happened between the scenes of the play's five acts. In this way, characters only mentioned in the play could be brought to life and the show could become more populous. Eliza Doolittle, the cockney flower-seller whose accent and language so bothered Professor Higgins, would go home and see her dustman father, Doolittle, before appearing at Higgins's house the next day for her speech improvement. In the play the audience never saw the pronunciation lessons; Lerner and Loewe decided to use them. The tryout of Eliza's newly acquired cultural wings would not occur at a tea party, but would afford more dramatic possibilities at fashionable Ascot.

With Pascal gone, a producer was found in Herman Levin, who had shepherded *Call Me Mister* and *Gentlemen Prefer Blondes* to successful runs. Almost from the moment they began working, Lerner and Loewe had made the decision that they wanted Rex Harrison for the querulous Professor Higgins, in spite of his lack of a traditional singing voice. As Lerner related about the musical's development stage, "It would strain the credulity of the audience if Professor Higgins suddenly opened his mouth and poured forth a rich baritone."

In February 1955, by which time Lerner and Loewe had written seven songs for what they were then calling "My Lady Liza," they flew to London to convince Harrison he was the ideal Henry Higgins. It wasn't easy. It was "hard for Rex to reach a decision," Lerner said of him. "He studied a menu for twenty minutes before ordering his soup." But Rex finally capitulated, after being told songs would be written for him to sing in a nonsinging way.

Harrison, without a powerful voice, represented a new concept of a leading man in a musical play. "The trick was," Lerner related, "to write the lines for music exactly the way a nonsinging person says them. Once we'd done that, Rex could either say them or sing them, and all would be well." In the case of the Higgins song "I've Grown Accustomed to Her Face," Loewe wrote it the way a normal person would say the lines instead of singing them, with no drawn-out notes for any of the words.

At forty-one, Mary Martin was old for the role of Eliza, but nonetheless indicated her interest in playing it. Lerner and Loewe met with her and her husband and played five of the songs they had written, among them the "Ascot Gavotte," and "Just You Wait" (Henry Higgins), none of which she liked.

The next choice was Julie Andrews, a charming nineteen-year-old who had appeared in *The Boy Friend*, an imported British pastiche about the twenties. She was close to Eliza in age, and had a lovely soprano voice, but was kept waiting until no other important star possibility turned up. Meanwhile, Stanley Holloway, of English music-hall and musical-comedy fame, was tapped for Doolittle.

Moss Hart agreed to become the director as soon as he heard "Why Can't the English?" Cecil Beaton designed

Julie Andrews as Eliza, surrounded by Cockney friends and singing "Wouldn't It Be Loverly" as she dreams of a better life in *My Fair Lady* (1956).

elegant Edwardian costumes; Oliver Smith created the sets, one of them a stunning Ascot enclosure in black, gray, and white; and Hanya Holm signed on as choreographer. William Paley, the head of CBS, through Goddard Lieberson, of the same company's record division, became interested enough to propose backing the entire show, a quid pro quo being that Columbia Records would have the rights to the original cast album.

In spite of the tinkering done to the text by Lerner, the musical, now named *My Fair Lady*, stayed remarkably close to the play, even to much of its dialogue. Nary a kiss was exchanged, as in Shaw's version, and the only slight deviation was in the ending, similar to that of the 1938 movie, which Shaw had allowed. The audience could feel that, if nothing else, the relationship between Higgins and Eliza would continue.

During the tryout, word spread that a magical new hit was working its

Eliza again: Proper grammar and an upper-class accent appear to have done the trick!

Costume design for a Covent Garden flower-seller by Cecil Beaton.

BRILLIANCE IN MOTION

Jerome Robbins was a well-known soloist with the American Ballet Theatre, but an unknown choreographer, when his first ballet, *Fancy Free*, a kind of paean to Manhattan, was premiered at the Metropolitan Opera House in April of 1944. From then on, he was regarded as one of the most brilliant and original figures in the American theatre. *Fancy Free* soon after metamorphosed into the musical *On the Town*, with music by Leonard Bernstein and book by Betty Comden and Adolph Green. Robbins was born Jerome Rabinowitz in New York in 1918, and was brought up in Weehawken, New Jersey. At New York University his aim was to become a chemist, but a lack of money forced him to abandon his studies, and he turned to dance. In 1940 he joined the newly formed American Ballet Theatre, and found his interest increasingly engaged in choreography. He rebelled against the Russian school then dominating ballet in this country, and began experimenting with a new and freer kind of American dance expression. His influence

(continued on p. 187)

way toward Broadway. By its mid-March 1956 opening, long lines had been forming at the Mark Hellinger Theatre for three weeks. Mail orders for tickets flowed in so heavily that Lerner, Loewe, and everyone else concerned worried that too much was expected. There was no cause for worry. Walter Kerr called the show "miraculous," and Brooks Atkinson

decided he had seen "the greatest musical of the Twentieth Century."

My Fair Lady continues to stand as a truly landmark musical, rightfully showered with awards. It established a new record by staying on Broadway for six and a half years. There was hardly a country in the world where the show did not play, and recordings of the show were made in the language of every country in which it was performed. For its $400,000 investment, CBS made in the neighborhood of fifty million dollars.

The question has been asked often: Why the remarkable, long-lasting appeal of *My Fair Lady*? There are the songs, of course, graceful, witty, appropriate — "I Could Have Danced All Night," "On the Street Where You Live," and the riotous "The Rain in Spain" — which lingered on the charts for years. Qualities of effervescent wit, of style, and of taste were not necessarily guarantees of long-lasting popularity, nor was a literate story, or an intelligent, sense-making plot. All of these the show had in enough abundance to make it a succès d'estime. But the show's astounding success had to derive from a rare combination of the right talents coming together at the right time.

Another case in point: *West Side Story.*

On January 6, 1949, Jerome Robbins made a telephone call to Leonard Bernstein, and Bernstein made a note of what they had talked about. It was an idea for a *"Romeo and Juliet* set in the slums at the coincidence of Easter-Passover celebrations." Bernstein was interested, as was writer Arthur Laurents, but for the next several years the idea remained only in the backs of their minds.

When they first met to discuss it, Laurents objected that pitting Jew against Italian Catholic, as Robbins had proposed, reminded him of *Abie's Irish Rose* set to music, and he didn't want to have any part of it. Six years later,

Laurents and Bernstein met accidentally at the pool of the Beverly Hills Hotel. Much in the news in Los Angeles at the time was gang warfare in Mexican neighborhoods, and, in talking about it, they were reminded of the *Romeo and Juliet* idea. Laurents suggested, "What about doing it about the Chicanos?" That led them to a more timely approach: changing the milieu to the street gangs of New York's debilitated West Side, where whites clashed with more newly arrived Puerto Ricans.

"A solemn pact has been born," Bernstein recorded in his diary, after Robbins was notified and had heartily approved of the change. "Here we go. God bless us."

Bernstein originally planned to write both the lyrics and music, but the double task proved too difficult, and the youthful Stephen Sondheim joined

(continued from p. 186)
on dance and musical theatre has been both long and lasting.

Some forty-five years after *Fancy Free* and *On the Town*, his *Jerome Robbins' Broadway* came to the Imperial Theatre, a compilation of the most notable dance sequences he staged over a period of twenty years for some fifteen shows, several of which he also directed, most of them hits. The numbers included "New York, New York," from *On the Town*; a Mack Sennett bathing beauty ballet from *High Button Shoes*; "The Small House of Uncle Thomas" from *The King and I*; and the wedding dance from his last show on Broadway, *Fiddler on the Roof*. The highlight of his *Broadway* reprise, however, was the leaping, finger-snapping suite of dances he conceived for the classic *West Side Story*, still absolutely electrifying nearly thirty-five years later.

Hal Prince (left), producer, and Jerome Robbins, who conceived *West Side Story* and went on to direct and choreograph it.

TO BE OR
NOT TO BE OPERA

What is the difference between a musical and an opera? Critic Will Crutchfield of the *New York Times* asked the question about a recorded version of *West Side Story*, and in his view there was none. "I can see no reason," he wrote, "why the 'Tonight' ensemble should not be compared to the quartet from *Rigoletto* . . . piece for piece the Bernstein stacks up to the Verdi." Another critic, Clive Barnes, took the argument even farther, suggesting that the living future of opera — or serious musical theatre — belonged in the hands of such composers as Leonard Bernstein and Stephen Sondheim. The opera of the classically oriented composer was, in his words, "deader than a dodo . . . a superb fossilized art, the preserve of interpreters rather than creators." For him, *Porgy and Bess* was "grand opera and grand popular theatre." Often, it is in recordings that certain musicals — *Show Boat* being a case in point — reveal their operatic or near-operatic qualities, especially when sung by classically trained voices. The argument, however, continues, and there are those who warn that the closer the musical comes to the opera house, the heavier and more moribund it might become on stage.

the team. In paralleling the Shakespeare plot, Laurents posited two gangs — the white Jets and the Puerto Rican Sharks. The hero, Tony, is a former leader of the Jets, turned to more peaceable ways, who falls in love with a newly arrived Puerto Rican girl, Maria. Their ill-fated romance occurs against the violent street life of the West Side neighborhood, and their love is declared in song ("Tonight") not on a balcony, but on a tenement fire escape.

The product of the collaboration between four fiercely creative temperaments was a beautiful and uncompromising work, again attesting to the heights that Broadway theatre was capable of reaching. Later Robbins said, "We were feeding each other all the time. We would meet wherever we could, depending on our schedules. Arthur [Laurents] would come in with a scene, the others would say they could do a song on this material. I'd supply, 'How about if we did this as a dance.' There was this wonderful, mutual exchange going on."

Bernstein felt that creating *West Side Story* was like walking on a tightrope, constantly maintaining a balance between the demands of the music and the extraordinary dance conceptions of Robbins, who directed the entire show. In conceiving the "rumble," a dramatic set piece, Bernstein said, "If it had been too balletic, we would have fallen off on one side. And if it had been too realistic we would have fallen off on the other side. There would have been no poetry to it, no art."

Interestingly enough, a contributor to the story's final shape was Richard Rodgers. Laurents had written a

Carol Lawrence and Larry Kert, the ill-fated lovers of *West Side Story* (1957).

scene in which Maria, after her lover, Tony, has been killed by a rival gang member, commits suicide. Rodgers did not think the original had to be followed so rigorously. "She's dead already," he told Robbins, "after all this happens to her." So, in the end, Maria is left grieving over Tony's body.

Cheryl Crawford was originally slated to produce. Sensing that the show might well be an artistic success but a commercial failure, she asked for changes that alienated the authors. Earlier, several producers contacted had had similar concerns. Ultimately Roger Stevens came to the rescue, but did not feel he could handle the production by himself. The astute producing team of Harold Prince and Robert E. Griffith, who had earlier turned the show down, now changed their minds and joined Stevens.

Because the story was about young people in the slums, casting youth was an obvious prerequisite, which meant that the show would not be able to use older, established stars. Larry Kert, as Tony, came out of the chorus of the Sammy Davis, Jr. musical, *Mr. Wonderful.* A newcomer, Carol Lawrence, was chosen for Maria after an audition that mesmerized Bernstein and the others. Chita Rivera, also from *Mr. Wonderful*, was given the part of Anita, Maria's fiery girlfriend.

Although *West Side Story* played for two years on Broadway, it took some time before it was recognized as a precedent-setting achievement. The starkness of the story and the brutality of the characters bothered some. Walter Kerr thought the work masterly, but regarded its "heartless craftsmanship" as a major flaw. And, with its harsh tenderloin settings by Oliver Smith, it was hardly traditional musical entertainment. It energized with a coruscating number like "America!"; it had lovely sounds in songs like "Maria" and "Somewhere"; and it had some humor in "Gee, Officer Krupke," but throughout it tended much more to disturb than to amuse. What it did have in abundance was poetry, and drama that came as much from the explosive Robbins ballets as from the words and music.

Brooks Atkinson regretted the loss to the theatre when Bernstein took over the conducting reins of the New York Philharmonic. His score for *West Side Story*, he said, was "a harsh ballad of the city, taut, nervous, and flaring, the rhythms wild, swift, and deadly."

Some thirty years after its Broadway debut in September 1957, a music critic greeted a new recording of *West Side Story* by calling it "an occasion for celebrating one of the great operas of our century." By then, there was hot debate about whether such transcendent Broadway musical works as *Show Boat*, *Porgy and Bess*, and *West Side Story* should indeed be ranked not as musicals but as full-blown American operas.

According to the *New York Times* critic Will Crutchfield: "Mr. Bernstein's 1950's *Romeo and Juliet* answers the standards of variety, melodic richness, seriousness of intent, and musical sweep that the major operatic composers have taught us to set."

At the time of Bernstein's death in October 1990, the question of whether he should have devoted more of his time and talents to "serious music" as opposed to musicals persisted. Whatever the decision of history on that point, in *West Side Story* Broadway had surely extended its musical reach.

The company in the challenge dance that ignites a fatal West Side gang war.

(*overleaf*) Costumes, from left to right: Austrian dirndl worn by Mary Martin in *The Sound of Music* (1960). Top hat and vest worn by Joel Grey in *Cabaret* (1966). Tunic and crown worn by Richard Burton in *Camelot* (1960). Ball gown created by Cecil Beaton for *My Fair Lady* (1956). Plaid blanket coat worn by Ethel Merman in *Gypsy* (1959). Backdrop painted by Nolan Studios, NYC.

Mary Martin in the Mainbocher-designed wedding gown she wore in *The Sound of Music* (1960).

VII *Metaphor and the Musical, 1957–1966*

THE MUSIC MAN

GYPSY

THE SOUND OF MUSIC

CAMELOT

HELLO, DOLLY!

FIDDLER ON THE ROOF

CABARET

While some theatregoers were still complaining that *West Side Story* had deprived them of the kind of pleasure they normally expected from musicals, a nice, genial, warm, uncomplicated show arrived in late December 1957 like a welcome Christmas gift. The author of *The Music Man*, which largely concerned the forming of a boys' band in a small Iowa town in 1912, was Meredith Willson, whose memories provided the framework, details, and nostalgic feeling of the story.

Willson was very much a music man himself. As a boy in Mason City, Iowa, he was first taught piano, then took up the flute for the town's boys' band in the absence of anyone else to play it. Eventually he headed for New York City and the Juilliard School to pursue a professional music career. At age nineteen, a virtuoso flutist, he was hired for the John Philip Sousa band. Subsequently he joined the New York Philharmonic, and from there went on to become a composer and songwriter, and on radio a popular orchestra leader.

When among friends he liked to talk about his early days in Mason City — the picnics, parades, and neighborliness of small-town life — and on one of those occasions Frank Loesser suggested he use his memories for a musical, even outlining the shape it ought to take: the fire chief as the leader of the town band, and in the theatre pit a brass band instead of an orchestra.

After some time Willson changed the main character to a traveling salesman and con artist, Harold Hill, also known as "Professor Hill," who bounces into River City, Iowa, in 1912 to fast-talk the locals into buying their children band instruments and uniforms in the expectation he will provide the teaching. Actually, he plans to decamp as soon as the instruments arrive, but is thwarted when he runs afoul of the suspicious local librarian and, to complicate matters, falls in love with her. Producers Cy Feuer and Ernest Martin were impressed enough with the script to promise a production, but then decided the story wasn't strong enough to carry a whole show. Willson rewrote the libretto with the help of playwright Franklin Lacey, but still needed a producer. After several failed attempts, he found one in Kermit Bloomgarden, who had co-produced Loesser's operatic *The Most Happy Fella*, a major success at the time. Loesser offered to serve as the associate producer.

Bloomgarden, in search of a director, went to Moss Hart, who had so brilliantly staged *My Fair Lady*. Hart thought the proposed musical bad, enough to make him think he perhaps ought to advise Bloomgarden to drop it, but instead he simply bowed out himself. Morton Da Costa took over and had the good fortune of staging one of the great musicals of the fifties — 1,375 performances on Broadway, and many, many more across the land and in Europe.

Danny Kaye and Gene Kelly were among those who turned down the role of Harold Hill, which finally fell to Robert Preston, a deep-voiced actor until then mostly in western movies. The pretty soprano Barbara Cook played opposite him as the town librarian.

Though a stranger to musicals,

(opposite)
The creative team of *The Music Man* (1957). From left: Rini Willson, Herbert Greene, musical director, Meredith Willson, Morton Da Costa, Kermit Bloomgarden, and Onna White, choreographer.

Preston brought enormous gusto to his role, especially when selling instruments and when forced, without knowing how to read music, to teach the young band members. The resulting "Seventy-six Trombones," a rousing but cacophonous echo of Willson's Sousa years, still was deeply satisfying to the proud parents of the town.

The Music Man's appeal to audiences lay in its rich local color, its likable characters — including Harold Hill — its comedy, and its charm. It was clearly a musician's show, from its plot situation that dealt with music to its musical range through ragtime, soft-shoe, ballad, march, even to a barbershop quartet, the Buffalo Bills, who mellowly sang the charms of someone called "Lida Rose." To further catch the atmosphere, Howard Bay provided sepia-print settings, and Raoul Pene du Bois designed costumes the shades of vanilla fudge ice cream and raspberry sundaes.

"The grace of the evening," Walter Kerr wrote in the *Herald Tribune*, "is in the beaming good nature of its people," yet with "a joyous time-bomb" of a trumpet blast "always on the point of exploding." "Nothing like it has ever been seen on Broadway," the awed critic for *Variety* reported after opening night at the Majestic Theatre, "and rarely has a first night audience let out a roar to equal the ovation accorded to Preston and the rest of the cast." It was one of those rare shows that appealed to just about everyone, as innocent and fresh, and as traditional as the Fourth of July.

The Music Man (1957): Barbara Cook, Marian the Librarian, and Robert Preston, who played the master of the musical con, Professor Harold Hill.

Just as *The Music Man* managed to avoid the traps of corniness and excessive sentimentality, so did *Gypsy* avoid a charge of overfamiliarity as it told the story of a frustrated stage mother who assuages her injured ego by pushing her daughters into performing careers. A vigorous, tough-minded and affecting musical that opened in May 1959, it brought a vivid glow to the last year of the supposedly somnolent fifties. It also provided convincing evidence that a new generation of gifted theatre people was claiming the center of the Broadway musical scene.

The names associated with *Gypsy* were already luminous: Arthur Laurents, author of the libretto, Jerome Robbins, director and choreographer, Stephen Sondheim, lyrics, and Jule Styne, the score. With them was the star, Ethel Merman, the sturdy representative of the "old guard," still attempting to convince doubters that she was just as much an

The children's band makes its debut before a group of slightly stunned townsfolk.

accomplished actress as she was a singer. After *Gypsy*, it can be said, nary a doubter remained.

Arthur Laurents needed convincing before agreeing to write the libretto based on the decidedly heightened memoirs of Gypsy Rose Lee, an ecdysiast known both for her statuesque proportions and her intellectual pretensions. David Merrick, a wily producer quick to sense hit potential, came across an excerpt from the book in *Harper's* magazine, and edged out other claimants for the stage rights. Irving Berlin and Cole Porter were approached and declined, after which Comden and Green were hired to do the book and lyrics, and Jule Styne the music. Comden and Green gave up when they saw no way to handle the character of Mama Rose, the invincible stage mother of the memoir.

By this time, Ethel Merman had indicated her interest in playing the role. In fact, while at a cocktail party in Gypsy Rose Lee's elegant Manhattan townhouse, she announced to her hostess: "I've read your book. I love it. I want to do it. I'm going to do it. And I'll shoot anyone else who gets the part."

Merrick was more than willing to have Merman, but to get her he had to join forces with Leland Hayward, to whom Merman owed her next commitment. Both Merrick and Hayward wanted Jerome Robbins and Arthur Laurents, fresh from their triumph of *West Side Story*; while Robbins was agreeable, Laurents couldn't get himself interested in the title character, who became the queen of strip-tease in America.

Jule Styne's career on Broadway goes back to *High Button Shoes*. In addition to Ethel Merman, he has written for such extraordinary stars as Judy Holliday (*Bells Are Ringing*), Carol Channing (*Gentlemen Prefer Blondes*), and Barbra Streisand (*Funny Girl*).

Leland Hayward was the one who kept after him. "You'll find a way," he told him. "One day," Laurents related later, "I heard a young woman talking about Gypsy Rose Lee's mother. She was apparently what they used to call a curvaceous plump blonde. Very sweet, and an absolute killer." He went to see Ethel Merman and did some straight talking. As he saw the role, he told her, Mama Rose Hovick would not be sympathetic. "This woman is a classic," he told her, "a mother who has to learn that if you try to live your children's lives you'll end up by destroying yourself. How far are you willing to go?" Merman assured him she would do whatever it was he wanted of her.

Thus inspired, Laurents wrote a taut, lean, pungent libretto in which the mother pushes her daughters headlong and unfeelingly into the tacky world of vaudeville. When one daughter, Baby June, decamps into marriage, and when the talkies ruin vaudeville, she forces her other daughter to learn the bumps and grinds of sleazy burlesque. She is a brassy woman who takes her daughters to a restaurant and sweeps the cutlery on the table into her pocketbook, saying, "We need silverware." When the waitress later comes around, the mother asks her sweetly if she may have a spoon for her tea. To get her ruthless way she makes promises, breaks them without a thought, then says, "I promise to keep my promise." Somehow, Merman made the character both believable and even, to a degree, lovable.

Laurents suggested young Stephen Sondheim for both the lyrics and the score, but Merman asserted her star

Mama Rose in her blanket coat with (left to right) Mort Marshall, Karen Moore, and Jacqueline Mayro.

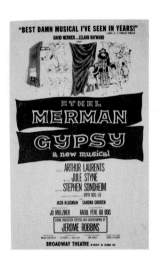

Original poster design for *Gypsy* (1959).

status and objected. She had had an unhappy experience with a relatively untried composer on her previous show and wanted someone else. As it turned out: Jule Styne. Sondheim was then asked to write the lyrics only, but was discomfited by the offer. He regarded himself first and foremost as a composer, and his lyric-writing as a sideline. Oscar Hammerstein had become sort of a patron and Dutch uncle to him, and advised him to take the assignment. The experience of writing a show for a star, he said, would be invaluable for him.

Styne had long been established as a composer of musicals. In 1947 he had written the music to Sammy Cahn's lyrics for *High Button Shoes*; in 1949, for the runaway hit *Gentlemen Prefer Blondes*;

and in 1956, *Bells Are Ringing*, in association with Comden and Green. Laurents worried, though, that Styne's work was too much in the pop song category, and that he might not be right for what he had conceived as a dramatic entity. Styne stifled his annoyance, offered to audition for him, and played several songs, after which Laurents was satisfied. The collaboration between Laurents, Sondheim, and Styne then proceeded harmoniously.

Laurents constructed the libretto so that almost every one of the scenes ended with a song and a blackout, to be immediately followed, seamlessly, by the next scene. Much of the show was a depiction of small-time show business in the twenties and thirties. Jo Mielziner's

199

Set design for *Gypsy* (1959) by Jo Mielziner.

Set design for backdrop and trim by Jo Mielziner.

sets emphasized the slatternly dressing rooms and garish stages of the old vaudeville houses and strip palaces in which Louise, played by Sandra Church, becomes, finally, the stripper Gypsy Rose Lee.

One number, "You Gotta Have a Gimmick," resulted directly from auditioning potential strippers. A veteran of the art, Faith Dane, showed up with a bugle, which she blew while undulating. The number was written in the show especially because of her and became a side-splitting trio when two other strippers were added: one wore flapping butterfly wings, and the third was literally electrified.

Another improvisation was the climactic number, originally planned as a ballet, in which Rose's past would come back to her in fleeting appearances like a nightmare. Robbins was persuaded that Merman needed a finale to herself because the blackout scene endings did not allow her to stay on stage and acknowledge applause. Substituted was an unconventional song, "Rose's Turn," that created the nightmare quality through words and music. Merman stood alone in a blaze of neon, still singing of her dream, now revealed as less for her daughters than for herself. As described by one critic, "The curtain descends on Miss Merman's most dazzling moment."

Another of Broadway's musical stars, Mary Martin, provided more dazzle — albeit of a cheerier sort — some six months later in the last of the Rodgers and Hammerstein shows, *The Sound of Music.*

It was at first envisioned as something quite different from what it turned out to be. A television director, Vincent J. Donehue, happened to see a German film about the Trapp Family Singers, adapted from the true story of Maria von Trapp, an Austrian novice nun sent as the governess for the seven children of a widower, the Baron Georg von Trapp. Maria and the baron fell in

Richard Rodgers (left) and Oscar Hammerstein II. *The Sound of Music* was their last show together.

love, and fled with the children when the Nazis marched into Austria. In America, and throughout much of the world, the Trapps gained fame from their concert appearances as a group of family singers.

Donehue thought it would make a wonderful musical for Mary Martin. So did she, and her husband, the producer Richard Halliday. Baron von Trapp had died by then and the family was scattered far and wide, so that it was all but impossible to find them and gain the needed consents, along with stage rights to the film. Leland Hayward became a partner in the enterprise when he offered to assume that burden.

BROADWAY!

Hayward also brought in Howard Lindsay and Russel Crouse to fashion a libretto. Their first idea for music was to use songs the Trapps sang at their concerts. Richard Rodgers was asked for advice, and to contribute one song. Rodgers felt that either the Trapp music be used throughout, or a completely new score be fashioned. Would he and Oscar consider . . . ? They would, if *The Sound of Music* could wait until their *Flower Drum Song* was off and running.

and, after an operation that occurred as the show went into rehearsal, he came back in time to write one last song, "Edelweiss."

Although *The Sound of Music* racked up the largest advance sale in the history of the theatre until then — well over two million dollars — it did not totally win over the critics. Many of the songs were vastly admired, and continued to be heard for many years, among them "Do-Re-Mi," "My Favorite

Mary Martin, Theodore Bikel, who played the Baron von Trapp, and the children sing "Edelweiss" in *The Sound of Music* (1960).

A year went by. Rodgers had successfully fought a cancer that lost him half of his lower jaw, but Hammerstein was having stomach problems — an ulcer, he thought. Actually it was cancer,

Things," and "Climb Every Mountain." Rodgers had in no way lost his magical way with melody, and Hammerstein's lyrics were touching in their cheerful simplicity. But for Walter Kerr of the

(opposite) Costume designs for the baron's ball by Lucinda Ballard.

The Sound of Music
SK#9

BODICE
SHEATH SKIRT
OVERSKIRT
LINING OF OVERSKIRT

BROADWAY!

The Sound of Music (1960): Set design for the von Trapp villa by Oliver Smith.

Herald Tribune, the "cascade of sugar" was a little too much. And he felt that Donehue, the director, had made the evening "suffer from little children."

"Must they bounce into bed in their nightgowns so often, and so charmingly?" he asked. "Must they wear so many different picture-book skirts, and fluff them so mightily, and smile so relentlessly?" Atkinson of the *Times* was kinder — he thought it a "bountiful musical evening" given a common touch and goodwill by Mary Martin's glowing personality, but was bothered by the conventional libretto of Lindsay and Crouse (Hammerstein had written lyrics only) that had the hackneyed feel of the kind of operetta Rodgers and Hammerstein had previously avoided.

A familiar phrase among theatre people when a show failed to gain critical respect was, "It's an audience show."

Apparently *The Sound of Music* was an audience show par excellence, because its patrons loved it and kept it running on Broadway for more than three years. Then, when the movie was made five years later, with Julie Andrews as Maria von Trapp, it was the largest moneymaker of its era, due in large part to the fact that parents could take their demanding children to see it again and again.

Hammerstein's cancer turned out to be incurable, and he died on August 23, 1960, less than eight months after the opening of *The Sound of Music*. That night, in silent tribute to him, all the lights on Broadway — and in London's West End theatre district, too — were dimmed for three minutes, the first time in theatre history that such a tribute had been paid.

While *My Fair Lady* was still enjoying its triumphant run on Broadway, Alan Jay Lerner and Frederick Loewe made another stab at glory with their Arthurian musical spectacle, *Camelot*. They had secured the rights to T. H. White's retelling of the legends of King Arthur and his court, *The Once and Future King*, and hoped to treat it with similar wit and gentle mockery.

Merely the announcement of the project was important theatre news. Several months before the show went into rehearsal, a full-page ad brought a deluge of ticket orders, and by the time the show arrived in New York, the advance sale — well over three million dollars — had eclipsed the record set by the previous year's *The Sound of Music*.

Much the same team from *My Fair Lady* was reassembled: Moss Hart as

204

director, Oliver Smith for settings, Hanya Holm for the stately dances, Julie Andrews for the role of Queen Guenevere, whose faithlessness to Arthur with Lancelot spins the triangular plot. Richard Burton, the boozy, mellow-voiced Welshman, and arguably the best of the new generation of English actors, agreed to play the king, although he had no formal musical training. Still, the Welsh are known for their musical voices, and, like so many others in Wales, as a boy Richard had participated in the traditional annual singing festivals.

By the time the musical reached Broadway, it was also being referred to as a "medical." Loewe had had a heart attack and had been cautioned against overwork. Lerner had suffered a near nervous breakdown when one of his many wives (serially speaking) left him while he was in the midst of fashioning the libretto and lyrics. The costume designer Adrian had died before completing his work. While shaping the show in Toronto at the acoustically deficient O'Keefe Centre, Lerner had landed in the hospital with bleeding ulcers. As he was leaving the hospital, Moss Hart arrived to take over his room: he had suffered a serious heart attack that ended his direction of the show. Lerner took over the show, and with the loyal help of Burton managed while on the road to carve it from four hours down to three — still very long. By that time

Costume design for Merlin by Adrian and Tony Duquette.

Richard Burton, Frederick Loewe, Alan Jay Lerner, and Julie Andrews, stars and authors of *Camelot* (1960).

mounting expenses had given the show another, less-glorious record — the most expensive musical ever produced on Broadway.

Nonetheless, expectations still ran high, and the opening-night audience at the Majestic Theatre on December 3, 1960, was as glittering a crowd of the notable and famous as had assembled on Broadway for a long time. Comparisons were inevitable, and *Camelot* was bound to suffer. Most critics agreed that the show was beautifully mounted, that its pageantry was impressive, its architecture and raiments royally lavish, that the great hall with its throne had grandeur, that Burton had a winning presence, that Julie Andrews was alternately girlish and regal and clear-voiced as ever. Robert Goulet's Lancelot was sung magnificently, and the score was filled with such treasures as the title song, "Camelot," "I Wonder What the King Is Doing Tonight," and "If Ever I Would Leave You."

After all the above, however, came the faint damns: a feeling of turgidity, especially in the second of the two acts; the relationships not well defined, the story-telling style unevenly veering between moments of enchantment and stodgy reality. Such humor as there was came from a stock numbskull in the figure of a deposed English king played by Robert Coote, the Colonel Pickering of *My Fair Lady.* In a more diabolical mood was the evil Mordred of Roddy McDowall.

In spite of its more than three-million-dollar advance sale it looked as though *Camelot* would not last the year that Burton had agreed to play in it.

Then, a few months after its opening, a sort of miracle occurred. One Sunday evening *The Ed Sullivan Show* was devoted to honoring Lerner and Loewe. By this time Moss Hart had recuperated enough to tinker with the show, to rerehearse it, cut two of its songs, and sharpen the libretto. Lerner cannily insisted that the last twenty minutes of Sullivan's show be devoted to *Camelot.* Newly rehearsed by Hart, Burton, Andrews, and Goulet sang several of the show's best songs, and Burton and Andrews charmed millions of viewers with their "What Do the Simple Folk Do?"

The following morning, the manager of the Majestic Theatre phoned Lerner and suggested he come down and look at something. What Lerner saw, instead of an empty sidewalk, was a line stretching around the block. The new audiences saw a livelier and more streamlined show than the one seen by the critics, and the word of mouth spread. *Camelot* became a hit that lasted on Broadway for more than two years, and became established enough for Lerner and Loewe to allow Burton out of his contract so that he could accept a well-paying role opposite Elizabeth Taylor in a film epic called *Cleopatra.* But that is another kind of history.

Apropos the show, during an interview for *Life* magazine soon after the assassination of President Kennedy, Mrs. Kennedy revealed that the late president liked to play records before going to sleep, and the song he loved most came at the end of a particular record. It was the ending of *Camelot,* when the saddened king urges a small boy to tell everyone that for "one, brief

Costume design for King Arthur by Adrian and Tony Duquette.

Oliver Smith's design for the closing scene of *Camelot* (1960).

shining moment" there was a spot "known as Camelot." Mrs. Kennedy went on to make her point about her husband's administration, saying, "There'll never be a Camelot again."

Camelot was playing in Chicago's Opera House at the time. Mrs. Kennedy's revelation made newspaper headlines everywhere, and all three thousand seats of the opera house were filled. When Louis Hayward, as the king, came to the final lines, the audience burst into tears. The play was stopped for five minutes before everyone's eyes — in the orchestra pit, on the stage, and in the wings — were dry enough to continue.

One more item: at the end of the first moon landing the astronauts left behind certain earthly artifacts. One was a gold-plated recording of *Camelot*.

Jack Kennedy's successor, Lyndon B. Johnson, had some reelection help from Broadway in the form of a rousing campaign song to the tune of "Hello, Dolly!" which came from producer David Merrick's musical version of Thornton Wilder's play *The Matchmaker*. Rechristened as *Hello, Dolly!*, it opened at the St. James Theatre on January 16, 1964, and ran for what seemed just about forever — edging, in fact, past *My Fair Lady*, to set a new record.

Merrick, a consummate promoter as well as a canny producer, saw that nothing but good could result from the

political use of the song, an electrifying show-stopper early in the second act. The number has widowed Dolly Levi, a marriage broker supposedly arranging a match for the wealthy Horace Vandergelder but actually interested in him herself, arriving at the ornate Harmonia Gardens, a favorite restaurant of hers in former times. All decked out in blondined hair, a plumed headdress, and glittering beads, she makes an entrance at the top of a wide, red-carpeted staircase, upon which the entire staff, joined by the patrons, heralds her return with a rousing rendition of the title song, and a march about the restaurant.

Jerry Herman, the writer of the song, was a young composer and lyricist who had written a few off-Broadway revues before embarking on Broadway with the well-regarded musical set in Israel, *Milk and Honey.* Hearing of Merrick's musical plans for *The Matchmaker*, he played some songs for him and got the job.

Carol Channing, who was offered the role of Dolly by Merrick after Ethel Merman had refused it, in an odd turn of events was also forced to audition. She had accepted on condition that Gower Champion direct the show, but he thought Carol — whose stage personality came, he felt, from her coy, mincing performance as Lorelei Lee in *Gentlemen Prefer Blondes* — was wrong for Dolly. Stars don't usually plead for auditions, but she did, and she was able to convince Champion that she would make an ideal Dolly. After eleven years with nary a hit, she changed her public persona literally overnight, becoming, in Champion's words, a conniving, shrewd busybody

who was nevertheless appealing and touching.

Out of town, playing to little enthusiasm in Detroit, the show almost foundered. Merrick considered closing it, but enough skilled carpentry was done on it to bring it to New York. The libretto by Michael Stewart was sharpened; three songs were cut, three new ones added, and help came from Charles Strouse and Lee Adams of the rock-and-roll satire *Bye, Bye, Birdie*, for a stirring first-act finale, "Before the Parade Passes By."

Oliver Smith designed sets that nostalgically evoked the New York City of 1890, and Champion filled the stage with gay colors for the ebullient "Put on Your Sunday Clothes" number at the Yonkers depot, during which the resplendent cast promenaded along a circular runway around the rim of the orchestra pit. For further embellishment, a railway car was pulled into the depot by a locomotive belching smoke and ashes.

Wilder's play never pretended to be much more than broad, good-natured farce, but swift-moving and lively direction, a good cast that included the amusing David Burns as Vandergelder and Eileen Brennan as the dressmaker he thinks he is wooing, won it critical approval as a triumph of staging and shrewd and successful showmanship over material that was not particularly extraordinary.

Neither did anyone think the title song extraordinary, certainly not that it would become one of the greatest of all show tunes. Herman wrote it in a single afternoon and later credited its enormous success to a recording of it made by Louis Armstrong. Unexpectedly, too,

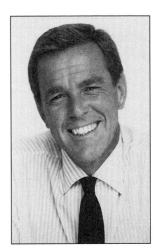

Gower Champion, director-choreographer of *Hello, Dolly!*

Carol Channing being greeted by admirers singing the title song from *Hello, Dolly!* (1964).

209

Costume design by Freddy Wittop for the evening gown worn by Mrs. Malloy, the young milliner befriended by Dolly. The role was originally played by Eileen Brennan.

Pearl Bailey, who starred in an all-black production of the show on Broadway in 1967.

came a suit over it for copyright infringement from Mack David, who claimed he had used the melody for a 1948 song called "Sunflower." Herman may or may not have heard the song; it may have stayed in the back of his mind; or it may have been a coincidence. The suit was settled out of court with a payment of half a million dollars, attesting to the kind of gold residing in a song that could catch the national consciousness as did "Hello, Dolly!"

It was clear to Howard Taubman, who had replaced Brooks Atkinson as the drama critic of the *New York Times*, that "the big noise on Broadway is the musical theatre," and that the audience for the musical was "much larger than for serious drama, humane comedy, or uproarious farce." Consequently, there was a scramble among producers, writers, and directors to find the kind of material that would bring the huge rewards now possible.

Taubman noted how far Broadway's musical had progressed from the "Graustarks and Monrovias that beguiled our forefathers." It had become able to support satire, literate laughter, and themes of social injustice and racial unrest. Raucous Tin Pan Alley had developed into a broad avenue of consummate stage ingenuity and, surprisingly often, serious artistry. Popular musical theatre seemed unaware of limitations, daring to venture far afield and perhaps face disaster while hoping for triumph. Yet, said Taubman, "Who would have guessed that the stories of Sholem Aleichem would be suitable for the musical stage?"

Librettist Joseph Stein and the song-writing team of Sheldon Harnick and Jerry Bock made such a guess as early as 1960 when they began thinking of a Sholem Aleichem musical, using as a basis the author's stories, written in Yiddish, of Tevye, an East European Jew, and his seven daughters. In constructing a story for the stage, Stein reduced the number of daughters to five, and focused on Tevye, a poor milkman living at the turn of the century in the Russian village of Anatevka. Each of the daughters has her marriage problems, which are resolved against the threat of pogroms and banishment of the villagers from their homes.

In seeking a producer, Bock, Harnick, and Stein went first to Harold Prince, who felt its ethnic nature too narrow, and that Jerome Robbins was the only director who could give the material the universality it needed. When approached, Robbins also had reservations. Harnick recalled, "He kept asking and hammering at us for months: 'What is this show about?' " It was about this dairy man and his daughters, they would reply. That wasn't enough, Robbins insisted. What had to be discovered was what gave the stories their power. Finally, one of them said, "It's about the dissolution of a way of life." Robbins's reluctance vanished at that point. He saw what the show needed — an opening number that would show the audience something of the traditional way of life that would eventually be lost.

After two other producers failed to get backing, Harold Prince took over what was not called *Fiddler on the Roof* until shortly before the start of rehearsals. The title came from a Marc Chagall painting, "The Green Violinist," depicting a violinist hovering over the roofs of a village. Stein used the image as an introduction and as a metaphor for the poverty-stricken Jews of Anatevka who adhered to their religious ways in the face of bigotry and persecution from the surrounding Christian society of Imperial Russia. Tevye, in explaining the presence of the fiddler perched precariously on the roof of his humble house, confides to the audience that

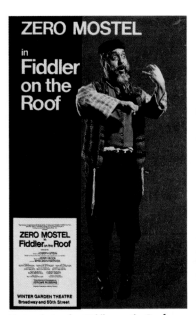

Poster design for *Fiddler on the Roof* (1964).

everyone in his village is, in a way, a fiddler on a roof. How do we keep our balance? he asks. "In a word — tradition!"

This allowed Robbins to employ his conception of an opening number that would be like a tapestry against which the entire show would be played: the villagers enter in appropriately shabby dress to dance a simple circular hora and chant of the traditions that bind them together, meanwhile being introduced one by one by Tevye. The important gentiles of the village are also introduced — his honor, the priest; his honor, the constable, etc. — but they ignore the circle and stride off after abrupt nods to the audience. When at the end of the show the families must leave the village, a similar circle forms and breaks, indicating that the exodus will irretrievably end a way of life.

Tevye, the much-put-upon dairyman, is a man of sly wit who communicates with God as easily as with the audience. He must pull his milkcart himself because his horse is lame, and his wife complains because he has not provided their five daughters with sufficient dowries. Why, he wonders, was it necessary for God to make him a poor man rather than a rich one, and wryly he sings of what he would do "If I Were a Rich Man."

Robbins, with the help of designer Boris Aronson's settings that suggested poverty but nevertheless had an atmospheric beauty, evoked the ceremonies, the simple joys, and eventually the malice (in the form of a pogrom) that would end a way of life. His dancers wore beards, the girls, babuchkas. Bock's flavorsome melodies managed to steer a course between the folk music of the shtetls and the more familiar sound of Broadway, leaving one critic (Walter Kerr) "slightly at sea." The turn-of-the-century milieu of Sholem Aleichem was suggested more than accurately realized, but audiences found pleasing such songs as the wistful "Matchmaker, Matchmaker," and the poignant "Sunrise, Sunset."

There was argument between Prince and Robbins about who should play Tevye, and Prince won out with his choice, Zero Mostel, who had recently reaped raves in the farcical *A Funny Thing Happened on the Way to the Forum.* His casting made it necessary for the songwriters, who had thought of Tevye as a pale, thin little man, to come up with songs more suitable to Mostel's

Costume designs for villagers in *Fiddler on the Roof* (1964) by Patricia Zipprodt.

Scene design for the wedding by Boris Aronson.

expansive frame. Thus, the resounding song "To Life." So penetrating, robust, and heartwarming was Mostel's Tevye, Taubman reported, "that you all but forget that it is a performance."

For a time the show's success after its opening in September 1964 was largely credited to Mostel's virtuoso performance, but when he left after nine months and was followed by Luther Adler, Herschel Bernardi, and several others over the years, it became clear that the show's qualities of humor, imagination, and compassion were most responsible for the more than 3,200 record-setting performances on Broadway, and its fervent acceptance just about everywhere else.

The insistence by Jerome Robbins on conceptualizing *Fiddler* in such a way

that the audience would be aware of the essential meaning behind the story may well have influenced Harold Prince with his direction and production of *Cabaret*. Prince spent three years looking for a

The death of tradition—the final scene of the show.

way to make a musical from the John van Druten play *I Am a Camera*, in turn based on a Christopher Isherwood story, "Sally Bowles," one of a group of stories about a young Englishman in Berlin who witnesses in microcosm the onset of Naziism. Inspiration came to Prince and his collaborators in fitful sparks rather than in one sudden flash, and when the fully formed show reached Broadway in November 1966, its startling and unique form broke through the mold of the so-called integrated musical — à la *Oklahoma!* — in which songs and musical numbers appeared to grow organically out of the story.

Prince was drawn to the material by what he saw as a parallel between the moral and spiritual bankruptcy of Germany in the late twenties and early thirties and the ugly racial turmoil here in the 1960s: the murders of Martin Luther King, Jr., Medger Evers, and three young civil rights workers in Mississippi. Isherwood's *Berlin Stories* (one of which was "Sally Bowles") subtly mirrored the decadence and corruption that accompanied the rise of the Nazis.

It was Joseph Masteroff, working with Prince as librettist, who first thought of a second-rate cabaret as a metaphor for the milieu of the story. This led Prince to remember a nightclub near where he had been stationed in Germany in 1951. "Whenever possible," Prince recalled, "I hung out around Maxim's. There was a dwarf MC, hair parted in the middle and lacquered down with brilliantine, his mouth made into a bright cupid's bow. . . ." He suggested such a figure for the master of ceremonies for the nightclub numbers which would

develop the decadent atmosphere in which the characters participate.

Borrowing more from Isherwood than van Druten, the story shows an American, Cliff Bradshaw, arriving by train in Berlin, taking a room in a boardinghouse run by Fräulein Schneider, and meeting the hedonistic Sally Bowles at the Kit Kat Klub, a cabaret of no particular distinction. Their relationship is marred by Sally's waywardness, and her disregard of any consequences for what might happen tomorrow. Another romance, between the landlady and a Jewish shopkeeper, is thwarted by the rising tide of anti-Semitism.

Prince held innumerable conferences with Masteroff and the lyricist-composer team, Fred Ebb and John Kander, searching for a look and form for the show. Realizing he had only "half a concept," he postponed it and did the unsuccessful *Superman* instead, after which he went to Moscow and found renewed impetus when he encountered

An early production meeting for *Cabaret* with (left to right) Jack Gilford, Jill Haworth, John Kander, Fred Ebb, and Joel Grey.

some innovative techniques at the Meyerhold-influenced Tagaganka Theatre. The main problem for the Isherwood musical was finding a unifying concept that would symbolically bind together the characters, and provide a menacing meaning to the events.

One of the ideas of Ebb and Kander was to put together five unrelated songs as part of a big musical number that would open the play and establish the atmosphere of the Berlin of 1930. Prince and Masteroff happened to stop by and listen to the songs. Then, said Ebb, "it happened."

"Why not use the songs *between* scenes," Prince suggested, "instead of lowering the curtain?"

It was then that the little MC that Prince remembered became the thread for the entire musical. The five songs would be dispersed randomly throughout the show as a metaphorical frame for the characters in the "book" scenes. More than that, they would be the show's musical numbers, with the Master of Ceremonies typifying the corrupt atmosphere and morality of the country. It was only after the collaborators had solidified their conception that the show was given its title, *Cabaret*.

The diminutive Joel Grey was an ideal choice for the MC and, made up similarly, became the living image of Prince's recollection. Most of the five songs of what would have been an opening number disappeared and only the first, "Willkommen," which the smirking MC sings as a grating welcome to the patrons of the Kit Kat Klub, was retained. The girls are all beautiful, all

Boris Aronson's set design for *Cabaret*.

virgins, he tells the audience. The bored-looking girls are anything but beautiful, and their revealed full, fleshy thighs were also reminiscent of the *"lumpen Fräuleins"* of the nightclub visited by Prince.

Another of the MC's numbers had its origin in a dream of Ebb's. In the dream he saw on the nightclub's stage Joel Grey with a gorilla in a pink tutu. From this image he thought of a song, and quickly telephoned Prince to see if it had validity. Prince thought it did, and a number was born, "If You Could See Her" (through my eyes), in which the MC assures the audience that they would also find the gorilla beautiful. The song, however, had a baneful last line meant to show the creeping anti-Semitism of the period. If they could see her through his eyes, the MC confides to the audience, "she doesn't look Jewish at all."

Unexpectedly, it was that line, which some took obtusely as comparing Jews to gorillas, that caused a crisis for the show. Prince was warned that unless

216

the line was taken out or changed, a good many of the theatre parties necessary to the show's success would be canceled. Over the objections of Ebb and the others, he had a new and innocuous line inserted.

The show, with its blaring nightclub scenes, its evil, prancing MC, its mood-establishing songs, and its innovative staging, was a large success and ran for three years. In fact, it was Joel Grey who, appearing sporadically, dominated the evening, overshadowing Jill Haworth as Sally, and Lotte Lenya as Fräulein Schneider. The theatre audience found itself brought into the show when it saw itself reflected in a distorting mirror on the stage in the nightclub scenes, a notion of the designer, Boris Aronson.

A few of the critics (perhaps failing to get the point,) thought the music reminiscent of early Kurt Weill when it was, in fact, meant to echo the satiric cabaret music of 1930 Berlin, but Walter Kerr, for one, gave *Cabaret* his wholehearted approval. He described as brilliantly conceived its "marionette's-eye view of a time and place in our lives that was brassy, wanton, carefree and doomed to crumble." Richard Watts, Jr., in the *New York Post*, said, "It is the glory of *Cabaret* that it can upset you while it gives theatrical satisfaction."

Cabaret's distinction grew with the years as it became regarded as an important forerunner of what came to be known as "the concept musical," in which an overall style or metaphorical treatment overshadowed the plot elements. In this development, Prince would be an unquestioned leader, as he took the musical into areas previously unexplored.

Movies made from Broadway's musicals had usually failed to equal or improve on their originals, but the film version of *Cabaret*, directed in 1972 by Bob Fosse, was a remarkable Hollywood departure, fully as bitter as the Prince version, and in some ways more so. It starred Liza Minnelli, whom Prince had rejected for the role of Sally Bowles because she wasn't English. For the film Sally was simply made American, an expedient somehow overlooked by Prince. Her friend, Cliff, played by Michael York, had been made American by Prince but in the film was returned to his British background, as in the Isherwood stories.

Joel Grey recreated his role and, with Fosse's direction, won himself an Academy Award. The lurid nightclub scenes, viewed as though through a distorting mirror, provided a more overwhelming atmosphere of moral corruption than in the stage version, and one of its songs, "Tomorrow Belongs to Me," as treated by Fosse, was a tour de force. A handsome young man sings it sweetly at an open-air café, joined by other nice-looking young people, then older ones, as the camera reveals the Nazi symbols on the boy's shirt, as he puts on the beaked Nazi cap and as he raises his hand in a Hitlerian salute. Here the arts of the stage and film joined to create an image that reverberated with powerful significance.

(opposite)
The MC of the Kit Kat Klub, Joel Grey, leads his chorus of "beautiful virgins" in one of Ronald Field's dances.

217

Poster design for the Broadway production of *Hair* (1968).

VIII   *Broadway at Large, 1967–1991*

HAIR

COMPANY

FOLLIES

A LITTLE NIGHT MUSIC

A CHORUS LINE

ANNIE

SWEENEY TODD

DREAMGIRLS

EVITA

CATS

LES MISÉRABLES

THE PHANTOM OF THE OPERA

MISS SAIGON

"*H*air arrived in the nick of time," William Kloman exulted in the drama section of the Sunday *New York Times* when the "American tribal love-rock musical" came to the Biltmore Theatre on April 29, 1968. "Things," he went on, "are in such bad shape on Broadway that the Drama Critics Circle couldn't find a big-budget musical there to give its award to this year, and had to go off-Broadway — to *Your Own Thing* — for the first time." He foresaw vast changes because of the new musical's influence on Broadway.

True, the 1967–68 theatre season had produced little in the musical category that was noteworthy. "A parade of mediocrities," one historian noted. *Your Own Thing*, playing downtown at the Orpheum Theatre, was a clever contemporary rock-music adaptation of Shakespeare's *Twelfth Night*.

A youth rebellion was well under way, propelled by opposition to the war in Vietnam and the ever-surging rock music that was bolstered by the arrival of the Beatles on these shores in 1964. All around the country young people "dropped out," "turned on," and advocated "making love, not war." "Flower power" was extolled, and Bob Dylan and Joan Baez announced that "The Times They Are A-Changing." The hair of both sexes grew long and wild; beards proliferated. Necks and chests were decorated with beads, chains, and oriental amulets believed to have mystical powers. Drug use was not only common among the disenchanted and the dropouts, but regarded as important to the proper practice of meditation, sexual

activity, and listening to rock — not necessarily in that order. Against this background, *Hair* came to Broadway — belatedly, some said, because Flower Power had peaked a few years before.

It was not a good thing in the eyes of youth to be over thirty, and those who were older strove to be "with it" by adopting the counterculture mode of dress. A Broadway playwright, on meeting with his long- and gray-haired fifty-five-year-old producer who was wearing beads, modishly faded blue jeans with ragged cuffs, and a black studded motorcycle jacket, said accusingly, "You are a traitor to your generation!" But perhaps this explains why the critics were uncommonly warm and kind to *Hair*, an exuberant, anarchic musical with little in the way of recognizable story, and notoriously featuring, at one point, a dimly lit display of its cast in the nude.

The cheeky show began its life off-Broadway at Joseph Papp's Public Theatre, and soon moved to a huge midtown discotheque, the Cheetah. There a canny Chicago millionaire, Michael Butler, saw possibilities in it and brought it to Broadway, rewritten to make it even bolder, wilder, and more anti-establishment, and redirected to emphasize these qualities by Tom O'Horgan, until then a downtown theatre guru.

The show's "hero" in the minuscule story is a dropout on his way to dropping in to the army, although what he really wants, he says in a moment of profound illumination, is "to eat mushrooms. I want to sleep in the sun." Clive Barnes, who reviewed it in

(opposite)
Singing of the coming Age of Aquarius in *Hair* (1968).

In *Hair*, peace, love, and brotherhood take to the barricades.

the *New York Times*, warned readers about its many four-letter words, only one of which he could print in his family newspaper: love. Several forms of the latter, including the perverse, were celebrated by the cast's long-haired hippies and scruffy flower children. They also opposed the draft, opted for peace and clean air, and in general mocked and scorned the standards of behavior common to the "square" establishment.

The music by Galt MacDermot had its charms — notably the songs "Aquarius," "Good Morning, Starshine," and "Let the Sunshine In." Supported heartily by, in the main, a prosperous establishment audience, *Hair* played more than 1,800 performances in its downtown and uptown manifestations. A revival some ten years later failed to fulfill the above-mentioned William Kloman's prophecy that *Hair* would bring

Broadway into "a brave new world of sensory enrichment." The show, now sadly dated, closed in less than two months.

During *Hair*'s heyday, producer Harold Prince and songwriter-lyricist Stephen Sondheim combined to reflect another and reasonably civilized view of contemporary life with their *Company*, a spare and brilliant musical that examined five live-in relationships — marital and otherwise — in Manhattan. The stories of the couples were at first contained in a lengthy series of one-act plays by George Furth. Three of those plays were used for the musical, and two new ones were written by Furth.

Under Prince's guidance it also became a story of Robert — a friend to all five couples, living alone, but himself involved with women friends. These fourteen people, made members of an acting company, comprised the entire cast, a small one for a musical. For a framework, a series of parties for Robert's thirty-fifth birthday are thrown by the couples, each different in kind and mood. Each member of the company danced, under choreographer Michael Bennett's guidance, and sang as they moved through the "rooms" of Boris Aronson's remarkable setting of aluminum and plastic, which included two transparent working elevators. During the loosely joined episodes they spoke and joked of love and loneliness inside and outside of marriage, while Sondheim's songs commented wittily, and often sardonically, on the happenstances of their daily lives.

The critics reacted favorably, for the most part, to the show's innovative qualities. Both *Newsweek*'s and *Time*'s critics called it "a landmark," while Henry Hewes in *The Saturday Review* said it "has remarkably distilled the essence of today's middle generation New York life." On the other hand, Clive Barnes in the *New York Times* thought its characters "are just the kind of people you expend hours each day trying to escape from," but praised Sondheim's "sophisticated" lyrics and music. Walter Kerr found much that was praiseworthy in the show — Prince's "immaculate" staging, for instance — but he just didn't seem to like it very much. Audiences did, though, enough to keep *Company* alive on Broadway for twenty months.

For Prince and Sondheim it was another year, another unusual show. Their memory-laden *Follies* opened,

The company of *Company* (1970). From left: John Cunningham, Dean Jones, Elaine Stritch, Harold Prince, Barbara Barrie, and Michael Bennett. Stephen Sondheim is at the piano.

almost a year to the day after *Company*, on April 4, 1971, at the Winter Garden Theatre. And again they demonstrated their nonadherence to traditional patterns of the musical.

The idea, which came from a newspaper item about a reunion of former Ziegfeld girls, had been around since 1965, when writer James Goldman and Stephen Sondheim began working on what they called "The Girls Upstairs." At first conceived melodramatically as the stories of two couples — former *Follies* performers — with reasons to kill someone, it was optioned and dropped by other producers before Prince took on its production and co-directed it with

Boris Aronson's spare, metallic setting for *Company* enhanced the feeling of contemporary angst that ran through the show.

Poster design for *Follies*.

PRINCE OF BROADWAY

Both as producer and director, Harold Prince has long been Broadway's most dynamic and daring creator of musicals. Born in New York City on January 30, 1928, he was educated in a city private school and at the University of Pennsylvania. He first attempted to write plays, but settled for an assistant's job with George Abbott. He then went on to produce, in association with Robert Griffith, *The Pajama Game* and *Damn Yankees*. With such successes as the innovative *West Side Story*, *Fiddler on the Roof*, and the Pulitzer Prize–winning *Fiorello!*, he appeared to have a magic touch. His reputation reached a new height, however, when he took on the dual roles of director and producer for the ground-breaking shows *Cabaret*, *Company*, *Follies*, and *Sweeney Todd*. But he had his flops, too, such as *Merrily We Roll Along*, his musical "sequel" to Ibsen in *A Doll's Life*, and *Rosa*. With his direction of the controversial *Evita*, he formed an association with the new English breed of composers and lyricists, one which resulted in his greatest success as a director, *The Phantom of the Opera*.

Michael Bennett, who also choreographed.

As might have been expected once Prince was involved, the concept changed. He wanted young people on stage to balance the older people who, in the first version, remembered but did not relive their past lives. The melodrama was dispensed with. Prince wanted the show to be "Fellini-like," audacious and somewhat abstract in form, and this led to what Sondheim later described as "a dream play, a memory piece" in which the younger "shadow" selves of the characters also emerged on stage.

In what plot there was, a Ziegfeld-like impresario, Dimitri Weismann of the once-famous "Weismann Follies," throws a reunion party for his old-time performers on the stage of his theatre just before it is to be demolished and turned into a parking lot. Two middle-aged couples among those who attend were good friends some thirty years earlier when the wives were "Follies" chorus

Hal Prince (left) and Stephen Sondheim, producer and writer-composer of *Follies* (1971).

girls. In those days, Sally, who married Buddy, had loved Ben, who married Phyllis but loved himself the more. Now the lives of all four are empty, even though Ben has become rich and famous and supports Phyllis in luxurious style. Sally's mundane middle-class existence is marred by Buddy's infidelities.

While the party goes on, Sally and Ben attempt to recapture their lost love for each other, while others of the cast recall past glories and woesome

Three-dimensional model of Boris Aronson's set design for *Follies*.

failures. By the end of the evening, as their "ghosts" assist them in re-enacting the past, it looks as though a marital reshuffle might occur, but no, it doesn't.

None of that romantic stuff for Prince and Sondheim. Not only is the theatre being wrecked, but marriages, hopes, and dreams, too. "The *Follies*," said Prince, referring to the Ziegfeld variety, "represented a state of mind between the two World Wars." America during that period was idealistic and hopeful and was going to lead the world. "Now you see the country is a riot of national guilt, the dream has collapsed, everything has turned to rubble underfoot."

The show, then, was about dreams that turned to rubble, although this wasn't always easy for audiences to discern, since the story wandered between life's reality and theatre's unreality, complicated further by those shadow alter egos of the four principals who, given lines to speak, became intrusive and eventually disruptive — all this taking place on a skeletal Boris Aronson set reminiscent of a theatre stage in dissolution.

Clive Barnes in the *New York Times* noted that Sondheim's music "comes in two flavors — nostalgic and cinematic." The nostalgic kind were deliberate and gentle parodies of such composers of yesteryear as Kern, Gershwin, Porter, and Arlen, but, as Barnes regretted, "with none of the heart." As for the cinematic music, he doubted that anyone would be parodying it in thirty or forty years. On the other hand, he thought the lyrics "as fresh as a daisy. His words are a joy to listen to, even when his music is

sending shivers of indifference up your spine."

The carefully chosen cast had its own nostalgic value: the still-statuesque Alexis Smith was brought back from film limbo for the affluent Phyllis; popular singer Dorothy Collins portrayed the woebegone Sally; Yvonne DeCarlo was a

CANDIDE REDUX

Leonard Bernstein's collaboration with Lillian Hellman on a musical version of Voltaire's *Candide* in 1956 was a failure, dogged by a pedestrian book and ineffectual staging by Tyrone Guthrie, and in spite of its witty and graceful score. Then, nearly two decades later, Harold Prince took on the challenge of not only restaging the piece, but reinventing it. Hellman's libretto was abandoned (at her wish) and Hugh Wheeler wrote his own comic version of Candide's constantly unfortunate adventures. Stephen Sondheim added new lyrics, and Prince gave it a circus-like production in an arena setting at the Chelsea Theatre loft of the Brooklyn Academy of Music. Its success there was such that it was moved to the Broadway Theatre, remodeled to allow for intimacy between audience and actors. Clive Barnes, cheering the new production, said: "Mr. Prince has given Broadway nothing so gaudy, glittering and endearing as this . . . a show that takes off like a rocket and never comes down." It ran for seventeen months. In 1982, Prince redirected *Candide* for the proscenium stage of the New York City Opera's New York State Theatre. There it retains an honored place in the opera company's repertory.

Choreographer and co-director of *Follies*, Michael Bennett, chooses a quiet corner in which to plan his next move.

Alexis Smith, of *Follies* (1971), in her dressing room.

Glynis Johns and Laurence Guittard of *A Little Night Music* (1973), Stephen Sondheim's lyrical examination of the many ages of love.

blowsy but still-seductive movie star. In a final and dazzling "Loveland" sequence, the stage is flooded with light and transformed into pastel archways through which come the showgirls of old

in all their airy frivolity and fantastic costuming. Somehow during these late festivities the cast members managed to come to terms with themselves.

There were critics who found *Follies* monumental in its daring and complicated conception; but Walter Kerr cautioned that "ingenuity without inspiration quickly becomes wearing and we are not too long in our seats before we realize that no one on the creative staff has had an idea for the evening capable of sustaining its weight in silvered feathers." However, when a new concert recording of *Follies* was issued in 1985, critic Stephen Holden in the *New York Times* saw (or rather, heard) it as "summing up a 60 year old musical tradition while rejecting its fundamentally optimistic philosophy . . . the show today seems almost diabolically conceived as 'the musical to end all musicals.' "

Rest assured, it did not. A key member of the *Follies* creative staff, Michael Bennett, had something in mind about hopes and dreams that, after a labyrinthine process of conception, became the longest-running musical in all of theatre history: *A Chorus Line*.

Before the show reached Broadway on July 25, 1975, however, Sondheim and Prince had continued their high-culture musical mission by adapting their *A Little Night Music* from the ruefully sophisticated *Smiles of a Summer Night*, a rare cinematic gem by the renowned Swedish filmmaker, Ingmar Bergman.

Done in operetta style, with three-quarter time employed throughout, the plot was easily understandable, as it followed Bergman's elegantly Swedish group of lovers through a wryly comic series of mix-ups and infidelities. From the show came the haunting "Send in the Clowns," Sondheim's best-known and most popular hit, for which he wrote both words and music.

While *A Little Night Music* had style, grace, and a modicum of intellectuality, the same could not be said for other musicals in that period in our history when the Watergate hearings and the first departure of a president through resignation captured the nation's avid attention. A few run-of-the mill shows became hits — in the case of *Pippin* largely through the staging and choreography of Bob Fosse — but, as Alan Jay Lerner said of the 1973–74 period, its musical offerings "were too embarrassing to discuss at the dinner table." He pointed, more or less specifically, to *Grease*, a fifties rock burlesque of pomaded hairstyles, teeny-boppers, drive-ins, and fusses about who goes with whom to the prom. Predominantly younger audiences found it fun, so much so that it became, to the consternation of Lerner and others, the all-time long-run champion — that is, until dislodged by *A Chorus Line*.

Michael Bennett, born in Buffalo, and trained as a dancer from the age of three, was himself a veteran of the dancing chorus before he became a choreographer for *Coco* and *Company*, and co-director of *Follies*. He claimed that *A Chorus Line* grew originally from his reaction to "the falsehood and apathy that seemed to grip the country during that period. I wanted to do something on

stage that would show people being honest with each other."

He had also been thinking of a show peopled entirely by dancers, and it was from this impulse that he met on a weekend in January 1974 with twenty-four dancers — "gypsies," as they were known in Broadway dance parlance — for a workout and a talk session. His idea was little more than a germ at the time. But he knew from his own experience the work and discipline needed for professional performance, the odds against being cast for a show, and, even when successful, the brief span of a dancer's career. Why did they do it, he wanted to know, what kept their hopes alive? The thirty hours of tape recordings of that session and following ones made Bennett realize "that what those kids had been doing was auditioning their lives for me."

From this developed the story of thirty-one dancers competing with each other for eight jobs in a chorus line. During the winnowing-down process, the contestants are forced by the director to reveal their life stories and secrets of their psyches to help him make his final choices. Eventually the selected ensemble, until then in rehearsal costume, shows itself off marvelously in satin and top hat chorus costumes in a vigorous step-kicking finale.

Much of what happened on stage came from the taped "autobiographies" of the dancers, put into script form by Bennett and his dancer friend Nicholas Dante, after selecting the most heart- and gut-wrenching of the confessionals. Joseph Papp was impressed enough to sponsor a workshop production at his

THE PASSIONATE JOSEPH PAPP

A vital force in New York's theatre for more than three decades, the founder of the New York Shakespeare Festival and the Public Theatre, the producer of *A Chorus Line*, Broadway's longest-running show ever, Joseph Papirofsky was born in 1921 to immigrant parents in Brooklyn, New York. He struggled through the depression hawking newspapers, selling pretzels, and shining shoes to help pay the family rent. Attracted to theatre at an early age, first as an actor, he developed a love for Shakespeare. In the navy, in World War II, he put on shows on the flattops of aircraft carriers; after the war, taking advantage of the G.I. Bill, he studied at the leftish Actors Laboratory in Hollywood. In New York he worked for CBS as a television stage manager, but was fired when he balked, on principal, over testifying at a congressional hearing on un-American activities.

After directing and occasionally producing off-Broadway plays in the early fifties, Papp, in 1954, began a Shakespeare workshop, which developed, with almost no funding, into his Shakespeare Festival. From then on, a dynamo of activity, Papp founded his Public Theatre in downtown Manhattan, home to a cadre of new American

(continued on p. 228)

(continued from p. 227)

playwrights, including Sam Shepard, John Guare, and David Rabe, experimental productions, classics, and the first production of the musical *Hair*. Volatile, opinionated, he managed to stay through four ruffled years of producing at Lincoln Center's troubled Beaumont Theatre in the 1970s. With *A Chorus Line*, first presented at the Public Theatre in 1975, and its steady tax-free golden box-office stream, Papp had the wherewithal to extend his range, to use theatre, as he expressed it, as "a societal force," to allow theatre to embrace "the disenchanted and the disenfranchised." In pursuit of this aim, he has battled the National Endowment for the Arts, and attempted to oust from his theatres such not always supportive critics as Walter Kerr and John Simon.

Program for *A Chorus Line*, in its original 1975 production at the Public Theatre.

```
                     New York Shakespeare Festival
                     P U B L I C    T H E A T E R

                       Produced by Joseph Papp

                             presents


                       A   C H O R U S   L I N E


                  Conceived, Choreographed and Directed
                            by Michael Bennett


                  Book by James Kirkwood and Nicholas Dante
                        Music by Marvin Hamlisch
                        Lyrics by Edward Kleban
                        Co-choreographer Bob Avian

                        Setting by Robin Wagner
                     Costumes by Theoni V. Aldredge
                       Lighting by Tharon Musser

                          Orchestrations by
              Bill Byers, Hershey Kaye and Jonathan Tunick
                   Music Coordinator Robert Thomas

          Music Direction and Vocal Arrangements by Don Pippin

                 Associate Producer Bernard Gersten

                              CAST
                      (in alphabetical order)
```

Roy	Scott Allen
Kristine	Renee Baughman
Sheila	Carole Bishop
Val	Pamela Blair
Mike	Wayne Cilento
Butch	Chuck Cissel
Larry	Clive Clerk
Maggie	Kay Cole
Richie	Ronald Dennis
Tricia	Donna Drake
Tom	Brandt Edwards
Judy	Patricia Garland
Lois	Carolyn Kirsch
Don	Ron Kuhlman
Bebe	Nancy Lane
Connie	Baayork Lee
Diana	Priscilla Lopez
Zach	Robert LuPone
Mark	Cameron Mason
Cassie	Donna McKechnie
Alan	Don Percassi
Barbara	Carole Schweid
Frank	Michael Serrecchia
Greg	Michel Stuart
Bobby	Thomas J. Walsh
Paul	Sammy Williams
Vicki	Crissy Wilzak

```
        A CHORUS LINE will be performed without an intermission.


                            An Audition
                     Time: Now    Place: Here

        The characters portrayed in "A Chorus Line" are, for the
        most part, based upon the lives and experiences of Broadway
        dancers. This show is dedicated to anyone who has ever
        danced in a chorus or marched in step...anywhere.

        This production is made possible in part by a special grant
        from the Shubert Foundation.
```

Public Theatre. Bennett, meanwhile, had persuaded composer Marvin Hamlisch to leave his Hollywood assignments and work up a score, which he did with Edward Kleban, a relatively unknown lyricist — in fact, he had to audition to get the job. During the workshop process, James Kirkwood, a playwright and former actor, was added to the creative team to sharpen the libretto.

The show opened at the Newman Theatre (part of Papp's Public Theatre complex) in April 1975, and won public enthusiasm before the reviews were in. After another hundred performances it moved uptown on July 25 to the Shubert Theatre, after which it won Tonys galore and a Pulitzer Prize. Papp's Shakespeare Festival, which sponsored the show, would, after a run of nearly fifteen years, earn a profit of nearly forty million dollars, enabling it to continue its free performances of Shakespeare in Central Park, and to produce several shows of limited commercial appeal.

According to some theatre people, though, the more lasting influence of *A Chorus Line* was its effect on the musical form itself, by changing, expanding, and freeing concepts. The workshop process by which it was developed became influential, too, and in succeeding years many shows, before venturing on to Broadway, were ironed out over long periods in workshop testing, through agreements with Actors' Equity. Producers benefited, too, by a consequent lessening of risk, as costs of musical theatre production rose to astronomical heights. Even *A Chorus Line*, with its simple bare stage and a mirrored back wall, incurred costs of more than a million dollars on its way to Broadway.

It was almost to be expected, in view of the musical's unparalleled success, that rancor would develop among members of the original company. (Over the years, more than five hundred performers appeared in it.) After all, it was *their* lives, *their* experiences, *their* dreams, that had provided the raw material. Cast members had been persuaded to sign away their rights to the merchandising of the show, and their profit participation was minimal to the extreme. Resented by some, too, were the continual accolades bestowed on Michael Bennett for its conception, direction, and resounding success, in spite of creative contributions to the show made by others. Yet, no one doubted that it was his special vision that had made it possible.

While *A Chorus Line* played on and on, the Tony Award committee during the dry 1977 season was desperately seeking a new musical worthy of being showcased during the annual televised ceremony. Just in time, an old comic strip, brightly and tunefully packaged, came to the rescue and won the prize.

How could it possibly miss, Alan Rich wondered, in his review of *Annie* in *New York* magazine, when it had "six pre-teen foundlings as chorus line, a mongrel dog, a love song to New York City, and a Christmas tree"? Similarly, Clive Barnes, in the *New York Times*, regarded any animosity toward the show as "tantamount to disliking motherhood, peanut butter, friendly mongrel dogs, and nostalgia." Aside from these mildly apologetic disclaimers, both critics loved it.

Michael Bennett, age twenty-one, in the chorus of *Bajour*.

Members of the chorus line in gold finale costumes.

It was Martin Charnin, a lyricist and director, who had the idea. In fact, he had it for five years before he got anywhere with it. He had bought a collection of "Little Orphan Annie" comic strips, and seeing in his mind's eye a musical based on the waif's adventures, asked two friends — writer Thomas Meehan and composer Charles Strouse — to help him bring it into being. Though both at first said, "Ughh," they were taken with Charnin's plan to use only Annie, her rich befriender, Daddy Warbucks, and Sandy, her dog, and to invent freely thereafter.

Meehan thought of Dickens and an earlier successful musical, *Oliver!*, and possibly the pluck and luck of Horatio Alger. One of his inventions was Miss Hannigan, the nefarious matron of an orphanage who keeps pursuing Annie, "a metaphorical figure standing for innate decency, courage, and optimism in the face of hard times." He set the tale in the first year of Roosevelt's presidency, with the country trying to rise from its economic depression.

None of the show's authors shared the ultra-conservative political philosophy of Harold Gray, the strip's creator, who hated Roosevelt so venomously that he had rich Daddy Warbucks commit suicide rather than face a future with him. (Warbucks was rescued later, though, when it turned out he took the wrong pill.) In Meehan's fable, Warbucks, just about the richest and kindliest man in the world in that era, takes Annie to visit the president and his cabinet — at which juncture Annie jumps on a table, sings "Tomorrow," and thereby inspires the New Deal.

Annie (1977): Annie, played by Andrea McArdle, together with Sandy and the orphans. They moved off the pages of the comics, and America was charmed by cute kids, a wistful mutt, and old-fashioned optimism.

The show was thought unworthy of Broadway by most of the producers approached, and it took until 1976 before Michael P. Price, who ran the Goodspeed Opera House in Connecticut, put it on to an encouraging response. But even then it needed help from Mike Nichols, who assumed the title of producer, and gave it expert shaping in Washington on its way to 2,377 performances in New York.

Just about all the critics reacted warmly, but *Time* magazine saw it as the season's most significant and prayed-for musical event: "*Annie* is an incredible achievement . . . drenching its audiences in tears of sentimental ecstasy as they flee from a confused reality to a warm fantasy of succor . . . a message of hope in a wounded country." One could hardly ask for more.

The original program for the Goodspeed Opera House production of *Annie*. As often happens on the road to Broadway, there were several subsequent cast changes, including Andrea McArdle moving out of the chorus of orphans to assume the title role.

Len Cariou, the barber, in an exultant moment in *Sweeney Todd* (1979).

(above right)

Angela Lansbury as Mrs. Lovett, whose unusual pies were possibly the worst in London.

If there were those at the Alvin Theatre who found *Annie*, with its brave little orphan girl and her lovable mutt, Sandy, too cloying, too sentimental, it wasn't very long before an antidote of sorts — *Sweeney Todd*, subtitled *The Demon Barber of Fleet Street* — was available at the neighboring Uris. In this dire chiller of a musical, Stephen Sondheim, the composer and lyricist, inserted a moment of parody when Angela Lansbury as Mrs. Lovett, a maker of meat pies, bewails the shortage of dog meat as she sings of "the worst pies in London." Unmistakable, as her voice soared, was a moment of melody from Annie's lyrical "Tomorrow."

For those in need of the blackest kind of humor, there was much, much more. Sondheim had been in London for a revival of *Gypsy*, when he came across a play version of *Sweeney Todd* by Christopher Bond, which had been

derived from a 1847 melodrama, *The String of Pearls, or The Fiend of Fleet Street*, in turn based on an old English ballad about a barber who slit the throats of his patrons, after which they were turned into meat pies by his friend, Mrs. Lovett. Bond's version was influenced by some twentieth-century sociology, in that Todd, who bloodily revenges himself after returning from an unjust prison sentence imposed by a judge who fancied his wife, was seen less as a monster than as a victim of the harshness inherent in England's nineteenth-century industrial revolution.

Sondheim's macabre sense of humor was stirred more by the Grand Guignol aspects of the story, while Hal Prince, who directed the musical version after some doubts about doing it, was stirred more by its social implications. The barber (played by Len Cariou) was, if not more to be pitied than censured, at least to be understood, no matter the maniacal heights of horror he reached. The differing points of view between Sondheim and Prince were discernible in the uneven blending of shocking mayhem, Victorian parody and sentiment, and diabolical humor.

To frame the grisly doings, virtually an entire Victorian foundry was erected on the Uris stage, the ironwork made from relics that came from old New England factories, and the interior filled with artifacts such as gauges, pulleys, and antiquated machinery which moved for little reason other than for atmospheric effect. The materials were purchased for $7,000, and it took another $100,000 to haul it all to New York. Light for the setting filtered in through an enclosure of sooty glass — Victorian workers, Prince pointed out in explaining the dimness, never saw the sun except through glass. (He did not mention whether this also applied to barbers.) Every now and then, for further aural symbolism, a steam whistle shrieked.

Sweeney's barbershop, within which he dispatched his customers and exacted his toll on the judge who had ravished his wife and stolen his infant daughter, was on a smaller set brought into the main set on rollers. It contained a barber chair and a chute beneath it, down which the customers slid, after their throats had been all too realistically cut, to land eventually as the ingredients for Mrs. Lovett's pies.

Fully eighty percent of this most strange musical tale was told operatically through melodic songs that were gruesomely comic and tender by turns — in the former case, "A Little Priest," in which Mrs. Lovett and Todd discuss the relative tastiness of the various types of upstanding gentlemen baked into her pies, and, in the latter, when Todd sings feelingly of his lost daughter Johanna while lathering a patron prior to a slide down the chute.

As might have been expected of a grim show about a crazed razor-wielding London barber, the responses varied. In spite of Len Cariou's fine and intense portrayal of Todd, only someone in a Charles Addams cartoon would have been able to find the demon barber a sympathetic protagonist. Angela Lansbury's Mrs. Lovett, however, was rather pathetic in her entrepreneurial innocence, and provided several moments of ghoulish comic relief. A few members of the audience had enough early on, and walked out, but most stayed on to cheer what they saw as a daring, unusual, and, for those with the stomach for it, enjoyable musical.

Among critics there was agreement that Sondheim and Prince had achieved a striking, even brilliant work, aside from a few too many throat-slittings and a social message that asserted itself only dimly through the prevailing gore. *Sweeney Todd* lasted a year on Broadway, and won both the Tony and the Drama Critics Circle awards for best musical. Five years after its debut in March 1979, its sheer musical artistry was cause enough for it to be restaged by Prince in more operatic form and to go into the repertory of the New York City Opera Company.

Michael Bennett, after following *A Chorus Line* with the anticipated but

THE SONDHEIM BREAKTHROUGH

Can one newspaper make a show as well as break it? A case in point is the treatment accorded Stephen Sondheim's musical (with James Lapine) *Sunday in the Park with George.* A month before its May 1984 opening, Samuel G. Freedman filled several pages of the *New York Times Magazine* on Sondheim's efforts to "transmute into words and music" the world of Georges Seurat's pointillist painting "A Sunday Afternoon on the Island of La Grand Jatte." The article was billed as "First in a Series on the Creative Mind."

Soon thereafter the musical was glowingly reviewed in the daily *Times* by its chief critic, Frank Rich, who prophesied that it would prepare "the stage for even more sustained theatrical innovations yet to come."

On June 10, *Times* critic Michiko Kakutani also went to bat for Sondheim and Lapine in the Sunday Arts and Leisure section by exploring the "dynamics of collaboration between two gifted artists . . . how a work of art evolves from a few phrases jotted down on a yellow legal pad into a fully realized show."

At the same time, the show had received much less glowing reviews from other critics. Clive Barnes of the *New York Post* was "nonplussed and disappointed." Douglas Watt of the *Daily News* advised that it "didn't bear looking at or listening to for very long," and *Variety*'s reviewer said its subject, "the creation of art, takes precedence over story and character. Audiences like shows about people. They're funny that way."

These churlish reactions may well have nettled Mr. Rich,

(continued on p. 234)

(continued from p. 233)
for, a few months later, he wrote a lengthy article in the *Times Sunday Magazine* entitled "A Musical Theatre Breakthrough," the subhead of which proclaimed "With *Sunday in the Park with George*, Stephen Sondheim has transcended four decades of Broadway history." If other critics didn't quite recognize transcendence when they saw it, a Pulitzer Prize committee did, and gave *George* its award for drama.

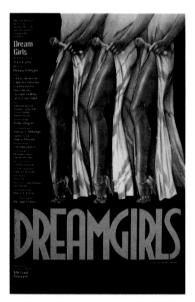

Poster design for *Dreamgirls* (1981).

disappointing *Ballroom*, returned to his more familiar backstage territory with *Dreamgirls*, a tale of a black singing group not unlike the Supremes, from which Diana Ross rose to her eminent star status. In the brilliantly staged musical, three girls from Chicago who call themselves the Dreamettes come to the Apollo Theatre in Harlem to compete in a talent contest. Thereafter, through forty numbers and twenty scenes, the Dreams, as they become known while being guided by their ambitious manager, encounter heartbreak, success, corruption, loves found and lost, and in the end lose the bright innocence with which they began their careers.

In true life, a member of the Supremes, Florence Ballard, was dropped because it was thought she didn't provide the right image, and Diana Ross emerged as the focus of the group. Ballard fell into obscurity and died young. In *Dreamgirls*, a not dissimilar character, the overweight Effie Melody White, is separated from the act, but manages not only to triumph on her own but to overcome the corrupt practices she meets on her way.

The show, like *A Chorus Line*, was developed through a workshop process, but did not begin with Bennett. Tom Eyen, an off-Broadway playwright, worked up the book and lyrics and, with Henry Krieger, who composed a score, showed the material to Bennett, who tested it with eight actors in three different workshops over a year's time in his studio. For eight hours a day the actors did exercises and improvisations, while the author and composer rewrote extensively until Bennett decided the show was ready for Broadway. Three

million dollars was raised with surprising ease, in view of the two-million-dollar failure of *Ballroom*. Apparently, investors sensed another *Chorus Line*.

Among the principals, Jennifer Holliday won particular praise as the overweight Effie, whose biggest moment came at the end of the first act when she is informed by her manager she must leave the group and screams out a song, "I Am Telling You I'm Not Going." The song's title was deceptive; she did go.

The staging also attracted accolades from the critics. Robin Wagner designed an extraordinary set of five floor-to-ceiling towers lined with stage lights and controlled by computers; these traveled about the stage in different configurations that denoted the playing spaces. Bridges rose or sank to reveal silhouetted figures on several levels. In pantomime, a striking moment occurred when shadowy figures showed the route of payola into the palms of disc jockeys.

However, when it came to the story and the Motown-influenced music, which had little variety, there was less enthusiasm, essentially because of the many plots and subplots that left little room or time to get to know and feel for the characters. The overall effect was dazzling, but for Walter Kerr and several others the show was too kaleidoscopic, had too much changing of colors and costume — all done efficiently, he said, "but all very remote." Audiences, though, were not bothered by such critical niceties. *Dreamgirls* sang on for more than 1,500 performances.

With *Cats*, in 1982, the British established a formidable beachhead in

Cats on stage at the Winter Garden Theatre in New York. Are these the "Practical Cats" of T. S. Eliot?

American musical theatre, one they refused to relinquish throughout the decade. Well before the song and dance rendering of T. S. Eliot's *Old Possum's Book of Practical Cats* arrived on these shores on October 7, its huge advance ticket sale, by far the largest in Broadway's history, guaranteed it as virtually — but not totally — impervious to critical sniping.

Word of the show, a raging success in London for more than a year, had crossed the ocean, but American anticipation was whetted further by an astute promotional campaign, one prominent feature being the black-painted billboard on Broadway from which for several months stared two pairs of yellow cat's eyes, and nothing else.

More help came from Barbra Streisand and Liza Minnelli, each of whom recorded "Memory," the show's most haunting song. On radio and television, for weeks on end, a voice on commercials asked: "Isn't the curiosity killing you?" Meanwhile, the façade of

GIRL SINGER

Early on, just about everyone knew that Barbra Streisand was headed for stardom. A nineteen-year-old lower Manhattan nightclub singer when she went into the musical version of Jerome Weidman's *I Can Get It for You Wholesale*, she stopped the otherwise lackluster show with the "Miss Marmelstein" number, in which she lamented her life as an unappreciated secretary. The star of the show was Elliott Gould, who later became her

(continued on p. 236)

(continued from p. 235)
husband. Two years later she was the star of *Funny Girl* (1964), a musical biography of Fanny Brice, whom she somewhat resembled in profile. Ignoring the temptation to use Brice's own material, Jule Styne gave a period flavor to some of his songs, but created others suited to Streisand's passionate from-the-gut style, which caused critic Stanley Kauffmann to refer to her at one point as Barbra Strident. All the other critics loved her, though, and applauded her acting, her comic gifts, as well as her heartfelt singing, especially of the hit "People." The show was troubled during its out-of-town tryouts, and Jerome Robbins had to be called in for rescue. Although *Funny Girl* did not differ much from other standard show-biz biographies, Streisand carried it to a long-running success, and with it, herself to a long and luminous film career, including two rather soppy screen renderings of Fanny Brice's triumphs and heartbreaks, *Funny Girl* and *Funny Lady.*

Andrew Lloyd Webber, composer of *Cats* (1982).

the Winter Garden Theatre was painted black, and, inside, new construction all but tore the theatre apart for renovations necessitated by the extraordinary setting.

When the show arrived at last, and critics had a chance to learn what the hullabaloo was all about, they were not entirely overwhelmed. "Less than purr-fect," one critic headlined his review. Frank Rich, in the *New York Times*, conceded that the show was neither brilliant nor emotionally powerful, but "it believes in purely theatrical magic, and on that it unquestionably delivers."

The theatrical magic did not happen in a flash. The first inspiration came to Andrew Lloyd Webber, the composer, who, when he read the *Practical Cats* poems, written by Eliot for his godchildren, was attracted by their irregular meter. In 1976 he began setting them to music, thinking they might make a television program, but first trying them out in a concert version at an informal music festival he held in summers at his home in the country. Eliot's widow mentioned some unpublished verses to him, and one of

these, about a faded beauty called "Grizabella, the Glamour Cat," suggested a theme and the wisp of a story to connect the songs.

Lloyd Webber was born into a musical background: his mother was a pianist and his father the dean of music at London University. In public school and at university an admirer of Richard Rodgers, he staged musicals, and while still in his early twenties, with the lyricist Tim Rice, wrote *Joseph and the Amazing Technicolor Dreamcoat* and *Jesus Christ Superstar.*

The latter began its life as a rock recording which sold millions of copies. Thus encouraged, Lloyd Webber and Rice decided to put it on the stage, with Tom O'Horgan as its director. When it opened on Broadway in 1971, several of the critics, failing to recognize a musical superstar-to-be in Lloyd Webber, regarded it as one more deviation from the cultural mainstream by rock-happy hippies. However, such runaway song hits as "I Don't Know How to Love Him" drew audiences in New York for a year and a half, and in London much longer. *Joseph* also reached Broadway, but through an off-Broadway route. And, by that time, there was *Evita.*

As with *Superstar*, a record album of *Evita*, based on the life and death of Eva Perón, the wife of the Argentine dictator, preceded the staged show, as did its most distinctive and hugely popular song, "Don't Cry for Me, Argentina." Lloyd Webber was averse to the restrictions of a libretto. He preferred the more operatic form of what he called "the sung-through" musical, in which plot was subordinate to music and spectacle.

Patti LuPone sings "Don't Cry for Me, Argentina," from *Evita* (1979).

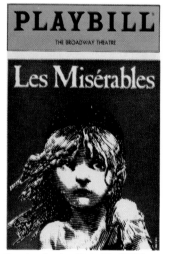

Program for *Les Misérables* (1987).

TO THE BARRICADES!

Les Misérables, the musical, owes its birth to Alain Boublil, a French songwriter, seeing *Jesus Christ Superstar* during a 1972 visit to New York. Captivated by the pop opera style of *Superstar*, Monsieur Boublil, with his compatriot Claude-Michel Schönberg, fashioned *La Revolution Française*, and then *Les Misérables*, a tableau-like musical first done as a recording and then staged as an arena spectacle in 1980 at the huge Palais des Sports in Paris.

The young British producer of *Cats*, Cameron Mackintosh, happened to hear the recorded version in 1982, and was excited enough by it to plan an English stage version. It took three years before the transference from French to English was accomplished and a production was mounted under the aegis of the Royal Shakespeare Company. The French production had to be entirely restructured, and a new synopsis fashioned from the twelve hundred pages of the monumental Victor Hugo novel by a pair of directors, Trevor Nunn and John Caird.

When *Les Misérables* opened at London's Barbican *(continued on p. 239)*

In the hands of director Harold Prince, the spectacle in *Evita* helped mask the lack of substance. Lloyd Webber's music, though, had broadened into more variety, with echoes of tangos, waltzes, marches, and parodies of Latin love songs. Prince filled the stage with vivid billboards, violent-looking placards, banners, film clips, and crowd sound effects. The revolutionary Che Guevara, perhaps to balance the fascistic Peróns, was brought on as a critical commentator on Evita's life. London had loved *Evita*, but New York critics were mixed at best. Still, by the time *Cats* came to town in 1982, it was still going strong on Broadway, a good three years after its American premiere.

Because of the American O'Horgan's guidance of *Superstar*, and Prince's of *Evita*, realization came slowly that the British were on their way to dominance on the Broadway of the eighties. It made little difference to American theatre owners. The largest organization, the Shuberts, owned theatres in New York and around the country. Spending more than three million dollars to bring *Cats* to New York, their investment was already recouped by the time it arrived. The more extravagant the show, it seemed, the better — and it was Lloyd Webber, like another young genius in Hollywood, Steven Spielberg, to whom he would soon be compared, who apparently held the musical key to the audiences of the Reagan era.

The affluent Yuppies had arrived, and they didn't appear to mind paying fifty dollars and more for a ticket to a show. (By 1990, top seats for another long-awaited British arrival, *Miss Saigon*, were selling for as much as a hundred dollars.) And, since it had been well proven that a hit musical could run for years on Broadway, with ancillary income from road companies, recordings, and film rights, many millions could be risked to mount a production.

The restructuring of the Winter Garden Theatre for *Cats* was not done to allow for grand spectacle of the Ziegfeld type, but to enlarge the stage to look like a huge rubbish-filled junkyard reaching out to and enveloping the mezzanine rail. When staged, the audience was in an environmental composition of larger-than-life-size used tires, car parts, bicycle wheels, rotting boards, squeezed-out toothpaste tubes, discarded shoes, all glowing in multicolored hues, while overhead laser-produced stars pierced through clouds.

The dancers — huge "cats," all of them — were illuminated by gleams of moonlight and neon. They wore colored wigs and costumes of fur and satin, painted and hair-tufted leotards. Lloyd Webber's music was written as much for dancing as for singing. What story there was centered on the choice of one cat to ascend to what Eliot had called "the heaviside layer," to be reborn into one of its lives. Eliot had given his cats names and personalities: Gus, the old actor; Macavity, criminally inclined; Rum Tum Tugger, never satisfied; and the winner was: the once-glamorous but now faded Grizabella, who ascended to her cat heaven in a flaming truck tire.

The conception grew into its phantasmagorical form under the direction of Trevor Nunn, the artistic director of London's Royal Shakespeare Company. With John Napier doing sets and costumes, he worked out the theatrical staging, but not until after he had wondered whether it might better be done as a modest chamber piece. Lloyd Webber, though, opted for a spectacular feline fantasy filled with music, dance, and energetic movement. Choreographer Gillian Lynne created the writhing, clawing, leaping dances, while Nunn concentrated on finding character in characteristics. The result proved fascinating enough to theatregoers to stay on into the nineties, its longevity threatening to displace the record run set by *A Chorus Line*.

The British invasion of Broadway grew more pronounced in 1986 and 1987 with the cheerful fifty-year-old import, *Me and My Girl*, followed by a lavish Royal Shakespeare Company musical production of *Les Misérables* and Broadway's most expensive ever, *Starlight Express*, another Lloyd Webber monster musical performed by roller skaters masquerading as trains. The composer disclaimed ultimate responsibility for the transmutation of a children's tale about a toy train into the high-tech extravaganza that had its weirdly bedecked skaters zooming about on tracks on what appeared to be the world's largest Erector Set. While failing to recoup its eight-million-dollar Broadway cost, the *Express* continued to run full throttle in London.

Lloyd Webber also said that for years he had wanted to write a romantic musical, and in a reversion from cats and trains, he found what he wanted in *The Phantom of the Opera*, Gaston Leroux's

hoary story of the disfigured architect of the Paris Opera House who falls in love with Christine, a dancer with singing ambitions in the corps de ballet. As it happened, Lloyd Webber had taken as his second wife Sarah Brightman, who appeared in the London production of *Cats*, and he thought that the role of Christine would be perfect for her lush coloratura.

Harold Prince was soon intrigued enough to take on the direction of the adaptation, which, with several models to choose from, stayed closest to the Lon Chaney silent version of the mid-1920s. Prince, too, was becoming somewhat weary of musicals so dependent for their effects on modern technology, although expense would be no object — not with Lloyd Webber involved. By the time *Phantom* reached Broadway on January 27, 1988, its cost, too, had reached eight million dollars. However, some seventeen million was already in the till, and anyone who hadn't bought an advance ticket would have to wait at least a year to see what Lloyd Webber and Prince had wrought.

They would not see anything altogether unexpected, for it would have been almost heretical not to have a huge chandelier menacing the audience, or an underground lake on which the Phantom would row his captive love, or that moment when Christine would steal up behind the organ-playing Phantom to snatch his mask for a long-awaited glimpse of his disfigurement.

There was all that and more in sumptuous late-Victorian settings, replete with draperies, designed by Maria Björnson. The basement of the

(continued from p. 238)
Theatre in October 1985, the critical response was decidedly mixed, but the public's reception was overwhelmingly favorable. By the time it came to New York's Broadway Theatre on March 12, 1987, it was a foregone hit, with an advance sale of over ten million dollars, a new record. It hardly needed the encomiums heaped upon it by the critics. Frank Rich in the *New York Times* saw its fusion of drama, music, character, design, and movement as "linked to the highest tradition of Broadway musical production." *Newsweek* heralded the power of its ensemble cast, and *Time* magazine lauded the music's blend of melody mixed with outrage — quite appropriate to the social messages embodied in the novel that began it all.

Program for *Miss Saigon* (1991).

FIRST MEGAHIT OF THE '90S

If *Phantom* had shown that escalating costs in staging a megamusical in the 1980s could be more than justified by increased advance sales, the upward spiral continued with the first megashow of the 1990s, *Miss Saigon*. Its advance sales of over thirty million dollars eclipsed the *Phantom* advance by considerably more than fifty percent.

239

venerable Majestic Theatre had to be excavated to accommodate scenery that included six giant candelabra that ascended to light the Phantom's private quarters. It took more alteration to make room for the rooftop across which the Phantom escapes at the end of the first act, and a marvel of ingenuity to create the catwalks to reach it. Computerized technology was used for what appeared to be candles with real flames — actually specially designed bulbs with filaments that flickered realistically. Another intricate operation brought the menacing chandelier over the heads of the audience and back to the stage where it eventually came down — too slowly, one critic complained.

Before coming to New York, and while the show was enjoying a phenomenal success in London, a crisis occurred when the Actors' Equity Association at first refused Sarah Brightman permission to recreate her star role here. Michael Crawford as the Phantom had already received his clearance, but Equity was upset that the two roles would rule out star-creating chances for American artists. Lloyd Webber, the producer with Cameron Mackintosh, was naturally upset and, indeed, threatened to withhold the production from New York, but the matter was eventually resolved, giving Ms. Brightman the opportunity to have her singing and acting ability evaluated by the New York critics. Some liked her, some were less than enthusiastic, but in the way of things a show already so hugely successful before its opening night would be bound to encounter some catty detractors. The all-but-superfluous

critics nevertheless proceeded to put their thoughtful views on paper. One critic was upset by the revealed face of the Phantom. It seemed to him no worse than a bad case of acne.

Lloyd Webber, by now so rich that estimates of his wealth rose each day like a booming stock market — in fact, he did sell stock in his companies — had his share of detractors as well as admirers. His music was popular, in one view, because his music was not written for the head, but was broadly emotional. His shows had little lyrical wit or character development. What he gave the audience was wall-to-wall music with no real need for them to listen to the words. Some regarded his music as derivative — they heard snatches of Puccini here, a bit of Rodgers there, a touch of Mozart, even Bach. When he had first thought of doing *Phantom* as a musical, he had considered using themes by nineteenth-century composers, but instead created his own lushly melodic pastiche.

Frank Rich in the *New York Times* mildly accused him of favoring "the decorative trappings of art over the troublesome substance of culture." In his view, Lloyd Webber was a "creature, perhaps even a prisoner of his time . . . ; he remakes La Belle Epoque in the image of our own gilded age."

Understandably, Lloyd Webber bridled at this sort of criticism and in turn accused Mr. Rich of attempting to foster his own ideas of the direction musicals ought to take. One thing is certain: Lloyd Webber had found a direction that his forebears as far back as *The Black Crook* had discovered. Audiences then had been enchanted by

THE MANY FACES OF THE PHANTOM

The *Phantom* came from the pen of Gaston Leroux in 1910. Lon Chaney, in a 1925 silent-screen version, was the first celluloid stalker — and the scariest — of the Paris Opera House. Audiences screamed at the sight of his horribly disfigured face. A version of the same film with dialogue sequences was released in 1930. The chandelier came crashing down again, with Claude Rains the culprit, in 1943, this time with good singing by Nelson Eddy. A British version in 1962 starred Herbert Lom, who frightened no one. Brian DePalma's 1974 rock version of the basic story, *Phantom of the Paradise*, starred Paul Williams. Television got on the bandwagon in 1983, with Maximilian Schell, and again with Charles Dance in 1990. British stage productions came along in 1975 and 1984, and *The Phantom*, a musical version, was produced Off-Broadway in 1984. If nothing else, all this proves that it doesn't take good looks to be a star.

Michael Crawford as the Phantom of the Opera.

an attraction that brought them fantasy, spectacle, song, dance, and a sort of story to hang it all on.

With all the wonders and terrors of the latter years of our century, what Lloyd Webber proved was the existence of a deep-seated desire to be transported into another realm, where emotions are spun out in music, words, and movement amid wondrous decor. So, perhaps Lloyd Webber's critics missed a point or two, and he was the one who was on the right track, attempting to restore musical theatre to what so much of the audience wanted it to be.

True, our musical stage needs a continual renewal of the energy that had created so distinctive a medium of artistic entertainment. Lost to us in the eighties were Gower Champion to cancer, the incandescent Bob Fosse to a heart attack, the innovative Michael Bennett to that new scourge, AIDS. Broadway, as always, keeps having its troubles: higher and higher costs; fewer and fewer shows able to bear the burden of those costs; a discouraging surrounding environment of porno shops, molding movie houses (which used to be fine theatres) showing trashy films, and streets haunted by prostitutes, dope peddlers, and underage runaways.

But all this will change, they tell us. Plans are under way, and have been for a long time, to rebuild the area with tall, new office buildings, and restore the theatres, including the New Amsterdam of *Ziegfeld Follies* fame. Still the plans, it must be said, are developing slowly.

Theatre, like every other entertainment form and industry, has had to adapt to the realities of the

(opposite)
The Phantom of the Opera (1988): The masquerade that gives the Phantom a rare chance to enter a world of light.

enormous media explosion in the last few decades of this century. The tasks of getting to and pleasing the Broadway audience have grown more difficult, ironically, perhaps, because the rewards can be so enormous. A hit musical in this age of instant communication is like a conglomerate that has mushroomed overnight, its effects felt around the world, creating offshoots into television, recording, and film and satellite productions ranging from Toronto to Tokyo. Inevitably this creates a blockbuster mentality, as prevalent on Broadway as in Hollywood, and producers go where the big money appears to be. Yet, we can still get a splendid revival of *Gypsy*, a brilliantly staged *Grand Hotel*, both of which had critic Walter Kerr deciding the musical wasn't moribund after all.

However, musical theatre doesn't depend on Broadway alone. Just a bit uptown there is Lincoln Center, which has revived musicals of the past. And, if on Broadway musical production is in decline, off-Broadway it is not, where many say the scene is at its most lively. The road is no longer a tour of stops of a night to a week, but often profitable lengthy pre- and post-runs in Washington's Kennedy Center, in Los Angeles, Chicago, and other cities. A show need no longer develop on Broadway, but can come from as far afield as a regional theatre, say, in Houston, or East Haddam, Connecticut. In fact, the workshop idea is perhaps more prevalent elsewhere, and Harold Prince is as likely to develop and try out a new show at a regional theatre or a university as in a Manhattan rehearsal hall.

Universities have become a hotbed of musical theatre, with productions of new and old shows, and new talent is bound to come from this field, as it has in the past. Broadway, it might be said, has spread its influence far and wide, and the musical theatre no longer lives by Broadway alone. But sooner or later there will be that inevitable renewal, for, as another of our lost great ones, Alan Jay Lerner, said, "Broadway cannot live without the musical theatre." And for those who sing, dance, compose, and write, they, it seems, cannot live a full life without Broadway. So they continue to come, to prepare, to audition, to hope, so that someday they may wonderfully entertain us.

The dancing chorus of *Anything Goes* (1934).

Index

Index